GW01246702

Professional Examination

Managerial Level

Paper P7

Financial Accounting and Tax Principles

Exam Kit

KAPLAN
PUBLISHING

CIMA

British Library Cataloguing-in-Publication Data

A catalogue record for this book is available from the British Library.

Published by Kaplan Publishing
Unit 2 The Business Centre
Molly Millars Lane
Wokingham
Berkshire
RG41 2QZ

ISBN 978-1-84710-447-2

© Kaplan Financial Limited, December 2007

Printed and bound in Great Britain

Acknowledgements

We are grateful to the Chartered Institute of Management Accountants, the Association of Chartered Certified Accountants and the Institute of Chartered Accountants in England and Wales for permission to reproduce past examination questions. The answers have been prepared by Kaplan Publishing.

INTRODUCTION

We have worked closely with experienced CIMA tutors and lecturers to ensure that our Kits are exam-focused and user-friendly.

This Exam Kit includes an extensive selection of questions that entirely cover the syllabus – this ensures that your knowledge is tested across all syllabus areas. Wherever possible questions have been grouped by syllabus topics.

All questions are of exam standard and format – this enables you to master the exam techniques. Section 1 contains Section A-type questions you will come across in your exam; Section 2 contains Section B-type questions and Section 3 contains Section C-type questions.

May and November 2007 exams are at the back of the book – try these under timed conditions and this will give you an exact idea of the way you will be tested in your exam.

KAPLAN PUBLISHING

CONTENTS

Section

INDEX TO QUESTIONS AND ANSWERS

SYLLABUS AND LEARNING OUTCOMES

Learning aims

This syllabus aims to test the student's ability to:

- describe the types of business taxation rules and requirements likely to affect a company (in respect of itself and its employees);

- describe and discuss how financial reporting can be regulated and the system of International Accounting Standards;

- prepare statutory accounts in appropriate form for a single company;

- assess and control the short-term financial requirements of a business entity.

Learning outcomes and syllabus content

A – PRINCIPLES OF BUSINESS TAXATION – 20%

Learning outcomes

On completion of their studies students should be able to:

- identify the principal types of taxation likely to be of relevance to an incorporated business in a particular country, including direct tax on the company's trading profits and capital gains, indirect taxes collected by the company, employee taxation, withholding taxes on international payments;

- describe the features of the principal types of taxation likely to be of relevance to an incorporated business in a particular country (e.g. in terms of who ultimately bears the tax cost, withholding responsibilities, principles of calculating the tax base);

- describe the likely record-keeping, filing and tax payment requirements associated with the principal types of taxation likely to be of relevance to an incorporated business in a particular country;

- describe the possible enquiry and investigation powers of taxing authorities;

- identify situations in which foreign tax obligations (reporting and liability) could arise and methods for relieving foreign tax;

- explain the difference in principle between tax avoidance and tax evasion;

- describe sources of tax rules and explain the importance of jurisdiction;

- explain and apply the accounting rules contained in IAS 12 for current and deferred taxation.

Syllabus content

- Concepts of direct versus indirect taxes, taxable person and competent jurisdiction.

- Sources of tax rules (e.g. domestic primary legislation and court rulings, practice of the relevant taxing authority, supranational bodies, such as the EU in the case of value added/sales tax, and international tax treaties).

- Direct taxes on company profits and gain:
  - The principle of non-deductibility of dividends and systems of taxation defined according to the treatment of dividends in the hands of the shareholder (e.g. classical, partial imputation and imputation).
  - The distinction between accounting and taxable profits in absolute terms (e.g. disallowable expenditure on revenue account, such as entertaining, and on capital account, such as formation and acquisition costs) and in terms of timing (e.g. deduction on a paid basis, tax depreciation substituted for book depreciation).
  - The nature of rules recharacterising interest payments as dividends.
  - Potential for variation in rules for calculating the tax base dependent on the nature or source of the income (schedular systems).
  - The need for rules dealing with the relief of losses.
  - The concept of tax consolidation (e.g. for relief of losses and deferral of capital gains on asset transfers within a group).

- Indirect taxes collected by the company:
  - In the context of indirect taxes, the distinction between unit taxes (e.g. excise duties based on physical measures) and ad valorem taxes (e.g. sales tax based on value).
  - The mechanism of value added/sales taxes, in which businesses are liable for tax on their outputs less credits for tax paid on their inputs, including the concepts of exemption and variation in tax rates depending on the type of output and disallowance of input credits for exempt outputs.

- Employee taxation:
  - The employee as a separate taxable person subject to a personal income tax regime.
  - Use of employer reporting and withholding to ensure compliance an assist tax collection.

- The need for record-keeping and record retention that may be additional to that required for financial accounting purposes.

- The need for deadlines for reporting (filing returns) and tax payments.

- Types of powers of tax authorities to ensure compliance with tax rules:
  - Power to review and query filed returns.
  - Power to request special reports or returns.
  - Power to examine records (generally extending back some years).
  - Powers of entry and search.
  - Exchange of information with tax authorities in other jurisdictions.

- International taxation:
  - The concept of corporate residence and the variation in rules for its determination across jurisdictions (e.g. place of incorporation versus place of management).
  - Types of payments on which withholding tax may be required (especially interest, dividends, royalties and capital gains accruing to non-residents).
  - Means of establishing a taxable presence in another country (local enterprise and branch).
  - The effect of double tax treaties (based on the OECD Model Convention) on the above (e.g. reduction of withholding tax rates, provisions for defining a permanent establishment).
  - Principles of relief for foreign taxes by exemption, deduction and credit.

- The distinction between tax avoidance and tax evasion, and how these vary among jurisdictions (including the difference between the use of statutory general anti-avoidance provisions and case law based regimes).

- Accounting treatment of taxation and disclosure requirements under IAS 12.

Note: Examples of general principles should be drawn from a 'benchmark' tax regime (e.g. the UK, USA, etc) or an appropriate local tax regime. Details of any specific tax regime will NOT be examined.

B – PRINCIPLES OF REGULATION OF FINANCIAL REPORTING – 10%

Learning outcomes

On completion of their studies students should be able to:

- explain the need for regulation of published accounts and the concept that regulatory regimes vary from country to country;

- explain potential elements that might be expected in a regulatory framework for published accounts;

- describe the role and structure of the International Accounting Standards Board (IASB) and the International Organisation of Securities Commissions (IOSCO);

- explain the IASB's *Framework for the Presentation and Preparation of Financial Statements*;

- describe the process leading to the promulgation of an International Accounting Standard (IAS);

- describe ways in which IASs can interact with local regulatory frameworks;

- explain in general terms, the role of the external auditor, the elements of the audit report and types of qualification of that report.

Syllabus content

- The need for regulation of accounts.

- Elements in a regulatory framework for published accounts (e.g. company law, local GAAP, review of accounts by public bodies).

- GAAP based on prescriptive versus principles-based standards.

- The role and structure of the IASB and IOSCO.

- The IASB's *Framework for the Presentation and Preparation of Financial Statements*.

- The process leading to the promulgation of a standard practice.

- Ways in which IASs are used: adoption as local GAAP, model for local GAAP, persuasive influence in formulating local GAAP.

- The powers and duties of the external auditors, the audit report and its qualification for accounting statements not in accordance with best practice.

C – SINGLE COMPANY FINANCIAL ACCOUNTS – 45%

Learning outcomes

On completion of their studies students should be able to:

*   prepare financial statements in a form suitable for publication, with appropriate notes;

*   prepare a cash flow statement in a form suitable for publication;

*   explain and apply the accounting rules contained in IASs dealing with reporting performance, tangible fixed assets and inventories;

*   explain the accounting rules contained in IASs governing share capital transactions;

*   explain the principles of the accounting rules contained in IASs dealing with disclosure of related parties to a business, construction contracts (and related financing costs), research and development expenditure, intangible fixed assets (other than goodwill on consolidation), impairment of assets, post-balance sheet events, contingencies, and leases (lessee only).

Syllabus content

*   Preparation of the financial statements of a single company, including the statement of changes in equity (IAS 1).

*   Preparation of cash flow statements (IAS 7).

*   Reporting performance: recognition of revenue, measurement of profit or loss, extraordinary items, prior period items, discontinuing operations and segment reporting (IAS 1, 8, 14, 18 & 35).

*   Property, Plant and Equipment (IAS 16): the calculation of depreciation and the effect of revaluations, changes to economic useful life, repairs, improvements and disposals.

*   Inventories (IAS 2).

*   Issue and redemption of shares, including treatment of share issue and redemption costs (IAS 32 and IAS 39), the share premium account, the accounting for maintenance of capital arising from the purchase by a company of its own shares.

*   The disclosure of related parties to a business (IAS 24).

*   Construction contracts and related financing costs (IAS 11 & 23): determination of cost, net realisable value, the inclusion of overheads and the measurement of profit on uncompleted contracts.

*   Research and development costs (IAS 38): criteria for capitalisation.

*   Intangible assets (IAS 38) and goodwill (excluding that arising on consolidation): recognition, valuation and amortisation.

*   Impairment of assets (IAS 36) and its effect on the above.

*   Post-balance sheet events (IAS 10).

*   Provisions and contingencies (IAS 37).

*   Leases (IAS 17) – operating and finance leases in the books of the lessee.

D – MANAGING SHORT-TERM FINANCE – 25%

Learning outcomes

On completion of their studies students should be able to:

- calculate and interpret working capital ratios for business sectors;
- prepare and analyse cash flow forecasts over a 12-month period;
- identify measures to improve a cash forecast situation;
- compare and contrast the use and limitations of cash management models and identify when each model is most appropriate;
- analyse trade receivable information;
- evaluate receivable and payable policies;
- evaluate appropriate methods of inventory management;
- identify alternatives for investment of short-term cash surpluses;
- identify sources of short-term funding;
- identify appropriate methods of finance for trading internationally.

Syllabus content

- Working capital ratios (e.g. receivable days, inventory days, payable days, current ratio, quick ratio) and the working capital cycle.
- Working capital characteristics of different businesses (e.g. supermarkets being heavily funded by payables) and the importance of industry comparisons.
- Cash flow forecasts, use of spreadsheets to assist in this in terms of changing variables (e.g. interest rates, inflation) and in consolidating forecasts.
- Variables that are most easily changed, delayed or brought forward in a forecast.
- The link between cash, profit and the balance sheet.
- The Baumol and Miller – Orr cash management models.
- The credit cycle from receipt of customer order to cash receipt.
- Evaluation of payment terms and settlement discounts.
- Preparation and interpretation of age analyses of receivables and payables.
- Establishing collection targets on an appropriate basis (e.g. motivational issues in managing credit control).
- The payment cycle from agreeing the order to make payments.
- Centralised versus decentralised purchasing.
- The relationship between purchasing and inventory control.
- Principles of the economic order quantity (EOQ) model and criticisms thereof.
- Types and features of short-term finance: trade payables, overdrafts, short-term loans and debt factoring.
- Use and abuse of trade payables as a source of finance.
- The principles of investing short term (i.e. maturity, return, security, liquidity and diversification).
- Types of investments (e.g. interest-bearing bank accounts, negotiable instruments including certificates of deposit, short-term treasury bills, and securities).
- The difference between the coupon on debt and the yield to maturity.
- Export finance (e.g. documentary credits, bills of exchange, export factoring, forfaiting).

REVISION GUIDANCE

Planning your revision

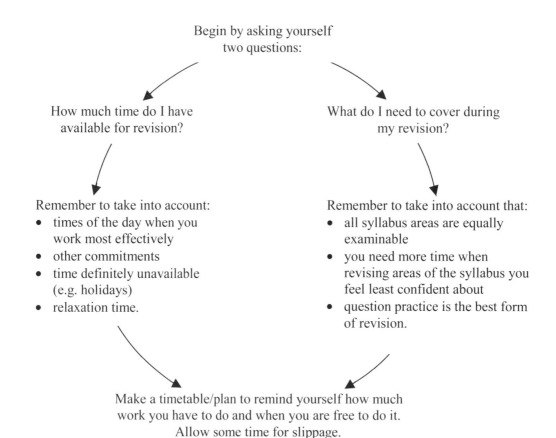

Begin by asking yourself
two questions:

How much time do I have
available for revision?

What do I need to cover during
my revision?

Remember to take into account:
- times of the day when you
  work most effectively
- other commitments
- time definitely unavailable
  (e.g. holidays)
- relaxation time.

Remember to take into account that:
- all syllabus areas are equally
  examinable
- you need more time when
  revising areas of the syllabus you
  feel least confident about
- question practice is the best form
  of revision.

Make a timetable/plan to remind yourself how much
work you have to do and when you are free to do it.
Allow some time for slippage.

Revision techniques

- Go through your notes and textbook **highlighting the important points**

- You might want to produce your own set of **summarised notes**

- **List key words** for each topic to remind you of the essential concepts

- **Practise exam-standard questions**, under timed conditions

- **Rework questions** that you got completely wrong the first time, but only when you think you know the subject better

- If you get stuck on topics, **find someone to explain** them to you (your tutor or a colleague, for example)

- **Read recent articles** on the CIMA website and in *Financial Management*

- **Read** good newspapers and professional journals

THE EXAM

Format of the exam

There will be a written exam paper of three hours, with the following sections: *Number of marks*

Section A	A variety of compulsory objective test questions, each worth 2 to 4 marks. Mini-scenarios may be given, to which a group of questions relate.	40
Section B	Six compulsory short answer questions, each worth 5 marks. Short scenarios may be given to which some or all of the questions relate.	30
Section C	From May 2007 one compulsory question worth 30 marks covering the preparation of at least two of the three key financial reporting statements – the income statement, balance sheet and cash flow statement.	30
	Total:	100

About the exam

- You are allowed **20 minutes' reading time** before the examination begins.

- Where you have a **choice of question**, decide which questions you will do. Unless you know exactly how to answer the question, spend some time **planning** your answer.

- **Divide the time** you spend on questions in proportion to the marks on offer. One suggestion is to allocate 1½ minutes to each mark available, so a 10-mark question should be completed in 15 minutes.

- Stick to the question and **tailor your answer** to what you are asked.

- If you do not understand what a question is asking, **state your assumptions**. Even if you do not answer in precisely the way the examiner hoped, you should be given some credit, if your assumptions are reasonable.

- If you **get completely stuck** with a question, leave space in your answer book and **return to it later.**

- Spend the last **five minutes** reading through your answers and **making any additions or corrections**.

- You should do everything you can to make things easy for the marker. The marker will find it easier to identify the points you have made if your **answers are legible.**

- **Objective test questions** include true/false questions, matching pairs of text and graphic, sequencing and ranking, labelling diagrams and single and multiple numeric entry, but

could also involve paragraphs of text which require you to fill in a number of missing blanks, or for you to write a definition of a word or phrase, or to enter a formula. With multiple-choice questions you have to choose the correct answer (and there is only *one* correct answer) from a list of possible answers.

- **Essay questions**: Your essay should have a clear structure. It should contain a brief introduction, a main section and a conclusion. Be concise. It is better to write a little about a lot of different points than a great deal about one or two points.

- **Computations**: It is essential to include all your workings in your answers. Many computational questions require the use of a standard format: company profit and loss account, balance sheet and cash flow statement for example. Be sure you know these formats thoroughly before the examination and use the layouts that you see in the answers given in this book and in model answers.

- **Scenario-based questions:** read the scenario carefully, identify the area in which there is a problem, outline the main principles/theories you are going to use to answer the question, and then apply the principles/theories to the scenario.

- **Reports, memos and other documents**: some questions ask you to present your answer in the form of a report or a memo or other document. So use the correct format – there could be easy marks to gain here.

MATHEMATICAL TABLES AND FORMULAE

Present value table

Present value of one unit of currency i.e. that is $(1 - r)^{-n}$ where r = interest rate; n = number of periods until payment or receipt.

Periods	Interest rates (r)									
(n)	1%	2%	3%	4%	5%	6%	7%	8%	9%	10%
1	0.990	0.980	0.971	0.962	0.952	0.943	0.935	0.926	0.917	0.909
2	0.980	0.961	0.943	0.925	0.907	0.890	0.873	0.857	0.842	0.826
3	0.971	0.942	0.915	0.889	0.864	0.840	0.816	0.794	0.772	0.751
4	0.961	0.924	0.888	0.855	0.823	0.792	0.763	0.735	0.708	0.683
5	0.951	0.906	0.863	0.822	0.784	0.747	0.713	0.681	0.650	0.621
6	0.942	0.888	0.837	0.790	0.746	0705	0.666	0.630	0.596	0.564
7	0.933	0.871	0.813	0.760	0.711	0.665	0.623	0.583	0.547	0.513
8	0.923	0.853	0.789	0.731	0.677	0.627	0.582	0.540	0.502	0.467
9	0.914	0.837	0.766	0.703	0.645	0.592	0.544	0.500	0.460	0.424
10	0.905	0.820	0.744	0.676	0.614	0.558	0.508	0.463	0.422	0.386
11	0.896	0.804	0.722	0.650	0.585	0.527	0.475	0.429	0.388	0.350
12	0.887	0.788	0.701	0.625	0.557	0.497	0.444	0.397	0.356	0.319
13	0.879	0.773	0.681	0.601	0.530	0.469	0.415	0.368	0.326	0.290
14	0.870	0.758	0.661	0.577	0.505	0.442	0.388	0.340	0.299	0.263
15	0.861	0.743	0.642	0.555	0.481	0.417	0.362	0.315	0.275	0.239
16	0.853	0.728	0.623	0.534	0.458	0.394	0.339	0.292	0.252	0.218
17	0.844	0.714	0.605	0.513	0.436	0.371	0.317	0.270	0.231	0.198
18	0.836	0.700	0.587	0.494	0.416	0.350	0.296	0.250	0.212	0.180
19	0.828	0.686	0.570	0.475	0.396	0.331	0.277	0.232	0.194	0.164
20	0.820	0.673	0.554	0.456	0.377	0.312	0.258	0.215	0.178	0.149

Periods	Interest rates (r)									
(n)	11%	12%	13%	14%	15%	16%	17%	18%	19%	20%
1	0.901	0.893	0.885	0.877	0.870	0.862	0.855	0.847	0.840	0.833
2	0.812	0.797	0.783	0.769	0.756	0.743	0.731	0.718	0.706	0.694
3	0.731	0.712	0.693	0.675	0.658	0.641	0.624	0.609	0.593	0.579
4	0.659	0.636	0.613	0.592	0.572	0.552	0.534	0.516	0.499	0.482
5	0.593	0.567	0.543	0.519	0.497	0.476	0.456	0.437	0.419	0.402
6	0.535	0.507	0.480	0.456	0.432	0.410	0.390	0.370	0.352	0.335
7	0.482	0.452	0.425	0.400	0.376	0.354	0.333	0.314	0.296	0.279
8	0.434	0.404	0.376	0.351	0.327	0.305	0.285	0.266	0.249	0.233
9	0.391	0.361	0.333	0.308	0.284	0.263	0.243	0.225	0.209	0.194
10	0.352	0.322	0.295	0.270	0.247	0.227	0.208	0.191	0.176	0.162
11	0.317	0.287	0.261	0.237	0.215	0.195	0.178	0.162	0.148	0.135
12	0.286	0.257	0.231	0.208	0.187	0.168	0.152	0.137	0.124	0.112
13	0.258	0.229	0.204	0.182	0.163	0.145	0.130	0.116	0.104	0.093
14	0.232	0.205	0.181	0.160	0.141	0.125	0.111	0.099	0.088	0.078
15	0.209	0.183	0.160	0.140	0.123	0.108	0.095	0.084	0.079	0.065
16	0.188	0.163	0.141	0.123	0.107	0.093	0.081	0.071	0.062	0.054
17	0.170	0.146	0.125	0.108	0.093	0.080	0.069	0.060	0.052	0.045
18	0.153	0.130	0.111	0.095	0.081	0.069	0.059	0.051	0.044	0.038
19	0.138	0.116	0.098	0.083	0.070	0.060	0.051	0.043	0.037	0.031
20	0.124	0.104	0.087	0.073	0.061	0.051	0.043	0.037	0.031	0.026

Cumulative present value of one unit of currency

This table shows the present value of one unit of currency per annum, receivable or payable at the end of each year for n years $\dfrac{1-(1+r)^{-n}}{r}$

Periods (n)	Interest rates (r)									
	1%	2%	3%	4%	5%	6%	7%	8%	9%	10%
1	0.990	0.980	0.971	0.962	0.952	0.943	0.935	0.926	0.917	0.909
2	1.970	1.942	1.913	1.886	1.859	1.833	1.808	1.783	1.759	1.736
3	2.941	2.884	2.829	2.775	2.723	2.673	2.624	2.577	2.531	2.487
4	3.902	3.808	3.717	3.630	3.546	3.465	3.387	3.312	3.240	3.170
5	4.853	4.713	4.580	4.452	4.329	4.212	4.100	3.993	3.890	3.791
6	5.795	5.601	5.417	5.242	5.076	4.917	4.767	4.623	4.486	4.355
7	6.728	6.472	6.230	6.002	5.786	5.582	5.389	5.206	5.033	4.868
8	7.652	7.325	7.020	6.733	6.463	6.210	5.971	5.747	5.535	5.335
9	8.566	8.162	7.786	7.435	7.108	6.802	6.515	6.247	5.995	5.759
10	9.471	8.983	8.530	8.111	7.722	7.360	7.024	6.710	6.418	6.145
11	10.368	9.787	9.253	8.760	8.306	7.887	7.499	7.139	6.805	6.495
12	11.255	10.575	9.954	9.385	8.863	8.384	7.943	7.536	7.161	6.814
13	12.134	11.348	10.635	9.986	9.394	8.853	8.358	7.904	7.487	7.103
14	13.004	12.106	11.296	10.563	9.899	9.295	8.745	8.244	7.786	7.367
15	13.865	12.849	11.938	11.118	10.380	9.712	9.108	8.559	8.061	7.606
16	14.718	13.578	12.561	11.652	10.838	10.106	9.447	8.851	8.313	7.824
17	15.562	14.292	13.166	12.166	11.274	10.477	9.763	9.122	8.544	8.022
18	16.398	14.992	13.754	12.659	11.690	10.828	10.059	9.372	8.756	8.201
19	17.226	15.679	14.324	13.134	12.085	11.158	10.336	9.604	8.950	8.365
20	18.046	16.351	14.878	13.590	12.462	11.470	10.594	9.818	9.129	8.514

Periods (n)	Interest rates (r)									
	11%	12%	13%	14%	15%	16%	17%	18%	19%	20%
1	0.901	0.893	0.885	0.877	0.870	0.862	0.855	0.847	0.840	0.833
2	1.713	1.690	1.668	1.647	1.626	1.605	1.585	1.566	1.547	1.528
3	2.444	2.402	2.361	2.322	2.283	2.246	2.210	2.174	2.140	2.106
4	3.102	3.037	2.974	2.914	2.855	2.798	2.743	2.690	2.639	2.589
5	3.696	3.605	3.517	3.433	3.352	3.274	3.199	3.127	3.058	2.991
6	4.231	4.111	3.998	3.889	3.784	3.685	3.589	3.498	3.410	3.326
7	4.712	4.564	4.423	4.288	4.160	4.039	3.922	3.812	3.706	3.605
8	5.146	4.968	4.799	4.639	4.487	4.344	4.207	4.078	3.954	3.837
9	5.537	5.328	5.132	4.946	4.772	4.607	4.451	4.303	4.163	4.031
10	5.889	5.650	5.426	5.216	5.019	4.833	4.659	4.494	4.339	4.192
11	6.207	5.938	5.687	5.453	5.234	5.029	4.836	4.656	4.486	4.327
12	6.492	6.194	5.918	5.660	5.421	5.197	4.988	7.793	4.611	4.439
13	6.750	6.424	6.122	5.842	5.583	5.342	5.118	4.910	4.715	4.533
14	6.982	6.628	6.302	6.002	5.724	5.468	5.229	5.008	4.802	4.611
15	7.191	6.811	6.462	6.142	5.847	5.575	5.324	5.092	4.876	4.675
16	7.379	6.974	6.604	6.265	5.954	5.668	5.405	5.162	4.938	4.730
17	7.549	7.120	6.729	6.373	6.047	5.749	5.475	5.222	4.990	4.775
18	7.702	7.250	6.840	6.467	6.128	5.818	5.534	5.273	5.033	4.812
19	7.839	7.366	6.938	6.550	6.198	5.877	5.584	5.316	5.070	4.843
20	7.963	7.469	7.025	6.623	6.259	5.929	5.628	5.353	5.101	4.870

Formulae

VALUATION MODELS

(i)   Future value of S, of a sum X, invested for n periods, compounded at $r\%$ interest:

$$S = X [1 + r]^n$$

(ii) Present value of one unit of currency payable or receivable in n years, discounted at $r\%$ per annum:

$$PV = \frac{1}{[1+r]^n}$$

(iii) Present value of an annuity of one unit of currency per annum, receivable or payable for n years, commencing in one year, discounted at $r\%$ per annum:

$$PV = \frac{1}{r}\left[1 - \frac{1}{[1+r]^n}\right]$$

(iv) Present value of one unit of currency per annum, payable or receivable in perpetuity, commencing in one year, discounted at $r\%$ per annum:

$$PV = \frac{1}{r}$$

(v)   Present value of one unit of currency per annum, receivable or payable, commencing in one year, growing in perpetuity at a constant rate of $g\%$ per annum, discounted at $r\%$ per annum:

$$PV = \frac{1}{r-g}$$

INVENTORY MANAGEMENT

Economic Order Quantity

$$EOQ = \sqrt{\frac{2C_o D}{C_h}}$$

Where:

C_o	=	cost of placing an order
C_h	=	cost of holding one unit in inventory for one year
D	=	annual demand

CASH MANAGEMENT

(i)   Optimal sale of securities, Baumol model:

$$\text{Optimal sale} = \sqrt{\frac{2\times\text{Annual cash disbursements}\times\text{Cost per sale of securities}}{\text{Interest rate}}}$$

(ii) Spread between upper and lower cash balance limits, Miller-Orr model:

$$\text{Spread} = 3\left[\frac{\frac{3}{4}\times\text{Transaction cost}\times\text{Variance of cash flows}}{\text{Interest rate}}\right]^{\frac{1}{3}}$$

UPDATES

Introduction

CIMA examinations are set in accordance with relevant legislation and accounting standards issued up to and including 1 December preceding the examination concerned.

This section provides a brief summary of technical developments which have occurred since June 2006. Students are advised to refer to notices of examinable legislation published in the CIMA student magazine and on the CIMA website (www.cimaglobal.com/students/index.htm) to ensure that they are up to date.

The following technical developments are discussed in this section:

IFRS 8 *Operating Segments*
IAS 1 *Presentation of Financial Statements (Revised)*

Please note that neither of these standards will be examined until 2009.

IFRS 8 *Operating Segments*

IFRS 8 *Operating Segments* was issued in November 2006 as part of the IASB's short-term convergence project with the US Financial Accounting Standards Board (FASB). It replaces IAS 14 *Segment Reporting*.

IFRS 8 applies to listed entities (or those about to be listed) and any other entities that choose to disclose segment information.

The core principle

IFRS 8 requires an entity to disclose segment information to enable users of the financial statements to evaluate the nature and financial effects of the business activities in which it engages and the economic environments in which it operates.

IFRS 8 requires reportable segments (operating segments) to be identified on a different basis from that required by IAS 14. IAS 14 defined a reportable segment as a distinguishable component of an entity that is subject to risks and returns that are different from those of other segments. IFRS 8 defines an operating segment as a component of an entity:

(a)   that engages in business activities from which it earns revenues and incurs expenses;

(b)   whose operating results are regularly reviewed by the entity's chief operating decision maker to make decisions about resources to be allocated to the segment and assess its performance; and

(c)   for which discrete financial information is available.

Under IFRS 8 segment information reflects the way that the entity is actually managed. An entity's reportable segments are those that are used in its internal management reports.

In practice, many entities' reportable segments will probably not change. The IFRS 8 approach has several advantages:

(a) identifying segments may be less subjective than under IAS 14;

(b) there may be a saving in cost and time as the information will already be available in the management accounts.

A disadvantage of the managerial approach is that reportable segments may change if an entity changes its organisational structure.

Further points to note

(a) Under IFRS 8, a part of an entity that only sells goods to other parts of the entity is a reportable segment if management treats it as one. IAS 14 required a reportable segment to earn a majority of its revenue from external sales.

(b) IAS 14 required an entity to prepare two segmental reports: one based on business segments and one based on geographical segments. IFRS 8 only requires one segmental report. If management uses more than one set of segment information, it should identify a single set of components on which to base the segmental disclosures.

(c) As at present, an entity should report information about an operating segment if it meets any of the following size thresholds:

  - revenue is 10% or more of total revenue;
  - reported profit is 10% or more of the total reported profit of all operating segments;
  - reported loss is 10% or more of the total reported loss of all operating segments that reported a loss;
  - assets are 10% or more of total assets.

  As at present, at least 75% of the entity's external revenue should be included in reportable segments. Smaller segments can be combined into one reportable segment provided that they have similar characteristics.

Disclosure requirements

Much of the information required by IFRS 8 is very similar to the disclosures required by IAS 14.

General information

IFRS 8 requires disclosure of the following:

  - factors used to identify the entity's reportable segments, including the basis of segmentation (for example, whether segments are based on products and services, geographical areas or a combination of these);

  - types of products and services from which each segment derives its revenues.

Information about profit or loss and other segment items

For each reportable segment an entity should report:

- a measure of profit or loss;
- a measure of total assets;
- a measure of total liabilities (if such an amount is regularly used in decision making).

Note that unlike IAS 14, IFRS 8 does not define segment revenue, segment result (profit or loss) or segment assets.

The following amounts must be disclosed if they are included in the measure of segment profit or loss reviewed by the chief operating decision maker:

- revenues from external customers;
- revenues from inter-segment transactions;
- interest revenue;
- interest expense;
- depreciation and amortisation;
- material items of income and expense (exceptional items);
- interests in the profit or loss of associates and joint ventures accounted for by the equity method;
- income tax expense;
- material non-cash items other than depreciation or amortisation.

The following amounts must be disclosed if they are included in the measure of segment assets reviewed by the chief operating decision maker:

- investments in associates and joint ventures accounted for by the equity method;
- amounts of additions to non-current assets other than financial instruments.

As at present, entities must provide reconciliations of the totals disclosed in the segment report to the amounts reported in the financial statements.

Entity-wide disclosures

IFRS 8 also requires the following disclosures about the entity as a whole, even if it only has one reportable segment:

- the revenues from external customers for each product and service or each group of similar products and services;

- revenues from external customers split between the entity's country of domicile and all foreign countries in total;

- non-current assets split between those located in the entity's country of domicile and all foreign countries in total;

- if revenue from a single external customer amounts to 10% or more of an entity's revenue, that fact and the total amount of revenue from that customer (but the identity of the customer need not be disclosed).

IAS 14 did not require this information, although some entities disclose it in the Operating and Financial Review.

Measurement

IFRS 8 requires segmental reports to be based on the information reported to and used by management, even where this is prepared on a different basis from the rest of the financial statements. IAS 14 required segmental information to conform with the accounting policies used in the main financial statements.

Therefore an entity must provide explanations of the measurement of segment profit or loss, segment assets and segment liabilities, including:

- the basis of accounting for any transactions between reportable segments;

- the nature of differences between the measurement of segment profit or loss, assets and liabilities and the amounts reported in the financial statements. Differences could include accounting policies and policies for the allocation of common costs and jointly used assets to segments.

One of the weaknesses of IAS 14 was that it did not require entities to disclose information about the allocation of items and the effect of inter-segment sales. IFRS 8 does require this information, if it is necessary for an understanding of the segmental report.

IAS 1 *Presentation of Financial Statements*

In September 2007, the IASB issued a revised IAS 1 *Presentation of Financial Statements*.

The revised IAS 1 changes the titles of financial statements as they will be used in IFRSs:

- 'balance sheet' will become 'statement of financial position';
- 'income statement' will become 'statement of comprehensive income';
- 'cash flow statement' will become 'statement of cash flows'.

Entities are not required to use the new titles in their financial statements. All existing Standards and Interpretations are being amended to reflect the new terminology. The revised IAS 1 resulted in consequential amendments to 5 IFRSs, 23 IASs, and 10 Interpretations.

The main changes from the previous version of IAS 1 are to require that an entity must:

- Present all non-owner changes in equity (known as 'comprehensive income') either in one statement of comprehensive income or in two statements (a separate income statement and a statement of comprehensive income). Components of comprehensive income may not be presented in the statement of changes in equity.

- Present a statement of financial position (balance sheet) as at the beginning of the earliest comparative period in a complete set of financial statements when the entity applies an accounting policy retrospectively or makes a retrospective restatement.

- Disclose income tax relating to each component of other comprehensive income.

- Disclose reclassification adjustments relating to components of other comprehensive income.

The revised IAS 1 is effective for annual periods beginning on or after 1 January 2009. However, early adoption is permitted.

SECTION A-TYPE QUESTIONS

PRINCIPLES OF BUSINESS TAXATION

1   In no more than 15 words, define the meaning of 'competent jurisdiction'.   **(2 marks)**

2   In no more than 20 words, define a taxable person.   **(2 marks)**

3   Which of the following taxes are direct taxes?

    (i)   Tax on ownership of property

    (ii)   Tax on dividends received

    (iii)   Excise duty on tobacco

    A   Taxes (i) and (ii) only

    B   Taxes (i) and (iii) only

    C   Tax (ii) only

    D   Taxes (ii) and (iii) only   **(2 marks)**

4   In no more than 20 words, explain why income might be taxed under different Schedules.

    (2 marks)

5   Tax on an enterprise's trading profits could be referred to as:

    (i)   income tax

    (ii)   profits tax

    (iii)   indirect tax

    (iv)   direct tax

    (v)   earnings tax.

Which TWO of the above would most accurately describe tax on an enterprise's trading profits?

    A   (i) and (iii)

    B   (i) and (iv)

    C   (ii) and (iii)

    D   (iv) and (v)   **(2 marks)**

6 Which of the following types of taxes is regarded as an indirect tax?

A   Taxes on income

B   Taxes on capital gains

C   Taxes on inherited wealth

D   Sales tax (value added tax)   **(2 marks)**

7 In no more than 15 words, complete the following sentence:

'A direct tax is one that ….'   **(2 marks)**

8 List (using no more than five words per item) the four main sources of tax rules in a country.

(4 marks)

9 In no more than 30 words, define deferred taxation.   **(2 marks)**

10 A company purchased an item of plant on 1 July 20X2 for $600,000. This asset is eligible for tax depreciation (capital allowances) at 20% each year, calculated by the reducing balance method. In the financial accounts, the annual depreciation charge is $80,000. On 1 July 20X5, the plant was sold for $300,000. The rate of tax on company profits is 40%. The company's year end is 30 June.

By how much will the tax charge for the year be increased or reduced as a consequence of the asset disposal?   **(3 marks)**

11 Spencer has produced draft financial statements for the year ended 30 June 20X5. These financial statements include a deferred tax liability of $8 million. However, no account has been taken of the potential deferred tax implications of the following asset revaluations.

On 30 June 20X5, the company revalued all its properties and a surplus of $7 million was taken to the statement of changes in equity. The company has no intention of disposing of any of these properties in the foreseeable future.

What is the deferred tax liability of Spencer at 30 June 20X5 under the provisions of IAS 12 *Income Taxes* after taking account of this event? [Use a rate of tax of 30% where required.]

(2 marks)

12 **CY had the following amounts for 20X3 to 20X5:**

Year ended 31 December:	20X3	20X4	20X5
	$	$	$
Accounting depreciation for the year	1,630	1,590	1,530
Tax depreciation allowance for the year	2,120	1,860	1,320

At 31 December 20X2, CY had the following balances brought forward:

	$
Cost of property, plant and equipment qualifying for tax depreciation	20,000
Accounting depreciation	5,000
Tax depreciation	12,500

CY had no non-current asset acquisitions or disposals during the period 20X3 to 20X5.

Assume the corporate income tax rate is 25% for all years.

Calculate the deferred tax provision required by IAS 12 *Income Taxes* at 31 December 20X5.

(3 marks)

13 **On 31 March 20X6, CH had a credit balance brought forward on its deferred tax account of $642,000. There was also a credit balance on its corporate income tax account of $31,000, representing an over-estimate of the tax charge for the year ended 31 March 20X5.**

CH's taxable profit for the year ended 31 March 20X6 was $946,000. CH's directors estimated the deferred tax provision required at 31 March 20X6 to be $759,000 and the applicable income tax rate for the year to 31 March 20X6 as 22%.

Calculate the income tax expense that CH will charge in its income statement for the year ended 31 March 20X6, as required by IAS 12 *Income Taxes*. **(3 marks)**

14 **DZ recognised a tax liability of $290,000 in its financial statements for the year ended 30 September 20X5. This was subsequently agreed with and paid to the tax authorities as $280,000 on 1 March 20X6. The directors of DZ estimate that the tax due on the profits for the year to 30 September 20X6 will be $320,000. DZ has no deferred tax liability.**

What is DZ's income statement tax charge for the year ended 30 September 20X6?

A $310,000

B $320,000

C $330,000

D $600,000 **(2 marks)**

15 **From the following information, calculate the total tax charge for the year. Assume a tax rate of 30%.**

	$
Profit before taxation in the financial accounts	80,000
Over-provision of tax in the previous year	2,000
Depreciation charge in the accounts	60,000
Non-taxable income	5,000
Non-allowable expenditure	12,000
Tax depreciation (capital allowances)	70,000

The total tax charge for the year is _____ . **(3 marks)**

16 The tax year runs from 1 May to 30 April. A company's accounting year ends on 31 December. Its taxable profits for the year to 31 December 20X4 were $75,000.

The rate of tax chargeable on company profits is as follows:

Year to 30 April 20X4	20%
Year to 30 April 20X5	25%

On the basis of this information, what amount of tax is payable for the tax year to 30 April 20X5? **(2 marks)**

17 An item of plant cost $20,000. For tax purposes, depreciation of $6,000 has been deducted to date and the remaining cost will be deductible in future periods.

Revenue generated by using the machine is taxable, any gain on disposal of the machine will be taxable and any loss on disposal will be deductible for tax purposes. For accounting purposes, total depreciation to date is $2,000.

The company involved is charged tax at 30%.

Based on the principles of IAS 12, which of the following statements are correct?

Statement 1: The tax base of the asset is $14,000.

Statement 2: The amount of deferred taxation to date relating to the asset is $1,200.

Statement 3: The temporary difference is a 'deductible' temporary difference.

A Statements 1 and 2 only are correct

B Statements 1 and 3 only are correct

C Statements 2 and 3 only are correct

D All three statements are correct **(2 marks)**

18 E has an accounting profit before tax of $95,000. The tax rate on trading profits applicable to E for the year is 25%. The accounting profit included non-taxable income from government grants of $15,000 and non-tax allowable expenditure of $10,000 on entertaining expenses.

How much tax is E due to pay for the year? **(2 marks)**

19 In no more than 40 words, explain the difference between tax avoidance and tax evasion.

(3 marks)

20 Double tax relief is used to:

A ensure that you do not pay tax twice on any of your income

B mitigate taxing overseas income twice

C avoid taxing dividends received from subsidiaries in the same country twice

D provide relief where a company pays tax at double the normal rate **(2 marks)**

21   **A withholding tax is:**

    A   tax withheld from payment to the tax authorities

    B   tax paid less an amount withheld from payment

    C   tax deducted at source before payment of interest or dividends

    D   tax paid on increases in value of investment holdings   **(2 marks)**

22   **A company with 4 million shares in issue has paid dividends of $560,000 in the year. A partial imputation system is in operation. Profits are taxed at 30% and the tax credit on dividends to individuals is 25%.**

What is the taxable dividend income for the year of an individual shareholder with 240,000 shares in the company?   **(2 marks)**

23   **In a country where a partial imputation system for the taxation of dividends is in operation, the rate of tax on company profits is 40%, the tax credit on dividends to individuals is 25% and the normal rate of tax on the income of individuals is 30%.**

A company with taxable profits of $870,000 paid dividends of $630,000 out of those profits. All its shareholders are individuals paying tax at the normal rate.

What is the total amount of tax paid to the government on the profits and dividends of the company?   **(2 marks)**

24   **A full imputation system of corporate income tax is one where an entity is taxable on:**

    A   all of its income and gains whether they are distributed or not. The shareholder is liable for taxation on all dividends received

    B   all of its income and gains whether they are distributed or not, but all the underlying corporation tax is passed to the shareholder as a tax credit

    C   all of its income and gains whether they are distributed or not, but only part of the underlying corporation tax is passed to the shareholder as a tax credit

    D   its retained profits at one rate and on its distributed profits at another (usually lower) rate of tax   **(2 marks)**

25   **DR makes a taxable profit of $400,000 and pays an equity dividend of $250,000. Income tax on DR's profit is at a rate of 25%.**

Equity shareholders pay tax on their dividend income at a rate of 30%.

If DR and its equity shareholders pay a total of $175,000 tax between them, what method of corporate income tax is being used in that country?

    A   The classical system

    B   The imputation system

    C   The partial imputation system

    D   The split rate system   **(2 marks)**

26   **In no more than 40 words, explain the nature of thin capitalisation rules.**   **(3 marks)**

27 In no more than 20 words, suggest a tax rule that might be introduced to prevent transfer prices between international subsidiaries from being used to manipulate the profits of subsidiaries in each country.

(2 marks)

28 Trading losses in any period can be carried back and set off against profits in the previous 12-month period, and any unrelieved losses can be carried forward to set against profits in future years. Trading losses cannot be set off against capital gains. Capital losses can be set off against capital gains in the same tax year, but unrelieved capital losses cannot be carried back. Unrelieved capital losses may be carried forward and set against capital gains in future years.

QWE had the following taxable profits, gains and losses in years 1 to 4.

	Trading profits/(losses) $	Capital gains/(losses) $
Year 1	50,000	6,000
Year 2	(90,000)	(8,000)
Year 3	30,000	5,000
Year 4	70,000	6,000

What are its taxable profits and gains in each year?

Year 1 _____

Year 2 _____

Year 3 _____

Year 4 _____

(4 marks)

29 What is the nature of group loss relief?

A   Profits and losses of all companies in the same group are consolidated and taxed at the same rate

B   Losses of subsidiaries must be set off against the profits of the parent company in the group

C   Members of the group may surrender their losses to any other member of the group

D   Companies in the same group are required by the tax authorities to surrender their losses to any other subsidiary in the group

(2 marks)

30 An entity, DP, in Country A receives a dividend from an entity in Country B. The gross dividend of $50,000 is subject to a withholding tax of $5,000 and $45,000 is paid to DP. Country A levies a tax of 12% on overseas dividends.

Country A and Country B have both signed a double taxation treaty based on the OECD model convention and both apply the credit method when relieving double taxation.

How much tax would DP be expected to pay in Country A on the dividend received from the entity in Country B?

A $400

B $1,000

C $5,400

D $6,000

(2 marks)

31 **The effective incidence of a tax is:**

A   the date the tax is actually paid

B   the person or entity that finally bears the cost of the tax

C   the date the tax assessment is issued

D   the person or entity receiving the tax assessment

(2 marks)

32 **AC made the following payments during the year ended 30 April 20X5:**

	$000
Operating costs (excluding depreciation)	23
Finance costs	4
Capital repayment of loans	10
Payments for the purchase of new computer equipment for use in AC's business	20

AC's revenue for the period was $45,000 and the corporate income tax rate applicable to AC's profits was 25%. The computer equipment qualifies for tax allowances of 10% per year on a straight line basis.

Calculate AC's tax payable for the year ended 30 April 20X5.   **(3 marks)**

33 **AE purchases products from a foreign entity and imports them into a country A. On import, the products are subject to an excise duty of $5 per item and sales tax of 15% on cost plus excise duty.**

AE purchased 200 items for $30 each and after importing them sold all of the items for $50 each plus sales tax at 15%.

How much is due to be paid to the tax authorities for these transactions?

A $450

B $1,450

C $2,050

D $2,500   **(3 marks)**

34 **Which ONE of the following powers is a tax authority least likely to have granted to them?**

A   Power of arrest

B   Power to examine records

C   Power of entry and search

D   Power to give information to other countries' tax authorities   **(2 marks)**

35 The OECD model tax convention defines a permanent establishment to include a number of different types of establishments:

(i)   a place of management

(ii)   a warehouse

(iii)   a workshop

(iv)   a quarry

(v)   a building site that was used for nine months.

Which of the above are included in the OECD's list of permanent establishments?

A   (i), (ii) and (iii) only

B   (i), (iii) and (iv) only

C   (ii), (iii) and (iv) only

D   (iii), (iv) and (v) only   **(2 marks)**

36 In no more than 15 words, define a tax base.   **(2 marks)**

37 ASD is a company resident in Country X. It has declared a dividend of $3 million, of which $600,000 is payable to FGH, a company resident in Country Y that owns 20% of ASD's share capital. Country X and Country Y have a double taxation agreement based on the OECD Model Convention, and withholding tax is levied at the maximum rate permitted.

What is the amount of withholding tax that should be deducted from the dividend paid to FGH?

(2 marks)

38 D purchased a non-current asset on 1 April 20X1 for $200,000. The asset attracted writing down tax allowances at 25% on the reducing balance. Depreciation was 10% on the straight-line basis. Assume income tax is at 30%.

The deferred tax balance for this asset at 31 March 20X4 is:

A $9,000

B $16,688

C $27,000

D $55,625   **(2 marks)**

39 One of the bases for establishing a company's country of residence for tax purposes is place of incorporation.

What is the other base that might be used?   **(2 marks)**

40 Which of the following is an ad valorem indirect tax?

(i) Duty of $0.40 on a litre of gasoline (petrol)

(ii) Duty of 3% on the purchase of property

(iii) 20% sales tax

A Taxes (i) and (iii) only

B Tax (ii) only

C Taxes (ii) and (iii) only

D Tax (iii) only **(2 marks)**

41 BC, a small entity, purchased its only non-current tangible asset on 1 October 20X3. The asset cost $900,000, all of which qualified for tax depreciation.

BC's asset qualified for an accelerated first year tax allowance of 50%. The second and subsequent years qualified for tax depreciation at 25% per year on the reducing balance method.

BC's accounting depreciation policy is to depreciate the asset over its useful economic life of five years, assuming a residual value of $50,000.

Assume that BC pays tax on its income at the rate of 30%.

Calculate BC's deferred tax balance required in the balance sheet as at 30 September 20X5 according to IAS 12 *Income Taxes*. **(4 marks)**

42 Country B has a corporate income tax system that treats capital gains/losses separately from trading profits/losses. Capital gains/losses cannot be offset against trading profits/losses. All losses can be carried forward indefinitely, but cannot be carried back to previous years. Trading profits and capital gains are both taxed at 20%.

BD had no brought forward losses on 1 October 20X2. BD's results for 20X3 to 20X5 were as follows:

	Trading profit/(loss)	Capital gains/(loss)
	$000	$000
Year to September 20X3	200	(100)
Year to September 20X4	(120)	0
Year to September 20X5	150	130

Calculate BD's corporate income tax due for each of the years ended 30 September 20X3 to 20X5. **(3 marks)**

43   Country OS has a sales tax system where sales tax is charged on all goods and services. Entities registered for sales tax are allowed to recover input tax paid on their purchases.

Sales tax operates at different levels in OS:

- Standard rate 10%

- Luxury rate 20%

- Zero rate 0%

During the last sales tax period, an entity, BZ, purchased materials and services costing $100,000, excluding sales tax. All materials and services were at standard rate sales tax.

BZ converted the materials into two products Z and L; product Z is zero rated and product L is luxury rated for sales tax purposes.

During the sales tax period, BZ made the following sales, excluding sales tax:

	$
Z	60,000
L	120,000

At the end of the period, BZ paid the net sales tax due to the tax authorities.

Assuming BZ had no other sales tax-related transactions, how much sales tax did BZ pay?

(2 marks)

44   An entity sells furniture and adds a sales tax to the selling price of all products sold. A customer purchasing furniture from the entity has to pay the cost of the furniture plus the sales tax. The customer therefore bears the cost of the sales tax.

This is referred to as:

A   formal incidence

B   indirect incidence

C   effective incidence

D   direct incidence   **(2 marks)**

45   BM has a taxable profit of $30,000 and receives a tax assessment of $3,000.

BV has a taxable profit of $60,000 and receives a tax assessment of $7,500.

BM and BV are resident in the same tax jurisdiction.

This tax could be said to be:

A   a progressive tax

B   a regressive tax

C   a direct tax

D   a proportional tax   **(2 marks)**

46   List THREE possible reasons why governments set deadlines for filing returns and/or paying taxes.   **(3 marks)**

47   CU manufactures clothing and operates in a country that has a sales tax system. The sales tax system allows entities to reclaim input tax that they have paid on taxable supplies. Sales tax is at 15% of the selling price at all stages of the manufacturing and distribution chain.

CU manufactures a batch of clothing and pays expenses (taxable inputs) of $100 plus sales tax. CU sells the batch of clothing to a retailer CZ for $250 plus sales tax. CZ unpacks the clothing and sells the items separately to various customers for a total of $600 plus sales tax.

How much sales tax do CU and CZ each have to pay in respect of this one batch of clothing?

(2 marks)

48   Corporate residence for tax purposes can be determined in a number of ways, depending on the country concerned.

Which ONE of the following is NOT normally used to determine corporate residence for tax purposes?

A   The country from which control of the entity is exercised

B   The country of incorporation of the entity

C   The country where the management of the entity holds its meetings

D   The country where most of the entity's products are sold   **(2 marks)**

49   In 1776, Adam Smith proposed that an acceptable tax should meet four characteristics. Three of these characteristics were certainty, convenience and efficiency.

Identify the FOURTH characteristic.

A   Neutrality

B   Transparency

C   Equity

D   Simplicity   **(2 marks)**

Data for Questions 50 and 51

Country D uses a sales tax system whereby sales tax is charged on all goods and services at a rate of 15%. Entities registered for sales tax are allowed to recover input sales tax paid on their purchases.

Country E uses a multi-stage sales tax system, where a cumulative tax is levied every time a sale is made. The tax rate is 7% and tax paid on purchases is not recoverable.

DA is a manufacturer and sells products to DB, a retailer, for $500 excluding tax. DB sells the products to customers for a total of $1,000 excluding tax.

DA paid $200 plus sales tax for the manufacturing cost of its products.

---

50   Assume DA operates in Country D and sells products to DB in the same country.

Calculate the net sales tax due to be paid by DA and DB for the products.   **(2 marks)**

51   Assume DA operates in Country E and sells products to DB in the same country.

Calculate the **total** sales tax due to be paid on all of the sales of the products.   **(2 marks)**

PRINCIPLES OF REGULATION OF FINANCIAL REPORTING

52   What is the main function of the International Financial Reporting Interpretations Committee?

A   Issuing International Financial Reporting Standards

B   Withdrawing International Financial Reporting Standards

C   Overseeing the development of International Financial Reporting Standards

D   Interpreting the application of International Financial Reporting Standards   **(2 marks)**

53   In the organisation structure for the regulation and supervision of International Accounting Standards, which of the bodies listed below acts as the overall supervisory body?

A   International Accounting Standards Committee Foundation

B   International Accounting Standards Board

C   Standards Advisory Council

D   International Financial Reporting Interpretations Committee   **(2 marks)**

54   Which of the following gives the best description of the objectives of financial statements as set out by the International Accounting Standards Board's (IASB) *Framework for the Preparation and Presentation of Financial Statements*?

A   To fairly present the financial position and performance of an enterprise

B   To fairly present the financial position, performance and changes in financial position of an enterprise

C   To provide information about the financial position and performance of an enterprise that is useful to a wide range of users in making economic decisions

D   To provide information about the financial position, performance and changes in financial position of an enterprise that is useful to a wide range of users in making economic decisions   **(2 marks)**

55   The IASB's Framework for the *Preparation and Presentation of Financial Statements* defines a liability as:

A   an amount owed to another entity

B   a present obligation arising as a result of past events, the settlement of which is expected to result in an outflow of economic benefits

C   expenditure that has been incurred but not yet charged to the income statement

D   an obligation that may arise in the future   **(2 marks)**

56 Under the IASB's *Framework for the Preparation and Presentation of Financial Statements* the 'threshold quality' of useful financial information is:

A   relevance

B   reliability

C   materiality

D   understandability   **(2 marks)**

57 The International Accounting Standards Board's (IASB) *Framework for the Preparation and Presentation of Financial Statements* (*Framework*) provides definitions of the elements of financial statements. One of the elements defined by the *Framework* is 'expenses'.

In no more than 35 words, give the IASB *Framework's* definition of expenses.   **(2 marks)**

58 The IASB's *Framework for the Preparation and Presentation of Financial Statements* identifies two factors that restrict the extent to which financial information can be both relevant and reliable.

What are these two restricting factors?   **(2 marks)**

59 IAS 1 *Presentation of Financial Statements* sets out six accounting concepts. Three of the concepts are accruals, going concern and consistency of presentation.

The remaining three concepts in IAS 1 are:

A   materiality and aggregation, offsetting, entity

B   time interval, duality, money measurement

C   materiality and aggregation, offsetting, comparative information

D   entity, time interval, comparative information.   **(2 marks)**

60 According to the IASB's *Framework for the Preparation and Presentation of Financial Statements (Framework),* 'equity' is described as:

A   the amount paid into the enterprise by the owner

B   accumulated profits less amounts withdrawn

C   the residual interest in the assets less liabilities

D   owner's capital investment in the enterprise   **(2 marks)**

61 The IASB's *Framework* sets out the characteristics of useful information. According to the Framework, which THREE of the following are NOT sub-characteristics of 'reliability'?

(i)	Confirmatory value	(iv)	Consistency
(ii)	Completeness	(v)	Neutrality
(iii)	Prudence	(vi)	Predictive value

A (i), (iii) and (vi)

B (i), (iv) and (vi)

C (ii), (iv) and (v)

D (ii), (iii) and (v) **(2 marks)**

62 The IASB's *Framework for the Preparation and Presentation of Financial Statements* defines elements of financial statements.

In no more than 30 words define an asset. **(2 marks)**

63 IAS 1 requires that the accounting policies adopted by a company should comply with IASs in order to ensure that financial statements provide information which is:

A relevant and reliable

B true and fair

C understandable and reliable

D understandable and relevant **(2 marks)**

64 In connection with the role of the external auditor, which of the following statements are CORRECT?

(i) The auditor certifies that the financial statements of an enterprise give a true and fair view.

(ii) It is not a primary duty of the auditor to seek out fraud.

(iii) The directors, not the auditor have the primary responsibility for the preparation of annual financial statements and the setting up of a suitable internal control system.

(iv) The auditor has the right of access at all times to the books, records, documents and accounts of the company.

A All four statements

B (ii), (iii) and (iv) only

C (iii) and (iv) only

D (iv) only **(2 marks)**

65 When an external auditor is unable to agree the accounting treatment of a material item with the directors of an enterprise, but the financial statements are not seriously misleading, he will issue:

A   an unqualified audit report

B   an adverse opinion

C   a qualified audit report using 'except for'

D   an unqualified audit report using 'except for'

66 The term GAAP is used to mean:

A   generally accepted accounting procedures

B   general accounting and audit practice

C   generally agreed accounting practice

D   generally accepted accounting practice   **(2 marks)**

67 Which ONE of the following is responsible for governance and fundraising in relation to the development of International Accounting Standards?

A   International Accounting Standards Board

B   International Financial Reporting Interpretations Committee

C   International Accounting Standards Committee Foundation Trustees

D   Standards Advisory Council   **(2 marks)**

68 Financial statements prepared using International Standards and the International Accounting Standards Board's (IASB) *Framework for the Preparation and Presentation of Financial Statements (Framework)* are presumed to apply two of the following four underlying assumptions:

(i)   relevance

(ii)   going concern

(iii)   prudence

(iv)   accruals.

Which TWO of the above are underlying assumptions according to the IASB's *Framework*?

A   (i) and (ii) only

B   (ii) and (iii) only

C   (iii) and (iv) only

D   (ii) and (iv) only   **(2 marks)**

69 The IASB's Framework for the Preparation and Presentation of Financial Statements *(Framework)* lists the qualitative characteristics of financial statements.

Which THREE of the following are NOT included in the principal qualitative characteristics listed by the *Framework*?

(i)   Comparability   (v)   Understandability
(ii) Relevance   (vi) Matching
(iii) Prudence   (vii) Consistency
(iv) Reliability

A   (i), (iii) and (vii)

B   (i), (ii) and (v)

C   (iii), (vi) and (vii)

D   (iii), (iv) and (vi)   **(2 marks)**

70 An auditor disagrees with the accounting treatment adopted by a company. The impact of the item concerned is seen to be material, but not pervasive.

Which of the following types of audit opinion would be appropriate?

A   Unqualified opinion

B   'Except for' opinion

C   Disclaimer of opinion

D   Adverse opinion   **(2 marks)**

71 The setting of International Accounting Standards is carried out by co-operation between a number of committees and boards, which include:

(i)   International Accounting Standards Committee Foundation (IASC Foundation)

(ii) Standards Advisory Council (SAC)

(iii) International Financial Reporting Interpretations Committee (IFRIC).

Which of the above reports to, or advises, the International Accounting Standards Board (IASB)?

Reports to: *Advises:*

A   (i) and (iii)   (ii)

B   (i) and (ii)   (iii)

C   (iii)   (ii)

D   (ii)   (i)   **(2 marks)**

72 If an external auditor does not agree with the directors' treatment of a material item in the accounts, the first action they should take is to:

A   give a qualified opinion of the financial statements

B   give an unqualified opinion of the financial statements

C   force the directors to change the treatment of the item in the accounts

D   persuade the directors to change the treatment of the item in the accounts   **(2 marks)**

73   **The external auditor has a duty to report on the truth and fairness of the financial statements and to report any reservations. The auditor is normally given a number of powers by statute to enable the statutory duties to be carried out.**

List THREE powers that are usually granted to the auditor by statute.   **(3 marks)**

74   **The process leading to the publication of an International Financial Reporting Standard (IFRS) has a number of stages.**

List the THREE stages that normally precede the final issue of an IFRS.   **(3 marks)**

75   **The International Accounting Standards Board's *Framework for the Preparation and Presentation of Financial Statements* defines five elements of financial statements. Three of the elements are asset, liability and income.**

List the other TWO elements.   **(2 marks)**

SINGLE COMPANY FINANCIAL ACCOUNTS

76   **IAS 1 *Presentation of Financial Statements* encourages an analysis of expenses to be presented on the face of the income statement. The analysis of expenses must use a classification based on either the nature of expense, or its function, within the entity such as:**

(i)   raw materials and consumables used

(ii)   distribution costs

(iii)   employee benefit costs

(iv)   cost of sales

(v)   depreciation and amortisation expense.

Which of the above would be disclosed on the face of the income statement if a manufacturing entity uses analysis based on function?

A   (i), (iii) and (iv)

B   (ii) and (iv)

C   (i) and (v)

D   (ii), (iii) and (v)   **(2 marks)**

77   **IAS 1 states that either on the face of the balance sheet or in notes to the financial statements, line items required in the balance sheet should be disaggregated into sub-classifications. For example, property, plant and equipment should be shown in sub-classifications in accordance with IAS 16.**

List THREE of the sub-classifications of the balance sheet line item 'receivables'.   **(3 marks)**

78 Which of the following must be presented on the face of the income statement?

(i)   Finance charges

(ii) Profits, gains and losses relating to discontinued operations

A   (i) only

B   (ii) only

C   Both (i) and (ii)

D   Neither   **(2 marks)**

79 Which of the following is NOT required by IAS 1 as an item to include in the notes to the accounts?

A   A statement that the entity is a going concern

B   A statement of compliance with International Financial Reporting Standards

C   The dividends declared or proposed before the publication of the financial statements but not included in the statements as a distribution to shareholders in the period

D   The key sources of estimation uncertainty in the financial statements   **(2 marks)**

80 IAS 1 *Presentation of Financial Statements* requires some of the items to be disclosed on the face of the financial statements and others to be disclosed in the notes:

(i)   Depreciation

(ii) Revenue

(iii) Closing inventory

(iv) Finance cost

(v)   Dividends

Which TWO of the above have to be shown on the face of the income statement, rather than in the notes?

A   (i) and (iv)

B   (iii) and (v)

C   (ii) and (iii)

D   (ii) and (iv)   **(2 marks)**

81 Which of the following should be classified as 'current assets' in the balance sheet of an entity in a processing industry whose operating cycle is typically 18 months in length?

(i)   The current portion of an amortising bank loan

(ii) Inventories realisable within 18 months

(iii) Assets held for resale

A   (i) and (ii) only

B   (i) and (iii) only

C   (ii) and (iii) only

D   (iii) only   **(2 marks)**

82   An enterprise undertakes a revaluation of its freehold property during the current period. The revaluation results in a significant surplus over carrying value.

In which of the components of the current period financial statements required by IAS 1 would the revaluation surplus appear?

A   Balance sheet and statement of changes in equity

B   Statement of changes in equity and cash flow statement

C   Balance sheet and income statement

D   Balance sheet and cash flow statement   (2 marks)

83   In the cash flow statement of BKS for the year to 31 December 20X5 the net cash flow from operating activities is to be arrived at by the 'indirect method'.

The following information is relevant:

	$000
Profit before tax	12,044
Depreciation	1,796
Loss on sale of tangible non-current assets	12
Increase in inventories	398
Increase in receivables	144
Increase in payables	468

State, in $000s, the cash generated from operations for the period.   (3 marks)

84   At 30 September 20X5, BY had the following balances, with comparatives:

Balance sheet extracts:

As at 30 September	20X5	20X4
	$000	$000
Non-current tangible assets		
Property, plant and equipment	260	180
Equity and reserves		
Property, plant and equipment revaluation reserve	30	10

The income statement for the year ended 30 September 20X5 included:

Gain on disposal of an item of equipment	$10,000
Depreciation charge for the year	$40,000

Notes to the accounts:

Equipment disposed of had cost $90,000. The proceeds received on disposal were $15,000.

Calculate the property, plant and equipment purchases that BY would show in its cash flow statement for the year ended 30 September 20X5, as required by IAS 7 *Cash Flow Statements*.   (4 marks)

85   At 1 October 20X4, BK had the following balance:

Accrued interest payable $12,000 credit

During the year ended 30 September 20X5, BK charged interest payable of $41,000 to its income statement. The closing balance on accrued interest payable account at 30 September 20X5 was $15,000 credit.

How much interest paid should BK show on its cash flow statement for the year ended 30 September 20X5?

A $38,000

B $41,000

C $44,000

D $53,000   **(2 marks)**

86   There follows extracts from the financial statements of BET for the year to 31 March 20X5 (all figures are in $000).

Extract from the income statement

	$000	$000
Profit on ordinary activities before taxation		1,600
Taxation		
Income taxes – current year	460	
– over provision in 20X4	(30)	
Deferred taxation	20	
	——	(450)
		1,150

Extracts from the balance sheet as at 31 March

	20X4	*20X3*
Current liabilities – taxation	460	380
Non-current liabilities		
Deferred taxation	100	80

What amount (in $000) will appear in respect of income taxes in the cash flow statement for the year to 31 March 20X4?   **(3 marks)**

87   IAS 7 requires cash flows to be analysed into three categories by source: operating activities, investing activities and financing activities.

Which of the following should be included under the 'investing activities' heading?

(i)   Cash paid for the purchase of non-current assets

(ii)   Cash received from the sale of non-current assets

(iii)   Dividends received

(iv)   Repayment of borrowings

A   All four items

B   (i) only

C   (i) and (ii) only

D   (i), (ii) and (iii) only   **(2 marks)**

88   Which of the items listed below is required to be disclosed (together with specified further information) under IAS 14 for each 'reportable segment' for an enterprise's primary basis of reporting?

(i)   Revenue derived from other segments

(ii)   Revenue derived from external customers

(iii)   Carrying amount of segment assets

(iv)   Profit or loss

A   (ii), (iii) and (iv) only

B   (i), (ii) and (iii) only

C   (ii) and (iv) only

D   (i), (ii), (iii) and (iv)   **(2 marks)**

89   IAS 14 *Segment Reporting* requires that segment revenue should be:

A   analysed by business segments and geographical segments

B   analysed by business segments

C   analysed by geographical segments

D   analysed by business segment and type of customer   **(2 marks)**

90   An entity is preparing a segmental analysis in accordance with IAS 14 *Segment Reporting*. The directors have elected to disclose business segments as the primary reporting format, but are unsure which of the following items need disclosure:

(i)   external revenue

(ii)   cost of sales

(iii)   capital employed

(iv)   segment profit.

Which TWO of the above require separate disclosure under IAS 14 in respect of segments reported as primary segments?

A   (i) and (ii) only

B   (i) and (iv) only

C   (i) and (iii) only

D   (iii) and (iv) only   **(2 marks)**

91   IAS 14 *Segment Reporting* requires an entity to select a primary and secondary segment reporting format.

CL has a number of different product groups and most of its trade is in Europe.

CQ has one major product and trades in a wide range of countries and cultural environments.

Which ONE of the following will CL and CQ select as primary and secondary segment formats?

	Primary reporting format		Secondary reporting format	
	CL	*CQ*	*CL*	*CQ*
A	Business segments	Business segments	Geographical segments	Geographical segments
B	Geographical segments	Geographical segments	Business segments	Business segments
C	Geographical segments	Business segments	Business segments	Geographical segments
D	Business segments	Geographical segments	Geographical segments	Business segments

(2 marks)

92   IAS 14 *Segment Reporting* requires segment information to be disclosed by publicly quoted entities.

List THREE criteria identified by IAS 14 to define a reportable business or geographical segment.   **(3 marks)**

93   IAS 18 *Revenue Recognition* defines when revenue may be recognised on the sale of goods.

List FOUR of the five conditions that IAS 18 requires to be met for income to be recognised.   **(4 marks)**

94   According to IAS 8, how should a material error in the previous financial reporting period be accounted for in the current period?

A   By making an adjustment in the financial statements of the current period through the income statement, and disclosing the nature of the error in a note

B   By making an adjustment in the financial statements of the current period as a movement on reserves, and disclosing the nature of the error in a note

C   By restating the comparative amounts for the previous period at their correct value, and disclosing the nature of the error in a note

D   By restating the comparative amounts for the previous period at their correct value, but without the requirement for a disclosure of the nature of the error in a note

(2 marks)

95   Which ONE of the following would be regarded as a change of accounting policy under IAS 8 *Accounting Policies, Changes in Accounting Estimates and Errors?*

A   An entity changes its method of depreciation of machinery from straight line to reducing balance

B   An entity has started capitalising borrowing costs for assets under the alternative treatment allowed by IAS 23 *Borrowing Costs*. The borrowing costs previously had been charged to income statement

C   An entity changes its method of calculating the provision for warranty claims on its products sold

D   An entity disclosed a contingent liability for a legal claim in the previous year's accounts. In the current year, a provision has been made for the same legal claim

(2 marks)

96   According to IAS 8, under what TWO circumstances is a change in accounting policy permitted?   **(4 marks)**

97   N prepares financial statements to 31 December each year. On 30 November 20X4, N entered into a binding commitment to close a division on 31 January 20X5. The closure was completed on schedule and the following transactions occurred during January 20X5:

(i)   N incurred closure costs of $4.2 million. $3 million of this figure was direct costs and $1.2 million was apportioned head office costs.

(ii)   The division made a small operating profit of $300,000.

(iii)   The division sold plant and made a loss on sale of $1,000,000. This fall in value had occurred before 31 December 20X4.

(iv)   The division sold properties and made a profit on sale of $2,000,000.

The 20X4 financial statements were approved by the directors on 20 February 20X5.

What should be the amount reported in the income statement of N for the year ended 31 December 20X4 in respect of the closure of the division, in compliance with IFRS 5 *Non-Current Assets Held for Sale and Discontinued Operations?*   **(4 marks)**

Data for Questions 98 and 99

DOC purchased property for $320,000 exactly 10 years ago. The land included in the price was valued at $120,000. The property was estimated to have a useful economic life of 20 years.

DOC has now had the property revalued (for the first time) by a professional valuer. The total value had increased to $800,000, the land now being valued at $200,000. The useful economic life remained unchanged.

98   What is the amount that should be credited to DOC's revaluation reserve?   **(2 marks)**

99   What should be the annual depreciation charge on the property in future years?

(2 marks)

100 Which of the following gives the best definition of *Property, Plant and Equipment*, based on the provisions of IAS 16?

A   Any assets held by an enterprise for more than one accounting period for use in the production or supply of goods or services, for rental to others, or for administrative purposes

B   Tangible assets held by an enterprise for more than 12 months for use in the production or supply of goods or services, for rental to others, or for administrative purposes

C   Tangible assets held by an enterprise for more than one accounting period for use in the production or supply of goods or services, for rental to others, or for administrative purposes

D   Any assets held by an enterprise for more than 12 months for use in the production or supply of goods or services, for rental to others, or for administrative purposes

(2 marks)

101 Which of the following items of expenditure incurred on an item of property, plant and equipment subsequent to its purchase should not be added to the carrying value of the asset?

A   The cost of servicing and overhauling

B   Modification to extend the useful life

C   Upgrading parts to achieve a significant improvement in the quality of output

D   Adoption of new production processes enabling a substantial reduction in previously assessed operating costs **(2 marks)**

102 MVZ has carried out a review of its property, plant and equipment at the end of its financial year. It has decided that there has been a significant change in the pattern of consumption of the future economic benefits for a particular group of assets, and has therefore decided to change the method of depreciation for those assets.

How should the change in depreciation method be accounted for?

A   As a change in accounting estimate and applied for the current year and in future years

B   As a change in accounting estimate and applied retrospectively as well as in future years

C   As a change in accounting policy and applied for the current year and in future years

D   As a change in accounting policy and applied retrospectively as well as in future years

(2 marks)

103 When the revaluation model is used for property, plant and equipment, what is the carrying value of the assets? (Answer in no more than 30 words.) **(2 marks)**

104 **Which of the following statements is correct?**

Statement 1: If the revaluation model is used for property, plant and equipment, revaluations must subsequently be made with sufficient regularity to ensure that the carrying amount does not differ materially from the fair value at each balance sheet date.

Statement 2: When an item of property, plant and equipment is revalued, there is no requirement that the entire class of assets to which the item belongs must be revalued.

A   Statement 1 only is correct

B   Statement 2 only is correct

C   Both statements are correct

D   Neither statement is correct   **(2 marks)**

105 **F's year-end is 30 June. F purchased a non-current asset for $50,000 on 1 July 20X2.**

Depreciation was provided at the rate of 20% per annum on the straight-line basis. There was no forecast residual value.

On 1 July 20X4, the asset was revalued to $60,000 and then depreciated on a straight-line basis over its remaining useful economic life which was unchanged. On 1 July 20X5, the asset was sold for $35,000.

In addition to the entries in the non-current asset account and provision for depreciation account, which TWO of the following statements correctly record the entries required on disposal of the non-current asset?

(i)   Debit income statement with a loss on disposal of $5,000.

(ii)   Credit income statement with a gain on disposal of $25,000.

(iii) Transfer $60,000 from revaluation reserve to accumulated profits as a movement on reserves.

(iv)   Transfer $30,000 from revaluation reserve to accumulated profits as a movement on reserves.

(v)   Transfer $30,000 from revaluation reserve to income statement.

(vi)   Transfer $60,000 from revaluation reserve to income statement.

A   (i) and (iv)

B   (ii) and (iii)

C   (i) and (v)

D   (ii) and (vi)   **(2 marks)**

106 Which ONE of the following items would CM recognise as subsequent expenditure on a non-current asset and capitalise it as required by IAS 16 *Property, Plant and Equipment*?

A   CM purchased a furnace five years ago, when the furnace lining was separately identified in the accounting records. The furnace now requires relining at a cost of $200,000. When the furnace is relined it will be able to be used in CM's business for a further five years.

B   CM's office building has been badly damaged by a fire. CM intends to restore the building to its original condition at a cost of $250,000.

C   CM's delivery vehicle broke down. When it was inspected by the repairers it was discovered that it needed a new engine. The engine and associated labour costs are estimated to be $5,000.

D   CM closes its factory for two weeks every year. During this time, all plant and equipment has its routine annual maintenance check and any necessary repairs are carried out. The cost of the current year's maintenance check and repairs was $75,000.

(2 marks)

107 DS purchased a machine on 1 October 20X2 at a cost of $21,000 with an expected useful economic life of six years, with no expected residual value. DS depreciates its machines using the straight line basis.

The machine has been used and depreciated for three years to 30 September 20X5. New technology was invented in December 20X5, which enabled a cheaper, more efficient machine to be produced; this technology makes DS's type of machine obsolete. The obsolete machine will generate no further economic benefit or have any residual value once the new machines become available. However, because of production delays, the new machines will not be available on the market until 1 October 20X7.

Calculate how much depreciation DS should charge to its income statement for the year ended 30 September 20X6, as required by IAS 16 *Property, Plant and Equipment*.

(3 marks)

108 An item of plant and equipment was purchased on 1 April 20X1 for $100,000. At the date of acquisition its expected useful economic life was ten years. Depreciation was provided on a straight line basis, with no residual value.

On 1 April 20X3, the asset was revalued to $95,000. On 1 April 20X4, the useful life of the asset was reviewed and the remaining useful economic life was reduced to five years, a total useful life of eight years.

Calculate the amounts that would be included in the balance sheet for the asset's cost/valuation and provision for accumulated depreciation at 31 March 20X5.   **(4 marks)**

109 IAS 16 *Property, Plant and Equipment* provides definitions of terms relevant to non-current assets. Complete the following sentence, in no more than 10 words.

'Depreciable amount is...'   **(2 marks)**

110 On 1 July 20X4, Experimenter opened a chemical reprocessing plant. The plant was due to be active for five years until 30 June 20X9, when it would be decommissioned. At 1 July 20X4, the costs of decommissioning the plant were estimated to be $4 million. The company considers that a discount rate of 12% is appropriate for the calculation of a present value, and the discount factor at 12% for Year 5 is 0.567.

What is the total charge to the income statement (depreciation and finance charge) in respect of the decommissioning for the year ended 30 June 20X5?

A $453,600

B $725,760

C $800,000

D $2,268,000 (3 marks)

111 IAS 2 *Inventories* specifies expenses that should be included in year-end inventory values. These could include:

(i) marketing and selling overhead

(ii) variable production overhead

(iii) general management overhead

(iv) accounting and finance overhead allocated to production

(v) cost of delivering raw materials to the factory

(vi) abnormal increase in overhead charges caused by unusually low production levels due to the exceptionally hot weather.

Which THREE of the above are allowable by IAS 2 as expenses that should be included in the cost of finished goods inventories?

A (i), (iii) and (v)

B (i), (ii) and (vi)

C (ii), (iv) and (v)

D (iii), (iv) and (vi) (2 marks)

112 IAS 2 *Inventories* states that when inventory is valued at cost, specific cost, FIFO and weighted average cost (calculated on a periodic basis or at each additional shipment) is required.

In no more than 30 words, state the rules in IAS 2 about the use of the following cost formulae for inventory:

(a) standard cost

(b) the retail method

(c) LIFO. (3 marks)

113 Neville has only two items of inventory on hand at its balance sheet date.

Item 1– Materials costing $24,000 bought for processing and assembly for a customer under a 'one off' order which is expected to produce a high profit margin. Since buying this material, the cost price has fallen to $20,000.

Item 2 – A machine constructed for another customer for a contracted price of $36,000. This has recently been completed at a cost of $33,600. It has now been discovered that, in order to meet certain health and safety regulations, modifications at an extra cost of $8,400 will be required. The customer has agreed to meet half the extra cost.

What should be the total value of these two items of inventory in the balance sheet?

(3 marks)

114 An entity purchased an item of property for $6 million on 1 July 20X3. The value of the land was $1 million and the buildings $5 million. The expected life of the building was 50 years and its residual value nil. On 30 June 20X5 the property was revalued to $7 million (land $1.24 million, buildings $5.76 million). On 30 June 20X7, the property was sold for $6.8 million.

What is the gain on disposal of the property that would be reported in the income statement for the year to 30 June 20X7?

A   Gain $40,000

B   Gain $240,000

C   Gain $1,000,000

D   Gain $1,240,000   **(2 marks)**

Data for Questions 115 and 116

X acquired the business and assets from the owners of an unincorporated business: the purchase price was satisfied by the issue of 10,000 equity shares with a nominal value of $10 each and $20,000 cash. The market value of X shares at the date of acquisition was $20 each.

The assets acquired were:

•   net tangible non-current assets with a book value of $20,000 and a current value of $25,000

•   patents for a specialised process valued by a specialist valuer at $15,000

•   brand name, valued by a specialist brand valuer on the basis of a multiple of earnings at $50,000

•   publishing rights of the first text from an author that the management of X expects to become a best seller. The publishing rights were a gift from the author to the previous owners at no cost. The management of X has estimated the future value of the potential best seller at $100,000. However, there is no reliable evidence available to support the estimate of the management.

---

115 In no more than 30 words, explain the accounting treatment to be used for the publishing rights of the first text.   **(2 marks)**

116 Calculate the value of goodwill to be included in the accounts of X for this purchase.

(4 marks)

117 IAS 38 *Intangible Assets* sets out six criteria that must be met before an internally generated intangible asset can be recognised.

List FOUR of IAS 38's criteria for recognition. **(4 marks)**

118 **Which of the following statements does not comply with standard accounting practice in respect of the accounting treatment of purchased goodwill?**

   A   If there is an impairment in value of purchased goodwill, the amount of the impairment should be taken directly to the reserves and not through the income statement

   B   Purchased goodwill should not be revalued upwards

   C   Purchased goodwill, insofar as it has not been written off, should be shown as a separate item under non-current assets in the balance sheet

   D   Purchased goodwill should not be amortised **(2 marks)**

119 **The information below refers to three non-current assets of IDLE as at 31 March 20X5:**

	A	*B*	*C*
	$000	$000	$000
Carrying value	200	300	240
Net selling price	220	250	200
Value in use	240	260	180

What is the total impairment loss? **(3 marks)**

120 **CI purchased equipment on 1 April 20X2 for $100,000. The equipment was depreciated using the reducing balance method at 25% per year. CI's balance sheet date is 31 March.**

Depreciation was charged up to and including 31 March 20X6. At that date, the recoverable amount was $28,000.

Calculate the impairment loss on the equipment according to IAS 36 *Impairment of Assets*.

(3 marks)

121 **The following measures relate to a non-current asset:**

   (i)   net book value $20,000

   (ii)   net realisable value $18,000

   (iii) value in use $22,000

   (iv)   replacement cost $50,000.

The recoverable amount of the asset is:

   A $18,000

   B $20,000

   C $22,000

   D $50,000 **(2 marks)**

PAPER P7 : FINANCIAL ACCOUNTING AND TAX PRINCIPLES

122 On 1 January Year 1, an entity purchased an item of equipment costing $76,000. The asset is depreciated using the reducing balance method, at a rate of 20% each year. After three years, an impairment review establishes that the asset has a value in use of $30,000 and a disposal value (less selling costs) of $27,000.

What is the amount of the impairment loss that should be written off in the income statement for the year to 31 December Year 3? **(3 marks)**

123 A company has been carrying out work on the design and testing of a new product. The work began in May 20X1 and it is now the end of 20X3. From 31 December 20X1, the project to develop the new product met all the criteria in IAS 38 for the development costs to be recognised as an intangible asset.

The recoverable amount of the 'know-how' embodied in the development work has been estimated as follows:

At 31 December 20X1:	$400,000
At 31 December 20X2:	$1,500,000
At 31 December 20X3:	$2,000,000

The costs incurred on the project have been as follows:

Year to 31 December 20X1:	$500,000
Year to 31 December 20X2:	$1,000,000
Year to 31 December 20X3:	$1,200,000

For the year to 31 December 20X3, what expense should be charged in the income statement for the costs of the development project? **(3 marks)**

124 A publishing company is developing a new reference book on national art treasures. The project to produce and publish the book began on 1 April 20X4, with a planned publishing date of September 20X5. The book is expected to sell for at least three years after publication, and to be very profitable.

The accounting year of the company ends on 30 June. The following costs had been incurred on the project in the years to 30 June 20X4 and 20X5.

	Year to 30 June 20X4	Year to 30 June 20X5
	$	$
Author's advance fees	20,000	30,000
Editing	0	60,000
Artwork	5,000	20,000

What should be the value in the balance sheet of the work on developing the new book, in compliance with IAS 38?

A   Nil

B $85,000

C $110,000

D $135,000 **(2 marks)**

125 S announced a rights issue of 1 for every 5 shares currently held, at a price of $2 each. S currently has 2,000,000 $1 ordinary shares with a quoted market price of $2.50 each. Directly attributable issue costs amounted to $25,000.

Assuming all rights are taken up and all money paid in full, how much will be credited to the share premium account for the rights issue? **(2 marks)**

30

KAPLAN PUBLISHING

126 At 1 January 20X5 CR had 2,000,000 ordinary shares of 25 cents each in issue. The company's only reserve at this date was accumulated profits amounting to $500,000.

On 1 May 20X5 the company made a one for two bonus issue.

On 1 September 20X5 the company made a one for three rights issue at a price of 40c. All shares in the issue were taken up.

What figures will appear in the capital and reserves section of the balance sheet as at 31 December 20X4?

	Issued share capital	*Share premium*	*Retained profits*
A	$1,150,000	Nil	$250,000
B	$1,000,000	Nil	$400,000
C	$1,000,000	$150,000	$250,000
D	$1,000,000	$250,000	$150,000

(2 marks)

127 A company has issued share capital of 20 million shares of $1 each. The shares were all issued five years ago at a price of $2.25 per share. The company has now purchased 100,000 of its own shares in the stock market for $4 each, and has cancelled them.

Prior to the share repurchase, the accumulated profits of the company were $10,000,000. The national law requires that when equity shares are purchased and cancelled, the company must create a capital reserve equal to the nominal value of the shares cancelled, to maintain the company's capital.

What is the balance on the accumulated profits reserve account after this share repurchase transaction? **(4 marks)**

128 R issued 500,000 new $1 equity shares on 1 April 20X4. The issue price of the shares was $1.50 per share. Applicants paid $0.20 per share with their applications and a further $0.80 per share on allotment. All money was received on time.

A final call of $0.50 per share was made on 31 January 20X5. One holder of 5,000 shares failed to pay the call by the due date and the shares were forfeited. The forfeited shares were reissued for $1 per share on 31 March 20X5.

Which of the following is the correct set of accounting entries to record the re-issue of the forfeited shares?

	Investment in own shares account	*Bank account*	*Investment in own shares account*	*Share premium account*
A	$5,000 credit	$5,000 debit	$2,500 debit	$2,500 credit
B	$5,000 credit	$5,000 debit	0	0
C	$5,000 credit	$5,000 debit	$2,500 credit	$2,500 debit
D	$5,000 debit	$5,000 credit	$2,500 credit	$2,500 debit

(2 marks)

129 IAS 32 *Financial Instruments: Disclosure and Presentation* classifies issued shares as either equity instruments or financial liabilities. An entity has the following categories of funding on its balance sheet:

(i) A preference share that is redeemable for cash at a 10% premium on 30 May 20X5.

(ii) An ordinary share which is not redeemable and has no restrictions on receiving dividends.

(iii) A loan note that is redeemable at par in 20Y0.

(iv) A cumulative preference share that is entitled to receive a dividend of 7% a year.

Applying IAS 32, how would EACH of the above be categorised on the balance sheet?

	As an equity instrument	*As a financial liability*
A	(i) and (ii)	(iii) and (iv)
B	(ii) and (iii)	(i) and (iv)
C	(ii)	(i), (iii) and (iv)
D	(i), (ii) and (iii)	(iv)

(2 marks)

130 BN is a listed entity and has the following balances included on its opening balance sheet:

	$000
Equity and reserves:	
Equity shares, $1 shares, fully paid	750
Share premium	250
Retained earnings	500
	1,500

BN reacquired 100,000 of its shares and classified them as 'treasury shares'. BN still held the treasury shares at the year end.

How should BN classify the treasury shares on its closing balance sheet in accordance with IAS 32 *Financial Instruments: Disclosure and Presentation?*

A   As a non-current asset investment

B   As a deduction from equity

C   As a current asset investment

D   As a non-current liability **(2 marks)**

131 Which of the statements below gives the best explanation of the objective of IAS 24 *Related Party Disclosures*?

The objective of IAS 24 is to:

A   regulate the price at which transactions between related parties take place

B   draw attention to the possibility that the financial statements may have been affected by material transactions with related parties

C   place a limit on the number of related party transactions which may take place in an accounting period

D   ensure that companies disclose the number of related party transactions taking place during an accounting period **(2 marks)**

132 **Which ONE of the following would be regarded as a related party of BS?**

    A   BX, a customer of BS

    B   The president of the BS Board, who is also the chief executive officer of another entity, BU, that supplies goods to BS

    C   BQ, a supplier of BS

    D   BY, BS's main banker   **(2 marks)**

133 **IAS 24 *Related Party Disclosures* deals with related parties of an organisation.**

Which of the following would be presumed to be a related party of an enterprise?

    A   A major customer whose purchases account for 30% of the enterprise's annual sales

    B   A shareholder holding 25% of the enterprise's equity

    C   A manager of the bank providing a loan to the enterprise

    D   Employees of the enterprise   **(2 marks)**

134 **BL started a contract on 1 November 20X4. The contract was scheduled to run for two years and has a sales value of $40 million.**

At 31 October 20X5, the following details were obtained from BL's records:

	$m
Costs incurred to date	16
Estimated costs to completion	18
Percentage complete at 31 October 20X5	45%

Applying IAS 11 *Construction Contracts*, how much revenue and profit should BL recognise in its income statement for the year ended 31 October 20X5?   **(2 marks)**

Data for Questions 135 and 136

B entered into a three-year contract to build a leisure centre for an enterprise. The contract value was $6 million. B recognises profit on the basis of certified work completed. At the end of the first year, the following figures were extracted from B's accounting records:

	$000
Certified value of work completed (progress payments billed)	2,000
Cost of work certified as complete	1,650
Cost of work-in-progress (not included in completed work)	550
Estimated cost of remaining work required to complete the contract	2,750
Progress payments received from enterprise	1,600
Cash paid to suppliers for work on the contract	1,300

---

135 **How much profit should B recognise in its income statement at the end of the first year?**

                                                              (2 marks)

136 What values should B record for this contract as 'gross amounts due from customers' and 'current liabilities – trade and other payables'?

	Gross amounts due from customers	*Current liabilities – trade and other payables*
A	$950,000	$350,000
B	$950,000	$900,000
C	$1,250,000	$600,000
D	$2,550,000	$900,000

(2 marks)

Data for Questions 137 and 138

CN started a three-year contract to build a new university campus on 1 April 20X4. The contract had a fixed price of $90 million.

CN incurred costs to 31 March 20X6 of $77 million and estimated that a further $33 million would need to be spent to complete the contract.

CN uses the percentage of cost incurred to date to total cost method to calculate stage of completion of the contract.

137 Calculate revenue earned on the contract to 31 March 20X6, according to IAS 11 *Construction Contracts*.   (2 marks)

138 State how much gross profit/loss CN should recognise in its income statement for the year ended 31 March 20X6, according to IAS 11 *Construction Contracts*.   (2 marks)

139 Which of the following gives the best definition of *Events after the Balance Sheet Date* as set out in IAS 10 ?

A   Those events, both favourable and unfavourable, which occur between the balance sheet date and the date on which the financial statements are approved by the shareholders

B   Those events, both favourable and unfavourable, which occur between the balance sheet date and the date of the auditor's report

C   Those events, both favourable and unfavourable, which occur between the balance sheet date and the date on which the financial statements are authorised for issue

D   Those unfavourable events which occur between the balance sheet date and the date on which the financial statements are authorised for issue   (2 marks)

140 Which of the following events after the balance sheet date are likely to be 'adjusting' events?

  (i) A write down of inventory held at the year-end

  (ii) Settlement of an insurance claim in the process of negotiation at the balance sheet date

  (iii) The issue of additional share capital

  (iv) The acquisition of a new business

  A (i) and (ii) only

  B (iii) and (iv) only

  C All four of the events

  D None of the events   **(2 marks)**

141 In the context of IAS 37 *Provisions, Contingent Liabilities and Contingent Assets*, which of the following statements are correct?

  (i) Provisions may be recognised for future operating losses.

  (ii) If a contingent asset is considered to be 'probable', disclosure should be made in a note.

  (iii) If a contingent liability is considered to be 'probable', a disclosure should be made in a note.

  A Statement (i) only

  B Statement (ii) only

  C Statements (ii) and (iii) only

  D Statement (iii) only   **(2 marks)**

142 List the THREE criteria set out in IAS 37 *Provisions, Contingent Liabilities and Contingent Assets* for the recognition of a provision.   **(3 marks)**

143 AP has the following two legal claims outstanding:

  • A legal action claiming compensation of $500,000 filed against AP in March 20X4.

  • A legal action taken by AP against a third party, claiming damages of $200,000 was started in January 20X3 and is nearing completion.

  In both cases, it is more likely than not that the amount claimed will have to be paid.

  How should AP report these legal actions in its financial statements for the year ended 31 March 20X5?

	Legal action against AP	*Legal action by AP*
A	Disclose by a note	No disclosure
B	Make a provision	No disclosure
C	Make a provision	Disclosure as a note
D	Make a provision	Accrue the income

                                                          (2 marks)

144 Which ONE of the following would be treated as a non-adjusting event after the balance sheet date, as required by IAS 10 *Events after the Balance Sheet Date*, in the financial statements of AN for the period ended 31 January 20X5? The financial statements were approved for publication on 15 May 20X5.

A   Notice was received on 31 March 20X5 that a major customer of AN had ceased trading and was unlikely to make any further payments.

B   Inventory items at 31 January 20X5, original cost $30,000, were sold in April 20X5 for $20,000.

C   During 20X4, a customer commenced legal action against AN. At 31 January 20X5, legal advisers were of the opinion that AN would lose the case, so AN created a provision of $200,000 for the damages claimed by the customer. On 27 April 20X5, the court awarded damages of $250,000 to the customer.

D   There was a fire on 2 May 20X5 in AN's main warehouse which destroyed 50% of AN's total inventory.   **(2 marks)**

145 Using the requirements set out in IAS 10 *Events after the Balance Sheet Date*, which of the following would be classified as an adjusting post balance sheet event in financial statements ended 31 March 20X4 that were approved by the directors on 31 August 20X4?

A   A reorganisation of the enterprise, proposed by a director on 31 January 20X4 and agreed by the Board on 10 July 20X4.

B   A strike by the workforce which started on 1 May 20X4 and stopped all production for 10 weeks before being settled.

C   A claim on an insurance policy for damage caused by a fire in a warehouse on 1 January 20X4. No provision had been made for the receipt of insurance money at 31 March 20X4 as it was uncertain that any money would be paid. The insurance enterprise settled with a payment of $1.5 million on 1 June 20X4.

D   The enterprise had made large export sales to the USA during the year. The year end receivables included $2 million for amounts outstanding that were due to be paid in US dollars between 1 April 20X4 and 1 July 20X4. By the time these amounts were received, the exchange rate had moved in favour of the enterprise and the equivalent of $2.5 million was actually received.   **(2 marks)**

146 Which ONE of the following would require a provision to be created by BW at its balance sheet date of 31 October 20X5?

A   The government introduced new laws on data protection which come into force on 1 January 20X6. BW's directors have agreed that this will require a large number of staff to be retrained. At 31 October 20X5, the directors were waiting on a report they had commissioned that would identify the actual training requirements.

B   At the balance sheet date, BW is negotiating with its insurance provider about the amount of an insurance claim that it had filed. On 20 November 20X5, the insurance provider agreed to pay $200,000.

C   BW makes refunds to customers for any goods returned within 30 days of sale, and has done so for many years.

D   A customer is suing BW for damages alleged to have been caused by BW's product. BW is contesting the claim and, at 31 October 20X5, the directors have been advised by BW's legal advisers it is very unlikely to lose the case.   **(2 marks)**

147 **DT's final dividend for the year ended 31 October 20X5 of $150,000 was declared on 1 February 20X6 and paid in cash on 1 April 20X6. The financial statements were approved on 31 March 20X6.**

The following statements refer to the treatment of the dividend in the accounts of DT:

(i)   The payment clears an accrued liability set up in the balance sheet as at 31 October 20X5.

(ii)   The dividend is shown as a deduction in the income statement for the year ended 31 October 20X6.

(iii)   The dividend is shown as an accrued liability in the balance sheet as at 31 October 20X6.

(iv)   The $150,000 dividend was shown in the notes to the financial statements at 31 October 20X5.

(v)   The dividend is shown as a deduction in the statement of changes in equity for the year ended 31 October 20X6.

Which of the above statements reflect the correct treatment of the dividend?

A   (i) and (ii)

B   (i) and (iv)

C   (iii) and (v)

D   (iv) and (v)   **(2 marks)**

148 **An item of machinery leased under a five-year finance lease on 1 October 20X3 had a fair value of $51,900 at date of purchase.**

The lease payments were $12,000 per year, payable in arrears.

If the sum of digits method is used to apportion interest to accounting periods, calculate the finance cost for the year ended 30 September 20X5.   **(3 marks)**

149 **Z entered into a finance lease agreement on 1 November 20X2. The lease was for five years, the fair value of the asset acquired was $45,000 and the interest rate implicit in the lease was 7%. The annual payment was $10,975 in arrears.**

The total amount owing under the lease at 31 October 20X4 was:

A $27,212

B $28,802

C $29,350

D $40,108   **(2 marks)**

150 **The definition of a finance lease under IAS 17 is:**

A   a lease under which the present value of the future lease payments is 90% or more of the fair value of the leased asset

B   a lease covering at least 75% of the useful economic life of the leased asset

C   a lease which contains an option to purchase the asset at the end of the lease period

D   a lease that transfers substantially all the risks and rewards incident to ownership of an asset   **(2 marks)**

Data for Questions 151 and 152

CS acquired a machine, using a finance lease, on 1 January 20X4. The machine had an expected useful life of 12,000 operating hours, after which it would have no residual value.

The finance lease was for a five-year term with rentals of $20,000 per year payable in arrears.

The cost price of the machine was $80,000 and the implied interest rate is 7.93% per year. CS used the machine for 2,600 hours in 20X4 and 2,350 hours in 20X5.

151   Using the actuarial method, calculate the non-current liability and current liability figures required by IAS 17 *Leases* to be shown in CS's balance sheet at 31 December 20X5.   **(3 marks)**

152   Calculate the non-current asset – property, plant and equipment net book value that would be shown in CS's balance sheet at 31 December 20X5. Calculate the depreciation charge using the machine hours method.   **(2 marks)**

MANAGING SHORT-TERM FINANCE

153   If an entity regularly fails to pay its suppliers by the normal due dates, it may lead to a number of problems:

(i)   having insufficient cash to settle trade payables

(ii)   difficulty in obtaining credit from new suppliers

(iii)   reduction in credit rating

(iv)   settlement of trade receivables may be delayed.

Which TWO of the above could arise as a result of exceeding suppliers' trade credit terms?

A   (i) and (ii)

B   (i) and (iii)

C   (ii) and (iii)

D   (iii) and (iv)   **(2 marks)**

154   A conservative policy for financing working capital is one where short-term finance is used to fund:

A   all of the fluctuating current assets, but no part of the permanent current assets

B   all of the fluctuating current assets and part of the permanent current assets

C   part of the fluctuating current assets and part of the permanent current assets

D   part of the fluctuating current assets, but no part of the permanent current assets

(2 marks)

155   ABC has produced the following sales forecast:

	$000
January	750
February	760
March	770
April	780
May	790
June	800

Currently 20% of customers pay in cash. Of the credit customers (excluding those who become irrecoverable debts), 60% pay in one month, 30% pay in two months and 10% in three months. Irrecoverable debts are 2%. This payment pattern is expected to continue.

What are the forecast cash receipts in April?   **(3 marks)**

156   If the current ratio for a company is equal to its acid test (that is, the quick ratio), then:

A   the current ratio must be greater than one

B   the company does not carry any inventory

C   trade receivables plus cash is greater than trade payables minus inventory

D   working capital is positive   **(2 marks)**

157   In October, a company made credit purchases of $18,000 and credit sales of $24,000. All sales are made on the basis of cost plus 25%. By how much will working capital increase in October as a result of these transactions?   **(2 marks)**

158   The following items have been extracted from a company's budget for next month:

	$
Sales on credit	240,000
Expected increase in inventory next month	20,000
Expected decrease in trade receivables next month	12,000

What is the budgeted receipt from trade receivables next month?   **(3 marks)**

159   DY had a balance outstanding on trade receivables at 30 September 20X6 of $68,000. Forecast credit sales for the next six months are $250,000 and customers are expected to return goods with a sales value of $2,500.

Based on past experience, within the next six months DY expects to collect $252,100 cash and to write off as irrecoverable debts 5% of the balance outstanding at 30 September 20X6.

Calculate DY's forecast trade receivables days outstanding at 31 March 20X7.   **(4 marks)**

160 A company has annual sales of $40 million, annual cost of sales of $30 million and makes annual purchases of $15 million. Its balance sheet includes among assets and liabilities the following:

Trade receivables $4 million
Trade payables $3 million
Inventory $8 million

What is its cash conversion cycle?

A   206.5 days

B   60.8 days

C   36.5 days

D   97.3 days   **(2 marks)**

161 XYZ's annual sales are $100m of which 95% are made on credit. Receivables at the beginning of the year were $10 million and at the end of the year total receivables were $12 million. 10% of receivables were non-trade related.

What is XYZ's average collection period?

A   36.5 days

B   40 days

C   38 days

D   46 days   **(2 marks)**

162 AC is a new company, whose directors have approached its bank for financial assistance. The bank has asked for draft income statement and balance sheet information to support the request for finance. The only information the directors have available is an estimate of sales for the first year, together with some industry averages for the current year.

	Industry averages
Cost of sales to sales	50%
Sales to capital employed	2.5 times
Non-current assets to capital employed	70%
Current ratio	1.5:1
Estimated sales for the year	$760,000

In the draft balance sheet for AC, what would be the total of current assets?   **(3 marks)**

163 The following items were extracted from a company's budget for next month:

	$
Purchases on credit	360,000
Expected decrease in inventory during the month	12,000
Expected increase in trade payables during the month	15,000

What is the budgeted payment to trade creditors for the month?

A $333,000

B $345,000

C $357,000

D $375,000   **(2 marks)**

164 The directors of J are applying for a bank overdraft facility. In the application the directors have to supply an estimate for their working capital needs. Forecasts are:

Gross profit to sales	30%
20X4 Purchases	$600,000
20X4 Opening inventory	2 months' worth of 20X4 purchases
20X4 Closing inventory	1½ times opening inventory
Average period for customers to pay	3 months
Average period to pay suppliers	1½ months

What is the forecast working capital at the end of 20X4? Ignore any holdings of cash or cash equivalents. **(3 marks)**

165 A company has a current ratio of 2:1. Due to having significant surplus cash balances, it has decided to pay its trade payable accounts after 30 days in future, rather than after 50 days as it has in the past.

What will be the effect of this change on the company's current ratio and its cash operating cycle?

	Current ratio	*Cash operating cycle*
A	Increase	Increase
B	Increase	Decrease
C	Decrease	Increase
D	Decrease	Decrease

(2 marks)

166 DX had the following balances in its trial balance at 30 September 20X6:

Trial balance extract at 30 September 20X6

	$000	$000
Revenue		2,400
Cost of sales	1,400	
Inventories	360	
Trade receivables	290	
Trade payables		190
Cash and cash equivalents	95	

Calculate the length of DX's working capital cycle at 30 September 20X6. **(4 marks)**

167 An enterprise commenced business on 1 April 20X2. Revenue in April 20X2 was $20,000, but this is expected to increase at 2% a month. Credit sales amount to 60% of total sales. The credit period allowed is one month. Irrecoverable debts are expected to be 3% of credit sales, but other customers are expected to pay on time. Cash sales represent the other 40% of revenue.

How much cash is expected to be received in May 20X2? **(3 marks)**

168   Which of the following is LEAST likely to characterise overtrading?

   A   Increased borrowing

   B   Increased cash balances

   C   Increased turnover

   D   Reduced working capital   **(2 marks)**

169   An aged creditors analysis (aged trade payables analysis) is:

   A   a listing of trade payables by date of invoicing

   B   a listing of trade payables with whom you are in arrears

   C   the proportion of purchases by value which are overdue

   D   a breakdown of trade payables according to length of time elapsing since the purchase
       was made   **(2 marks)**

170   Examine the validity of the following statements with respect to the Miller-Orr cash-management model.

   Statement 1: The greater the variability in cash flows, the greater is the spread between the upper and lower cash balance limits.

   Statement 2: The return point is the lower limit plus one-third of the spread.

	Statement 1	Statement 2
A	True	False
B	True	True
C	False	False
D	False	True

                                                                                   (2 marks)

171   XYZ maintains a minimum cash holding of $10,000. The standard deviation of its daily cash flows is $4,000. The transaction cost per sale or purchase of marketable securities is $40. The daily interest rate is 0.04% per day.

   Using the Miller-Orr cash management model, calculate the upper limit to the cash holdings of XYZ, to the nearest $1,000.   **(3 marks)**

172   CT uses the Miller-Orr cash management model to help manage cash flows. The management accountant has agreed with the directors that the lower limit for cash will be $2,500.

   The current rate of interest that CT pays is 0.025% per day. Each transaction costs CT $30. CT's daily cash flows have been measured and the variance calculated as $300,000.

   Calculate, for CT, the Miller-Orr return point and upper limit.   **(3 marks)**

173   A company uses the Baumol cash-management model. Cash disbursements are constant at $20,000 each month. Money on deposit earns 5% a year, while money in the current account earns a zero return. Switching costs (that is, for each purchase or sale of securities) are $30 for each transaction.

   What is the optimal amount (to the nearest $100) to be transferred in each transaction?

                                                                                   (2 marks)

174 WM's major supplier, INT, supplies electrical tools and is one of the largest companies in the industry, with international operations. Deliveries from INT are currently made monthly, and are constant throughout the year. Delivery and invoicing both occur in the last week of each month.

Details of the credit terms offered by INT are as follows:

Normal credit period	*Cash discount*	*Average monthly purchases*
40 days	2% for settlement in 10 days	$100,000

WM always takes advantage of the cash discount from INT.

Calculate the annual rate of interest (to two decimal places) implied in the cash discount offered by INT. Assume a 365-day year. **(3 marks)**

175 FGH requires a rate of return of 12.85% each year.

Two of FGH's suppliers, P and Q, are offering the following terms for immediate cash settlement:

Supplier	*Cash settlement discount*	*Normal settlement period*
P	1%	1 month
Q	2%	2 months

Which of the discounts should be accepted to achieve the required rate of return?

A   The discounts offered by both P and Q

B   The discount offered by P only

C   The discount offered by Q only

D   Neither of them   **(2 marks)**

176 What are the three main services provided by a without recourse factor?   **(3 marks)**

177 SK sells bathroom fittings throughout the country in which it operates. In order to obtain the best price, it has decided to purchase all its annual demand of 10,000 shower units from a single supplier. RR has offered to provide the required number of showers each year under an exclusive long-term contract.

Demand for shower units is at a constant rate all year. The cost to SK of holding one shower unit in inventory for one year is $4 plus 3% of the purchase price.

RR is located only a few miles from the SK main showroom. It has offered to supply each shower unit at $400 with a transport charge of $200 per delivery. It has guaranteed such a regular and prompt delivery service that SK believes it will not be necessary to hold any safety inventory (that is, buffer inventory) if it uses RR as its supplier.

Using the economic order quantity model (EOQ model), calculate the optimal order size, assuming that RR is chosen as the sole supplier of shower units for SK.   **(3 marks)**

178 Which of the following would be LEAST likely to arise from the introduction of a Just-in-Time inventory ordering system?

A   Lower inventory holding costs

B   Less risk of inventory shortages

C   More frequent deliveries

D   Increased dependence on suppliers   **(2 marks)**

179 Which of the following is LEAST relevant to the simple economic order quantity (EOQ) model for inventory?

A   Safety stock

B   Annual demand

C   Holding costs

D   Order costs   **(2 marks)**

180 A company uses the economic order quantity model (that is, the EOQ model) to manage inventory.

Situation 1 – interest rates rise.

Situation 2 – sales volumes increase.

What would happen to the economic order quantity in each of these two situations?

	Situation 1	*Situation 2*
A	Increase	Increase
B	Increase	Decrease
C	Decrease	Increase
D	Decrease	Decrease

                                                                                (2 marks)

181 PB uses 2,500 units of component X per year. Its production director has calculated that the cost of placing and processing a purchase order for component X is $185, and the cost of holding one unit of component X for a year is $25.

What is the economic order quantity (EOQ) for component X and, assuming a 52-week year, what is the average frequency at which purchase orders should be placed?

	EOQ	*Frequency of orders*
A	136 units	3 weeks
B	136 units	6 weeks
C	192 units	4 weeks
D	192 units	5 weeks

                                                                                (2 marks)

182 Calculate the economic order quantity (EOQ) for the following item of inventory:

- quantity required per year 32,000 items

- order costs are $15 per order

- inventory holding costs are estimated at 3% of inventory value per year

- each unit currently costs $40.   **(2 marks)**

183   Invoice discounting normally involves:

    A   offering a cash discount for early settlement of invoices

    B   selling an invoice to a discount house at a profit

    C   selling an individual invoice for cash to a factor organisation at a discount

    D   writing off an invoice, partly or in total, as an irrecoverable debt   **(2 marks)**

184   Four investments are available:

- Investment A pays interest of 1.6% every 3 months
- Investment B pays interest of 3.5% every 6 months
- Investment C pays interest of 5.2% every 9 months
- Investment D pays interest of 7.0% every 12 months

Which investment gives the best annual rate of return?

    A   Investment A

    B   Investment B

    C   Investment C

    D   Investment D   **(2 marks)**

185   **XYZ has $1 million to invest for one year. It can lock it away at a fixed rate of 7% for the full year, or invest at 6.5% for a three-month term, speculating on an increase in interest rates. Assume the rate available increases to 7.5% after three months and XYZ invests at this rate for the rest of the year.**

By how much is XYZ better off from its gamble on interest rates?

    A $2,500

    B $12,836

    C $73,414

    D $3,414   **(2 marks)**

186   Which ONE of the following statements about certificates of deposits is NOT true?

    A   Certificates of deposit are issued by banks

    B   Certificates of deposit will typically have maturity periods of between one month and five years

    C   Certificates of deposit are non-negotiable

    D   Certificates of deposit are issued in bearer form   **(2 marks)**

187   Which of the following are NOT true about bills of exchange?

    A   The payee must be a specified person

    B   A bill is made out by the drawer

    C   A bill must be paid by the drawee

    D   A bill can be discounted with a bank   **(2 marks)**

188 After a bill of exchange has been accepted, there are a number of possible actions that the drawer could take.

Which ONE of the following is NOT a possible course of action?

A Ask the customer for immediate payment

B Discount the bill with a bank

C Hold the bill until the due date and then present it for payment

D Use the bill to settle a trade payable   (2 marks)

189 The bank accepts the instrument drawn upon it by its customer, and then sells it into a secondary market at a discount, including a commission, passing the proceeds to its client. The bank then pays the bill at face value. Which description best describes this instrument?

A A letter of credit

B A forfaiting agreement

C An acceptance credit

D A commercial bill   (2 marks)

190 Which of the following most appropriately describes *forfaiting*?

A It is a method of providing medium-term export finance

B It provides short-term finance for purchasing fixed assets which are denominated in a foreign currency

C It provides long-term finance to importers

D It is the forced surrender of a share due to the failure to make a payment on a partly paid share   (2 marks)

191 List FOUR forms of short-term finance generally available to small entities.   (4 marks)

192 A bond with a coupon rate of 7% is redeemable in eight years' time for $100. Its current purchase price is $82. What is the percentage yield to maturity?   (4 marks)

193 AL's customers all pay their accounts at the end of 30 days. To try and improve its cash flow, AL is considering offering all customers a 15% discount for payment within 14 days.

Calculate the implied annual (interest) cost to AL of offering the discount, using compound interest methodology and assuming a 365-day year.   (3 marks)

194   The economic order quantity formula includes the cost of placing an order. However, the Management Accountant is unsure which of the following items should be included in 'cost of placing an order':

(i)   administrative costs

(ii)   postage

(iii)   quality control cost

(iv)   unit cost of products

(v)   storekeeper's salary.

Which THREE of the above would usually be regarded as part of the cost of placing an order?

A   (i), (ii) and (iii) only

B   (i), (iv) and (v) only

C   (ii), (iii) and (iv) only

D   (i), (ii) and (v) only   **(2 marks)**

195   An entity's working capital financing policy is to finance working capital using short-term financing to fund all the fluctuating current assets as well as some of the permanent part of the current assets.

The above policy is an example of:

A   an aggressive policy

B   a conservative policy

C   a short-term policy

D   a moderate policy   **(2 marks)**

196   BE has been offering 60-day payment terms to its customers, but now wants to improve its cash flow. BE is proposing to offer a 1.5% discount for payment within 20 days.

Assume a 365-day year and an invoice value of $1,000.

What is the effective annual interest rate that BE will incur for this action?   **(4 marks)**

197   CX purchased $10,000 of unquoted bonds when they were issued by Z. CX now wishes to sell the bonds to B. The bonds have a coupon rate of 7% and will repay their face value at the end of five years. Similar bonds have a yield to maturity of 10%.

Calculate the current market price for the bonds.   **(3 marks)**

198 The trade receivables ledger account for customer C shows the following entries:

		Debits	*Credits*
		$	$
Balance brought forward		0	
10 June X6	Invoice 201	345	
19 June X6	Invoice 225	520	
27 June X6	Invoice 241	150	
3 July X6	Receipt 1009 – Inv 201		200
10 July X6	Invoice 311	233	
4 August X6	Receipt 1122 – Inv 225		520
6 August X6	Invoice 392	197	
18 August X6	Invoice 420	231	
30 August X6	Receipt 1310 – Inv 311		233
7 September X6	Invoice 556	319	
21 September X6	Receipt 1501 – Inv 392		197
30 September X6	Balance	845	

Prepare an aged analysis showing the outstanding balance on a monthly basis for customer C at 30 September 20X6. **(4 marks)**

199 DK is considering investing in government bonds. The current price of a $100 bond with 10 years to maturity is $88. The bonds have a coupon rate of 6% and repay face value of $100 at the end of the 10 years.

Calculate the yield to maturity. **(4 marks)**

SECTION B-TYPE QUESTIONS

PRINCIPLES OF BUSINESS TAXATION

200 SALES TAX

A sales tax is collected by the businesses that sell the products or services subject to tax. Businesses are liable to the tax authorities for the sales tax on their outputs, less a credit for sales tax paid on their inputs.

Required:

Explain how this system ensures that the full burden of the sales tax falls on the end consumer, and explain how the system differs when the products or services sold by a business are:

(a)   taxed at 0%

(b)   exempt from the sales tax.   **(5 marks)**

201 TAX COLLECTORS FOR THE GOVERNMENT

You are the management accountant in an entity that has recently appointed a new non-executive director, who is unfamiliar with taxation and is surprised that the entity is involved in collecting tax as well as paying tax on its own profits.

Required:

Write a short memo to the non-executive director explaining:

(a)   the various ways in which a business might be required to assist the government in collecting tax

(b)   the reason or reasons why dividends paid to shareholders are non-allowable for tax purposes, whereas interest payments normally are.   **(5 marks)**

202 LOSS RELIEF

Explain why rules are needed for the relief of losses by business entities.   **(5 marks)**

203 EXCESS TAX

Explain why a business entity might provide for more tax in a particular year than it should actually be liable to pay, and how this excess provision of tax is dealt with:

(a)   by the tax authorities, and

(b)   in the financial statements of the business entity.   **(5 marks)**

204 DIVIDENDS

Taxit makes a profit of $5,000,000, out of which it pays a dividend of $2,400,000 to its shareholders. The taxation on profits is at the rate of 40%, and shareholders are taxed on their income at 40% income.

There are various different approaches to the taxation of dividends on business profits. These include:

(a)   the classical system

(b)   the full imputation system

(c)   the partial imputation system.

Required:

Explain the difference between these three taxation systems, illustrating your answer with reference to the profits and dividend payments of Taxit and assuming that, where a partial imputation system applies, the tax credit is 25% of the gross dividend.   **(5 marks)**

205 TAX ENTRIES (PILOT PAPER)

On 1 January 20X3, SPJ had an opening debit balance of $5,000 on its tax account, which represented the balance on the account after settling its tax liability for the previous year. SPJ had a credit balance on its deferred tax account of $1.6 million at the same date.

SPJ has been advised that it should expect to pay $1 million tax on its trading profits for the year ended 31 December 20X3 and increase its deferred tax account balance by $150,000.

Required:

Prepare extracts from the income statement for the year ended 31 December 20X3, balance sheet at that date and notes to the accounts showing the tax entries required.   **(5 marks)**

206 TAX CHARGE

The tax charge for an entity STP is $5 million on profits before tax of $35 million. This is an effective rate of tax of 14.3%. Another entity JNI has an income tax charge of $10 million on profit before tax of $30 million for the same period. This is an effective rate of tax of 33.3%. However, for both entities the same 25% rate of income tax is applicable to their profits. The cash flow statements also show that each entity paid the same amount of tax, $8 million, during the period.

Required:

Suggest the possible reasons why the income tax charge in the financial statements as a percentage of the profit before tax may not be the same as the applicable income tax rate, and why the tax paid in the cash flow statement may not be the same as the tax charge in the income statement.   **(5 marks)**

207 AB (MAY 05 EXAM)

AB acquired non-current assets on 1 April 20X3 costing $250,000. The assets qualified for accelerated first year tax allowance at the rate of 50% for the first year. The second and subsequent years were at a tax depreciation rate of 25% per year on the reducing balance method.

AB depreciates all non-current assets at 20% a year on the straight line basis.

The rate of corporate income tax applying to AB for 20X3-X4 and 20X4-X5 was 30%. Assume AB has no other qualifying non-current assets.

Required:

Apply IAS 12 *Income Taxes* and calculate:

(i)   the deferred tax balance required at 31 March 20X4

(ii)   the deferred tax balance required at 31 March 20X5

(iii)   the charge to the income statement for the year ended 31 March 20X5.   **(5 marks)**

208 DG (NOV 06 EXAM)

DG purchased its only non-current tangible asset on 1 October 20X2. The asset cost $200,000, all of which qualified for tax depreciation. DG's accounting depreciation policy is to depreciate the asset over its useful economic life of five years, assuming no residual value, charging a full year's depreciation in the year of acquisition and no depreciation in the year of disposal.

The asset qualified for tax depreciation at a rate of 30% per year on the reducing balance method. DG sold the asset on 30 September 20X6 for $60,000.

The rate of income tax to apply to DG's profit is 20%. DG's accounting period is 1 October to 30 September.

Required:

(i)   Calculate DG's deferred tax balance at 30 September 20X5.

(ii)   Calculate DG's accounting profit/loss that will be recognised in its income statement on the disposal of the asset, in accordance with IAS 16 *Property, Plant and Equipment*.

(iii)   Calculate DG's tax balancing allowance/charge arising on the disposal of the asset.

(5 marks)

209 DEFT

The Chief Accountant of Deft is in the process of drafting the annual report for the year ended 31December 20X4. He is currently preparing the note in respect of deferred tax.

The deferred taxation account had a credit balance of $1.5 million at 31 December 20X3. All of these amounts arose in respect of the difference between depreciation and capital allowances.

During the year ended 31 December 20X4, the company charged $18.0 million in depreciation and claimed $20.8 million in capital allowances.

The income tax current charge for the year is $4.7 million.

Assume an income tax rate of 30% throughout.

Required:

Prepare notes in respect of deferred taxation for Deft for the year to 31 December 20X4. These should be in a form suitable for publication.   **(5 marks)**

210   AVOIDANCE v EVASION (NOV 05 EXAM)

(a)   Explain the difference between tax avoidance and tax evasion.   **(2 marks)**

(b)   Briefly explain the methods that governments can use to reduce tax avoidance and tax evasion.   **(3 marks)**

(Total: 5 marks)

211   WITHHOLDING TAX (MAY 06 EXAM)

CW owns 40% of the equity shares in Z, an entity resident in a foreign country. CW receives a dividend of $45,000 from Z; the amount received is after deduction of withholding tax of 10%. Z had before tax profits for the year of $500,000 and paid corporate income tax of $100,000.

Required:

(a)   Explain the meaning of 'withholding tax' and 'underlying tax.'   **(2 marks)**

(b)   Calculate the amount of withholding tax paid by CW.   **(1 mark)**

(c)   Calculate the amount of underlying tax that relates to CW's dividend.   **(2 marks)**

(Total: 5 marks)

PRINCIPLES OF REGULATION OF FINANCIAL REPORTING

212   CONSULTATIVE PROCESS

A general manager in your enterprise has recently enrolled on a management course at the local college. She is studying a module on finance and accounting and is having some difficulty understanding the theory. She has asked you, the trainee management accountant, to explain the consultative process used to produce a new International Financial Reporting Standard (IFRS).   **(5 marks)**

213   DEVELOPMENT (MAY 06 EXAM)

C is a small developing country which passed legislation to create a recognised professional accounting body two years ago. At the same time as the accounting body was created, new regulations governing financial reporting requirements of entities were passed. However, there are currently no accounting standards in C.

C's government has asked the new professional accounting body to prepare a report setting out the country's options for developing and implementing a set of high quality local accounting standards. The government request also referred to the work of the IASB and its International Financial Reporting Standards.

Required:

As an advisor to the professional accounting body, outline THREE options open to C for the development of a set of high quality local accounting standards. Identify ONE advantage and ONE disadvantage of each option.   **(5 marks)**

214 FAIR PRESENTATION

IAS 1 *Presentation of Financial Statements* requires directors to present fairly the financial position of an enterprise.

Required:

Explain why this requirement can be difficult to fulfil and how the IASB's *Framework for the Preparation and Presentation of Financial Statements* can help overcome these difficulties. **(5 marks)**

215 WOT

A key part of the International Accounting Standards Board's *Framework for the Preparation and Presentation of Financial Statements* (Framework) is the definition of assets and liabilities.

The following transactions or events have arisen in relation to WOT, for the year to 31 March 20X5.

(1)   On 1 April 20X4 WOT purchased a new office building at a cost of $5 million. The building has an estimated life of 50 years, but it contains a sophisticated air conditioning and heating system (included in the price of the building), which will require replacement every 10 years at a cost of $500,000. WOT intends to depreciate the building at $60,000 per annum and provide a further $50,000 each year to facilitate the replacement of the heating system. The auditors have challenged the decision to provide for the replacement of the air conditioning and heating system.

(2)   WOT undertakes a considerable amount of research and development work. Most of this work is done on its own behalf, but occasionally it undertakes this type of work for other companies. Before any of its own projects progress to the development stage they are assessed by an internal committee, which carefully analyses all information relating to the project. This process has led to a very good record of development projects delivering profitable results. WOT intends to capitalise all development costs, but the auditors have challenged this decision.

Required:

Explain briefly whether these transactions or events give rise to assets or liabilities.

(5 marks)

216 LOSSES

In the current financial year, an entity began a long-term construction contract on behalf of a customer. The contract price is $5,000,000. At the end of the current financial year, costs incurred to date are $1,900,000 and estimates of further costs to completion are $3,400,000. The entity must therefore recognise a loss of $300,000 on the contract in the current financial year.

The IASB's *Framework for the Preparation and Presentation of Financial Statements* (Framework) effectively defines losses on individual transactions in such a way that they are associated with increases in assets or decreases in liabilities.

Required:

Explain how the definition of losses contained in the Framework could be used to justify the requirement of IAS 11 *Construction Contracts* to recognise losses in full on long-term contracts as soon as they can be foreseen. **(5 marks)**

217 DISAGREEMENT

The external auditors of Strand have challenged the proposed accounting treatment by the entity of the following transactions.

(a) Strand's largest customer placed an order during September 20X4 for all of the goods that it is likely to require during the year ending 30 September 20X5. Strand invoiced this customer for these goods during September 20X4. A total of $800 million was debited to trade receivables and credited to revenue in respect of this invoice. A provision for $300 million was created in respect of the estimated cost of manufacturing the invoiced goods.

(b) Strand's customer agreed to place the order referred to above only after receiving a number of written assurances from Strand's Directors. The goods themselves will be delivered at times and in quantities decided by the customer. The customer will pay for the goods in accordance with Strand's normal credit terms after delivery. The customer can cancel the order without penalty at any time and any remaining balance on the invoice will be cancelled immediately.

Strand's external auditors have examined the documentation and disagree with the Directors' decision to treat this transaction as a sale.

The International Accounting Standards Board's *Framework for the Preparation and Presentation of Financial Statements* (Framework) effectively defines profits on individual transactions in terms of increases in net assets. This means that profits are normally associated with an increase in the value of assets, where an asset is defined as 'a resource controlled by the enterprise as a result of past events and from which future economic benefits are expected to flow to the enterprise'.

Required:

Explain whether Strand is justified in treating the transaction in the scenario as a sale.

(5 marks)

218 EXTERNAL AUDIT (NOV 06 EXAM)

DC is carrying out three different construction contracts. The balances and results for the year to 30 September 20X6 were as follows:

Contract	1	2	3
Contract end date	30 Sept 20Y0	31 Dec 20X7	30 Sept 20X7
	$m	$m	$m
Profit/(loss) recognised for year	2	2.3	(0.6)
Expected total profit/(loss) on contract	12	5	(3)

DC's management has included $3.7m profit in the income statement for the year ended 30 September 20X6.

No allowance has been made in the income statement for the future loss expected to arise on contract 3, as the managements consider the loss should be offset against the expected profits on the other two contracts.

EA & Co are DC's external auditors. EA & Co consider that the profit in relation to long-term contracts for the year ended 30 September 20X6 should be $1.3m, according to IAS 11 *Construction Contracts*. Assume that EA & Co have been unable to persuade DC's management to change their treatment of the long-term contract profit/loss.

Required:

(a) Explain the objective of an external audit.

(b) Identify, with reasons, the type of audit report that would be appropriate for EA & Co to use for DC's financial statements for the year ended 30 September 20X6. Briefly explain what information should be included in the audit report in relation to the contracts.

Your answer should refer to appropriate International Standards on Auditing (ISA).

(5 marks)

219 ACCEPTABLE ACCOUNTING POLICY

The chairman of the audit committee has been recently appointed. He is concerned about the possibility that the external auditors might give a qualified audit report. He has been informed that, in the previous year, there were disagreements between the auditors and the board of directors about the acceptability of one of the accounting policies that the directors wanted to adopt.

Required:

Prepare a memo for the audit committee chairman, explaining the main considerations that an external auditor uses in deciding whether an accounting policy is acceptable. **(5 marks)**

220 ELEMENTS OF FINANCIAL STATEMENTS (MAY 05 EXAM)

List the FIVE elements of financial statements defined in the IASB's *Framework* and explain the meaning of each. **(5 marks)**

221 QUALITATIVE CHARACTERISTICS (NOV 05 EXAM)

The International Accounting Standards Board's (IASB's) *Framework for the Preparation and Presentation of Financial Statements* (*Framework*) identifies four principal qualitative characteristics of financial information.

Required:

Identify and explain EACH of the FOUR principal qualitative characteristics of financial information listed in the IASB's *Framework*. **(5 marks)**

SINGLE COMPANY FINANCIAL ACCOUNTS

222 DF (NOV 06 EXAM)

You are in charge of the preparation of the financial statements for DF. You are nearing completion of the preparation of the accounts for the year ended 30 September 20X6 and two items have come to your attention.

(1) Shortly after a senior employee left DF in April 20X6, a number of accounting discrepancies were discovered. With further investigation, it became clear that fraudulent activity had been going on. DF has calculated that, because of the fraud, the profit for the year ended 30 September 20X5 had been overstated by $45,000.

(2)   On 1 September 20X6, DF received an order from a new customer enclosing full payment for the goods ordered; the order value was $90,000. DF scheduled the manufacture of the goods to commence on 28 November 20X6. The cost of manufacture was expected to be $70,000. DF's management wants to recognise the $20,000 profit in the income statement for the year ended 30 September 20X6. It has been suggested that the $90,000 should be recognised as revenue and a provision of $70,000 created for the cost of manufacture.

DF's income statement for the year ended 30 September 20X5 showed a profit of $600,000. The draft income statement for the year ended 30 September 20X6 showed a profit of $700,000. The 30 September 20X5 accounts were approved by the directors on 1 March 20X6.

Required:

Explain how the events described above should be reported in the financial statements of DF for the years ended 30 September 20X5 and 20X6.   **(5 marks)**

223   TAB SEGMENTS

TAB, a UK company, has recently acquired four large overseas subsidiaries. These subsidiaries manufacture products that are totally different from those of the parent company. The parent company manufactures paper and related products whereas the subsidiaries manufacture the following:

	Product	*Location*
Subsidiary 1	Car products	Spain
Subsidiary 2	Textiles	Korea
Subsidiary 3	Kitchen utensils	France
Subsidiary 4	Fashion garments	Thailand

The directors have purchased these subsidiaries in order to diversify their product base but do not have any knowledge on the information that is required in the financial statements, regarding these subsidiaries, other than the statutory requirements. The directors of the company realise that there is a need to disclose segment information but do not understand what the term means or what the implications are for the published financial statements.

Required:

Explain to the directors the criteria that should be used to identify the separate reportable segments. You should illustrate your answer by reference to the above information.

(5 marks)

224   CHANGE

Beta is a supplier of electricity. During Year 8, Beta changed its accounting policy for the treatment of interest costs on borrowing that are directly attributable to the new electricity generating plant that is under construction for use by Beta. In previous years, Beta's policy has been to capitalise the borrowing costs and include them in the cost of the asset under construction. Beta has now decided to treat these costs as an expense of the period in which they are incurred, and not to capitalise them. Management believes that this change in policy is desirable because it results in a more relevant treatment of borrowing costs and is also compatible with local industry practice, so that the change will make Beta's financial statements more comparable.

Beta has capitalised $500,000 of borrowing costs in Year 7 on new plant under construction, and $900,000 in periods before Year 7. During Year 8, Beta has made a profit before interest and taxation of $6,000,000: interest costs have been $1,000,000 and tax is $1,500,000.

In Year 7, Beta reported:

	$000
Profit before interest and taxation	4,500,000
Interest expense	0
Profit before taxation	4,500,000
Taxation	1,200,000
Profit after taxation	3,300,000

Taxation on profits is at the rate of 30%.

The generating plant is still under construction, and Beta has not yet begun to charge depreciation on the asset.

Required:

(a) Explain how Beta should report, in its financial statements for the year to 31 December Year 8, the change to charging interest on borrowing costs as an expense.

(b) Prepare an extract from the income statement for Year 8 and Year 7, showing how the relevant figures should be stated. **(5 marks)**

Note: You should assume that the change will have no impact on Beta's Year 7 tax liability.

225 INCOME STATEMENT (MAY 06 EXAM)

The following is an extract from the trial balance of CE at 31 March 20X6:

	$000	$000
Administration expenses	260	
Cost of sales	480	
Interest paid	190	
Interest bearing borrowings		2,200
Inventory at 31 March 20X6	220	
Property, plant and equipment at cost	1,500	
Property, plant and equipment, depreciation to 31 March 20X5		540
Distribution costs	200	
Revenue		2,000

Notes:

(i) Included in the closing inventory at the balance sheet date was inventory at a cost of $35,000, which was sold during April 20X6 for $19,000.

(ii) Depreciation is provided for on property, plant and equipment at 20% per year using the reducing balance method. Depreciation is regarded as cost of sales.

(iii) A member of the public was seriously injured while using one of CE's products on 4 October 20X5. Professional legal advice is that CE will probably have to pay $500,000 compensation.

Required:

Prepare CE's income statement for the year ended 31 March 20X6 down to the line 'profit before tax'. **(5 marks)**

226   BJ (NOV 05 EXAM)

BJ is an entity that provides a range of facilities for holidaymakers and travellers. At
1 October 20X4 these included:

- a short-haul airline operating within Europe, and

- a travel agency specialising in arranging holidays to more exotic destinations, such as
  Hawaii and Fiji.

BJ's airline operation has made significant losses for the last two years. On 31 January
20X5, the directors of BJ decided that, due to a significant increase in competition on short
haul flights within Europe, BJ would close all of its airline operations and dispose of its fleet
of aircraft. All flights for holiday-makers and travellers who had already booked seats would
be provided by third party airlines. All operations ceased on 31 May 20X5.

On 31 July 20X5, BJ sold its fleet of aircraft and associated non-current assets for $500
million; the carrying value at that date was $750 million.

At the balance sheet date, BJ was still in negotiation with some employees regarding
severance payments. BJ has estimated that, in the financial period October 20X5 to
September 20X6, it will agree a settlement of $20 million compensation.

The closure of the airline operation caused BJ to carry out a major restructuring of the entire
entity. The restructuring has been agreed by the directors and active steps have been taken to
implement it. The cost of restructuring to be incurred in year 20X5/20X6 is estimated at $10
million.

Required:

Explain how BJ should report the events described above and quantify any amounts required
to be included in its financial statements for the year ended 30 September 20X5. (Detailed
disclosure notes are not required.)   **(5 marks)**

227   TANGIBLE NON-CURRENT ASSETS

Diva has tangible non-current assets in its balance sheets at 31 December 20X4 and
31 December 20X5 as follows:

	At 31 December 20X5	At 31 December 20X4
	$000	$000
Property, plant and equipment at carrying amount	8,417	6,228

The following information is also available:

(1)

	31 December 20X5	31 December 20X4	
	Cost or valuation	Cost or valuation	Accumulated depreciation/ amortisation
	$000	$000	$000
Land	3,520	2,743	0
Buildings	3,703	3,177	612
Plant, machinery and equipment	2,653	1,538	671
Assets under construction	0	53	0

(2)   The land was revalued by $375,000 on 31 December 20X5.

(3)   During the year, machines were disposed of for net sales proceeds of $20,000. The
machines originally cost $125,000 and accumulated depreciation on the assets at the
date of disposal was $111,000.

(4)   *Depreciation charge*:

Depreciation charges for the year are as follows:

Buildings: $75,000

Plant and machinery: $212,000

(5)   Assets under construction refer to a contract, started in November 20X4, to build and supply C with new machinery. The machinery was installed and testing was completed by 31 September 20X5. Production began early October 20X5. The balance on the assets under construction account was transferred to the plant and machinery account on 31 December 20X5. The amount transferred was $350,000.

Required:

Prepare the disclosure note for property, plant and equipment for the year ended 31 December 20X5, in the form prescribed by International Accounting Standards.**(5 marks)**

228   **DW**

The following problems and issues have arisen during the preparation of the draft financial statements of DW for the year to 30 September 20X5:

The following schedule of the movement of plant has been drafted:

	Cost $m	Depreciation $m
At 1 October 20X4	97.20	32.50
Additions at cost excluding		
Leased assets (see (1) and (2) below)	22.50	–
Depreciation charge for year	–	19.84
Disposal (see (2) below)	(5.00)	
Balance 30 September 20X5	114.70	52.34

Notes:

(1)   The addition to plant is made up of:

	$m
Basic cost from supplier	20.00
Installation costs	1.00
Pre-production testing	0.50
Annual insurance and maintenance contract	1.00
	22.50

(2)   The disposal figure of $5 million is the proceeds from the sale of an item of plant during the year which had cost $15 million on 1 October 20X1 and had been correctly depreciated prior to disposal. Dawes charges depreciation of 20% per annum on the cost of plant held at the year end.

Required:

Prepare a corrected schedule of the movements of the cost and depreciation of plant.

(5 marks)

229   BI (NOV 05 EXAM)

BI owns a building which it uses as its offices, warehouse and garage. The land is carried as a separate non-current tangible asset in the balance sheet.

BI has a policy of regularly revaluing its non-current tangible assets. The original cost of the building in October 20X2 was $1,000,000; it was assumed to have a remaining useful life of 20 years at that date, with no residual value. The building was revalued on 30 September 20X4 by a professional valuer at $1,800,000.

BI also owns a brand name which it acquired 1 October 20X0 for $500,000. The brand name is being amortised over 10 years.

The economic climate had deteriorated during 20X5, causing BI to carry out an impairment review of its assets at 30 September 20X5. BI's building was valued at a market value of $1,500,000 on 30 September 20X5 by an independent valuer. A brand specialist valued BI's brand name at market value of $200,000 on the same date.

BI's management accountant calculated that the brand name's value in use at 30 September 20X5 was $150,000.

Required:

Explain how BI should report the events described above and quantify any amounts required to be included in its financial statements for the year ended 30 September 20X5.

(5 marks)

230   REVALUATION (NOV 06 EXAM)

DV purchased two buildings on 1 September 20W6. Building A cost $200,000 and had a useful economic life of 20 years. Building B cost $120,000 and had a useful economic life of 15 years. DV's accounting policies are to revalue buildings every five years and depreciate them over their useful economic lives on the straight line basis. DV does not make an annual transfer from revaluation reserve to retained profits for excess depreciation.

DV received the following valuations from its professionally qualified external valuer:

31 August 20X1	Building A	$180,000
	Building B	$75,000
31 August 20X6	Building A	$100,000
	Building B	$30,000

Required

Calculate the gains or impairments arising on the revaluation of Buildings A and B at 31 August 20X6 and identify where they should be recognised in the financial statements of DV.   **(5 marks)**

231 USEFUL ECONOMIC LIFE (PILOT PAPER)

A new type of delivery vehicle, when purchased on 1 April 20X0 for $20,000, was expected to have a useful economic life of four years. It now appears that the original estimate of the useful economic life was too short, and the vehicle is now expected to have a useful economic life of six years from the date of purchase. All delivery vehicles are depreciated using the straight-line method and are assumed to have zero residual value.

Required:

As the trainee management accountant, draft a memo to the transport manager explaining whether it is possible to change the useful economic life of the new delivery vehicle. Using appropriate International Accounting Standards, explain how the accounting entries relating to the delivery vehicle should be recorded in the income statement for the year ended 31 March 20X3 and the balance sheet at that date. **(5 marks)**

232 DECOMMISSIONING (PILOT PAPER)

NDL drilled a new oil well, which started production on 1 March 20X3. The licence granting permission to drill the new oil well included a clause that requires NDL to 'return the land to the state it was in before drilling commenced'.

NDL estimates that the oil well will have a 20-year production life. At the end of that time, the oil well will be decommissioned and work carried out to reinstate the land. The cost of this decommissioning work is estimated to be $20 million.

Required:

As the trainee management accountant, draft a memo to the production manager explaining how NDL must treat the decommissioning costs in its financial statements for the year to 31 March 20X3. Your memo should refer to appropriate International Accounting Standards. **(5 marks)**

233 HOTELS

AH owns three hotels. It has employed a firm of surveyors to revalue some of its properties during the past year. The directors have decided that the valuations should be incorporated into the entity's financial statements.

This is the first time that such a revaluation has taken place and the accountant responsible for the preparation of the non-current asset note in the balance sheet is unsure of the correct treatment of the amounts involved. The entity's year end is 30 September 20X4.

The accountant has extracted the following table from the report prepared by the surveyors:

	Original cost	Depreciation to 30 September 20X3	Market value at 1 January 20X4	Estimated useful life from 1 January 20X4
	$000	$000	$000	Years
Hotel G	400	96	650	50
Hotel H	750	56	820	30
Hotel K	500	70	320	40

Depreciation for the first three months of the year is to be based on the entity's original valuation of its hotels. Depreciation for the remaining nine months of the year to 30 September 20X4 is to be based on the new valuations and the estimated useful remaining lives in the surveyor's report.

Required:

Prepare a memo giving an answer to the following questions from the accountant. You should explain the principles of the accounting treatments, and you are **not** required to provide calculations or figures for the actual valuations.

(a)   The book value of Hotel K has fallen as a result of the revaluation. How should this decrease be reflected in the financial statements?

(b)   Does *all* of the depreciation based on the revalued amounts for Hotels G and H have to be charged to the income statement for the year to 30 September 20X4, or can a proportion be offset against the revaluation reserve instead?

(c)   What should be the carrying amount or net book value for the hotels in the balance sheet as at 30 September 20X4?   **(5 marks)**

234   OAK

OAK has recently purchased an item of plant from Plantco. The details of this are:

	$	$
Basic list price of plant		240,000
Trade discount applicable to OAK		12.5% on list price
Related costs:		
Shipping and handling costs		2,750
Estimated pre-production testing		12,500
Maintenance contract for three years		24,000
Site preparation costs:		
Electrical cable installation	14,000	
Concrete reinforcement	4,500	
Own labour costs	7,500	
	———	26,000

OAK paid for the plant (excluding the related costs) within four weeks of order, thereby obtaining an early settlement discount of 3%.

OAK had incorrectly specified the power loading of the original electrical cable to be installed by the contractor. The cost of correcting this error of $6,000 is included in the above figure of $14,000.

The plant is expected to last for 10 years. At the end of this period there will be compulsory costs of $15,000 to dismantle the plant and $3,000 to restore the site to its original use condition.

Required:

Calculate the amount at which the initial cost of the plant should be measured. (Ignore discounting.)   **(5 marks)**

235   DEVELOPMENT COSTS (MAY 06 EXAM)

CD is a manufacturing entity that runs a number of operations including a bottling plant that bottles carbonated soft drinks. CD has been developing a new bottling process that will allow the bottles to be filled and sealed more efficiently. The new process took a year to develop. At the start of development, CD estimated that the new process would increase output by 15% with no additional cost (other than the extra bottles and their contents). Development work commenced on 1 May 20X5 and was completed on 20 April 20X6. Testing at the end of the development confirmed CD's original estimates.

CD incurred expenditure of $180,000 on the above development in 20X5/X6.

CD plans to install the new process in its bottling plant and start operating the new process from 1 May 20X6.

CD's balance sheet date is 30 April.

Required:

(a)   Explain the requirements of IAS 38 *Intangible Assets* for the treatment of development costs.   **(3 marks)**

(b)   Explain how CD should treat its development costs in its financial statements for the year ended 30 April 20X6.   **(2 marks)**

(Total: 5 marks)

236   SLY

SLY is a manufacturing company. It held its annual inventory count on 31 March 20X5, the entity's year end. The accounts department is currently working its way through the inventory sheets placing a value on the physical inventories.

Work-in-progress

The cost of work-in-progress includes an element of overheads. The following table of figures has been prepared in order to assist in the calculation of the overhead absorption:

	$
Fixed costs	
Factory rent, rates and insurance	150,000
Administration expenses	190,000
Factory security	110,000
Variable costs	
Factory heat, light and power	300,000
Sales commissions and selling costs	120,000
Depreciation of machinery	200,000
Depreciation of delivery vehicles	76,000

Overheads are usually absorbed on the basis of labour hours. The inventory sheets suggest that 500 labour hours have been included in work-in-progress. A total of 80,000 hours have been worked by production staff during the year. This figure is, however, much lower than the normal figure of 95,000 hours.

Required:

(a)   Explain how IAS 2 requires overheads to be treated in the valuation of closing inventories.

(b)   Calculate the value of overheads to be absorbed into the closing work-in-progress.

(5 marks)

237 PREFERENCE SHARES

The issued capital section of some balance sheets is complicated by the fact that it is possible to issue a range of different types of share, some of which are more like loan instruments than ordinary shares. Preferred shares are a relatively simple example of this.

An entity has three classes of preference shares in issue:

(a) Irredeemable 3% preference shares of $1 each

(b) Redeemable 5% preference shares of $1 each, redeemable in three years' time

(c) Convertible 4% preference shares of $1 each, convertible into ordinary shares in four years' time at the rate of one new ordinary share for every three preference shares.

Required:

Explain why different types of share capital should be classified separately.   **(5 marks)**

238 REDEEMABLE SHARES (MAY 06 EXAM)

CR issued 200,000 $10 redeemable 5% preference shares at par on 1 April 20X5. The shares were redeemable on 31 March 20Y0 at a premium of 15%. Issue costs amounted to $192,800.

Required:

(a) Calculate the total *finance* cost over the life of the preference shares.   **(2 marks)**

(b) Calculate the annual charge to the income statement for finance expense, as required by IAS 39 *Financial Instruments: Recognition and Measurement*, for each of the five years 20X6 to 20Y0. Assume the constant annual rate of interest as 10%.   **(3 marks)**

(Total: 5 marks)

239 NEWCARS

Newcars sells both new and good quality second-hand cars. The company is large and has a large number of shareholders. The only large block of shares is held by Arthur, who owns 25% of Newcars. Arthur is a member of Newcars' board of directors and he takes a keen interest in the day-to-day management of the company.

Arthur also owns 25% of Oldcars. Oldcars sells inexpensive second-hand cars which are either relatively old or have a high mileage. Arthur is also a member of the board of directors of Oldcars.

Apart from Arthur, Newcars and Oldcars have no shareholders in common. The only thing that they have in common, apart from Arthur's interest in each, is that Newcars sells a large number of cars to Oldcars. This usually happens when a customer of Newcars has traded in a car that is too old to be sold from Newcars' showroom. Most of these cars are immediately resold to Oldcars and go into Oldcars' normal trading inventories. These sales account for approximately 5% of Newcars' revenue. Oldcars acquires approximately 20% of its cars from Newcars.

Required:

(a) Suggest, with reasons, whether Newcars and Oldcars are related parties in terms of the requirements of IAS 24 *Related Party Disclosures*.

(b) Assuming that Newcars and Oldcars are related parties, describe the related parties' disclosures that would have to be made in the companies' financial statements in respect of the sale and purchase of cars between the two companies.   **(5 marks)**

240 CB IMPORTERS (MAY 06 EXAM)

CB is an entity specialising in importing a wide range of non-food items and selling them to retailers. George is CB's president and founder and owns 40% of CB's equity shares:

- CB's largest customer, XC, accounts for 35% of CB's revenue. XC has just completed negotiations with CB for a special 5% discount on all sales.

- During the accounting period, George purchased a property from CB for $500,000. CB had previously declared the property surplus to its requirements and had valued it at $750,000.

- George's son, Arnold, is a director in a financial institution, FC. During the accounting period, FC advanced $2 million to CB as an unsecured loan at a favourable rate of interest.

Required:

Explain, with reasons, the extent to which each of the above transactions should be classified and disclosed in accordance with IAS 24 *Related Party Disclosures* in CB's financial statements for the period. **(5 marks)**

241 CIVIL ENGINEERING COMPANY

SVL is a civil engineering company. It started work on a long-term project during the year ended 31 December 20X4. The following figures relate to this project at the balance sheet date.

	Rottenrow Centre $000
Contract price	8,000
Costs incurred to date	2,900
Estimated costs to completion	5,200
Value of work certified to date	3,000
Cash received from the customer	3,400

An old mineshaft has been discovered under the site for the Rottenrow Centre and the costs of dealing with this have been taken into account in the calculation of estimated costs to completion. C's lawyers are reasonably confident that the customer will have to bear the additional costs which will be incurred in stabilising the land. If negotiations are successful then the contract price will increase to $10 million.

C recognises revenue and profits on long-term contracts on the basis of work certified to date.

Required:

Calculate the figures which would appear in C's financial statements in respect of this project. **(5 marks)**

242 AE (MAY 05 EXAM)

AE has a three-year contract which commenced on 1 April 20X4. At 31 March 20X5, AE had the following balances in its ledger relating to the contract:

	$000	$000
Total contract value		60,000
Cost incurred up to 31 March 20X5:		
Attributable to work completed	21,000	
Inventory purchased for use in 20X5/6	3,000	24,000
Progress payments received		25,000
Other information:		
Expected further costs to completion		19,000

At 31 March 20X5, the contract was certified as 50% complete.

Required:

Prepare the income statement and balance sheet extracts showing the balances relating to this contract, as required by IAS 11 *Long-Term Contracts*. **(5 marks)**

243 NEW PRODUCTS

Y provides packaging products to mail order and internet retailers. Y is the market leader in its sector and is trying to keep ahead of the competition by researching new packaging products. Y is about to launch a new type of packaging on to the market. The new product is expected to be commercially viable and Y has sufficient resources for the foreseeable future.

Y has developed this product from original research started three years ago. The research and development had three phases:

- Phase 1 – July 20X1 to May 20X2 – pure research into possible new types of material. Carried out by a local university department at a cost of $75,000.

- Phase 2 – June 20X2 to April 20X3 – consultancy fees incurred for the investigation of the commercial possibilities of the newly discovered material. Fees incurred $192,000.

- Phase 3 – June 20X3 to May 20X4 – costs of developing the product and preparing for product launch, $223,000.

Required:

Explain how Y should treat the research and development costs in its financial statements for the years ended 31 May 20X2, 20X3 and 20X4. Your explanation should include reference to relevant International Accounting Standards. **(5 marks)**

244   BRAND NAME

Z acquired the business and assets of Q, a sole trader, on 31 October 20X4. The fair value of the assets acquired from Q were:

	$000
Non-current intangible assets	
Brand QQ – brand name	220
Non-current tangible assets	
Plant and equipment	268
Inventory	5
	493
Cash paid to Q	523

Z's accounting policy on recognised non-current intangible assets is that brand names are amortised over 10 years.

On 31 October 20X5, the QQ brand name was valued by an independent valuer at $250,000.

Required:

Explain how Z should treat the QQ brand name in its balance sheet for the years ended 31 October 20X4 and 20X5. Your explanation should include reference to relevant International Accounting Standards. **(5 marks)**

245   SCOPE

Scope is a paper-producing company. In the year to 31 December 20X4, the following events occurred.

(a)   Scope paid the engineering department at Northtown University a large sum of money to design a new pulping process which will enable the use of cheaper raw materials. This process has been successfully tested in the University's laboratories and is almost certain to be introduced at Scope's pulping plant within the next few months.

Scope also paid a substantial amount to the University's biology department to develop a new species of tree which could grow more quickly and therefore enable the company's forests to generate more wood for paper manufacturing. The project met with some success in that a new tree was developed. Unfortunately, it was prone to disease and the cost of the chemical sprays needed to keep the wood healthy rendered the tree uneconomic.

(b)   One of the company's employees was injured during the year. He had been operating a piece of machinery which had been known to have a faulty guard. The company's lawyers have advised that the employee has a very strong case, but will be unable to estimate likely financial damages until further medical evidence becomes available.

Required:

Explain how these matters should be dealt with in the financial statements of Scope for the year to 31 December 20X4. **(5 marks)**

246 LEGAL CLAIMS

The Chief Accountant of Z, a construction enterprise, is finalising the work on the financial statements for the year ended 31 October 20X5. She is considering the following matters that might require some adjustment or disclosure under the requirements of IAS 37.

(a) A customer has lodged a claim against Z for repairs to an office block built by the enterprise. The roof leaks and it appears that this is due to negligence in construction. Z is negotiating with the customer and will probably have to pay for repairs that will cost approximately $100,000.

(b) The roof in (a) above was installed by a subcontractor employed by Z. Z's lawyers are confident that the enterprise would have a strong claim to recover the whole of any costs from the subcontractor. The Chief Accountant has obtained the subcontractor's latest financial statements. The subcontractor appears to be almost insolvent with few assets.

Required:

As assistant to the Chief Accountant, prepare a memo explaining how each of these contingencies should be accounted for. Assume that all amounts stated are material.

(5 marks)

247 EVENTS

Explain how each of the following events should be reported in the financial statements of FRG for the year to 31 December 20X4.

(a) A claim has been made against a company for injury suffered by a pedestrian in connection with building work by the company. Legal advisers have confirmed that the company will probably have to pay damages of $200,000, but that a counter claim made against the building sub-contractors for $120,000 would probably be successful.

(b) A fire broke out at FRG's Westown factory on 4 February 20X5. This has destroyed the factory's administration block. Many of the costs incurred as a result of this fire are uninsured.

(c) A major customer went into liquidation on 27 January 20X5. The customer's balance at 31 December 20X4 remains unpaid. The receiver has intimated that unsecured payables will receive very little compensation, if any. **(5 marks)**

248 PROVISIONS (PILOT PAPER)

IAS 37 defines the meaning of a provision and sets out when a provision should be recognised.

Required:

Using the IAS 37 definition of a provision, explain how a provision meets the International Accounting Standards Board's *Framework for the Preparation and Presentation of Financial Statements* definition of a liability. **(5 marks)**

249   CLASSIFICATION OF LEASES

TR obtains cars for its sales force by means of leasing arrangements, made with a finance company though a car dealer. Six new cars were acquired recently under the following terms:

- a non-cancellable four-year lease

- a total of 16 payments, made one every three months in arrears

- each instalment to be $18,000 ($3,000 per car)

- the fair value of each car was $40,000. The present value of the lease payments equals the fair value of the cars at the inception of the lease

- TR will pay for all insurance, repairs and maintenance costs.

Required:

Explain the meaning of a 'finance lease', using the above to illustrate your answer. Identify whether the lease on TR's cars should be treated as an operating lease or a finance lease.

(5 marks)

250   FINANCE LEASE (1) (PILOT PAPER)

A lessee leases a non-current asset on a non-cancellable lease contract of five years, the details of which are:

- The asset has a useful economic life of five years.

- The rental is $21,000 per annum payable at the end of each year.

- The lessee also has to pay all insurance and maintenance costs.

- The fair value of the asset was $88,300.

The lessee uses the sum of digits method to calculate finance charges on the lease.

Required:

Prepare income statement and balance sheet extracts for years one and two of the lease.

(5 marks)

251   FINANCE LEASE (2) (MAY 05 EXAM)

A five-year finance lease commenced on 1 April 20X3. The annual payments are $30,000 in arrears. The fair value of the asset at 1 April 20X3 was $116,000. Use the sum of digits method for interest allocations and assume that the asset has no residual value at the end of the lease term.

Required:

In accordance with IAS 17 *Operating and Finance Leases*:

(a)   calculate the amount of finance cost that would be charged to the income statement for the year ended 31 March 20X5

(b)   prepare balance sheet extracts for the lease at 31 March 20X5.   **(5 marks)**

252 FLOODING

During April 20X5, excessive rain fell in the region where Z's main factory and warehouse facilities are situated. At the end of April 20X5, the rainfall caused heavy flooding and Z's factory and warehouse were standing in two metres of water. The factory plant and equipment were damaged but can be fully repaired. However, all of Z's inventory was badly damaged and was written off. Z's equipment repairs and inventory write-offs were insured and the insurance underwriter has agreed to pay for the repairs and the replacement of the inventory. As it will be some time before the factory is able to operate normally again, Z has decided to purchase finished goods inventory from outside suppliers during the period that the factory will be closed for repairs. During the period when Z is buying in inventory instead of manufacturing its own products, its profits will be reduced by a material amount.

Required:

Write a memo to your Chief Accountant explaining how Z should treat this situation in its financial statements for the year to 31 March 20X5. **(5 marks)**

MANAGING SHORT-TERM FINANCE

253 SPREADSHEET

Explain why spreadsheet models are used extensively for cash flow forecasting. **(5 marks)**

254 AM (MAY 05 EXAM)

AM is a trading entity operating in a country where there is no sales tax. Purchases are on credit, with 70% paid in the month following the date of purchase and 30% paid in the month after that.

Sales are partly on credit and partly for cash. Customers who receive credit are given 30 days to pay. On average 60% pay within 30 days, 30% pay between 30 and 60 days and 5% pay between 60 and 90 days. The balance is written off as irrecoverable. Other overheads, including salaries, are paid within the month incurred.

AM plans to purchase new equipment at the end of June 20X5, the expected cost of which is $250,000. The equipment will be purchased on 30 days' credit, payable at the end of July.

The cash balance on 1 May 20X5 is $96,000.

The actual/budgeted balances for the six months to July 20X5 were:

All figures $000	Actual			Budgeted		
	Feb	Mar	Apr	May	Jun	Jul
Credit sales	100	100	110	110	120	120
Cash sales	30	30	35	35	40	40
Credit purchases	45	50	50	55	55	60
Other overhead expense	40	40	40	50	50	50

Required:

Prepare a monthly cash budget for the period May to July 20X5 and assess the likelihood of AM being able to pay for the equipment when it falls due. (Round all figures to the nearest $000.) **(5 marks)**

255 CASH FORECASTING (PILOT PAPER)

HRD owns a number of small hotels. The room occupancy rate varies significantly from month to month. There are also high fixed costs. As a result, the cash generated each month has been very difficult to estimate.

Christmas is normally a busy period and large cash surpluses are expected in December. There is, however, a possibility that a rival group of hotels will offer large discounts in December and this could damage December trade for HRD to a significant extent.

January is a poor period for the industry and therefore all the company's hotels will close for the month, resulting in a negative cash flow. The Finance Director has identified the following possible outcomes and their associated probabilities:

	$000	Probability
Expected cash balance at 30 November 20X3	+ 175	1.0
Net operating cash flow in December 20X3	+ 700	0.7
	– 300	0.3
Net operating cash flow in January 20X4	– 900	1.0

Assume cash flows arise at month ends.

After January 20X4, trade is expected to improve, but there is still a high degree of uncertainty in relation to the cash surpluses or deficits that will be generated in each month.

Required:

Calculate the expected cash balance or overdraft of HRD at 31 January 20X4.

Explain why your answer may not be useful for short-term cash planning and outline alternative approaches that could be used. **(5 marks)**

256 MODELS

The treasurer of a local government department is reviewing her cash management procedures. She plans to introduce the use of cash management models and has asked you to investigate their applicability to the department. The following information is available.

- The department has agreed with its bank that it will maintain a minimum daily cash balance of $15,000. Severe financial penalties will apply if this balance is not maintained.

- A forecast of daily cash movements for the next 12 months shows a standard deviation of daily cash flows of $3,000.

- The daily interest rate is at present 0.0236% and this is not expected to change for the foreseeable future.

- The transaction cost for each sale or purchase is $25.

Required:

Write a brief memo to the treasurer which discusses how the Miller-Orr model would operate in practice, using the information given above. Your report should include calculations of the upper and lower limits for cash balances and the return point. Assume a spread of $26,820. **(5 marks)**

257 CASH MANAGEMENT MODELS (NOV 06 EXAM)

DJ maintains a minimum cash holding of $1,000. The standard deviation of its daily cash flows has been measured at $300 (variance is $90,000). DJ's annual cash outgoings are $420,000 spread evenly over the year. The transaction cost of each sale or purchase of treasury bills is $25. The daily interest rate is 0.02% (7.3% per year).

Required:

(a) Using the Baumol cash management model, calculate the optimum amount of treasury bills to be sold each time cash is required.

(b) Using the Miller-Orr cash management model, calculate the optimum amount of securities to sell when the cash holding reaches the lower limit.

(5 marks)

258 GOLF CLUBS

Eagle Golf operates 20 golf clubs throughout the country, where members play on high quality courses, with clubhouse facilities including bars and restaurants. The clubs have private membership and members pay annual subscriptions.

The cash management policy problems of the entity have been summarised by the chief executive officer as follows.

'Our cash inflow is very uneven, but we know when it is coming in. Members pay their subscriptions on 1 January each year, and this is most of our income, so we have surplus cash in January that tends to decrease as the year passes by, until the year end when we normally have an overdraft. This is then cleared by the receipt of subscriptions in January. We do have other sources of income, such as receipts from the restaurant, bars and shops, but these are fairly even over the year. The costs of maintaining the golf courses is seasonal with the highest cost being in the summer when the need to maintain the greens and fairways is greatest.'

Required:

As a member of the treasury team of Eagle Golf, write a memorandum to the board which:

(a) evaluates the cash management problems facing the entity, and

(b) analyses the way in which cash management might be improved. **(5 marks)**

259 DF

DF is a manufacturer of sports equipment that has recently won a major three-year contract to supply FF with a range of equipment. FF is a large company with over 100 sports shops.

The new contract is expected to double DF's existing total annual sales, but demand from FF will vary considerably from month to month.

The contract will mean a significant additional investment in current assets. In particular, the contract with FF will require orders to be delivered within two days. This delivery period gives DF insufficient time to manufacture items, therefore significant inventories need to be held at all times. Also, FF requires 90 days' credit from its suppliers. This will result in a significant additional investment in receivables by DF.

If DF borrows from its bank to finance current assets, either using a loan or an overdraft, it expects to be charged annual interest at 12%. Consequently, DF is considering offering a 3% cash discount to FF for settlement within 10 days rather than the normal 90 days.

Required:

Calculate the annual equivalent rate of interest implicit in offering a 3% cash discount to FF for settlement of debts within 10 days rather than 90 days.

Briefly explain the factors, other than the rate of interest, that DF would need to consider before deciding on whether to offer a cash discount. **(5 marks)**

260 FONT

FONT is a manufacturer of locks and household security fittings. Over the last 12 months it has encountered increasing problems with late payment by credit customers.

The last 12 months of credit sales of $67.5 million show an increase of 10% over the previous year, but FONT's bank overdraft, on which it is charged interest at 9% per year, has also increased (by $1.8 million) over the last year. The management wants to reduce FONT's working capital requirements by reducing the trade receivables collection period.

The management accountant has extracted a profile of unpaid receivables (an 'aged debtors' profile) which is shown below:

% of total payments of trade receivables (by value)	Average collection period (days)
5	30
28	45
10	60
30	75
16	90
11	120

Irrecoverable debts currently stand at $2 million per year.

FONT's management is considering whether to employ the services of a with recourse payments collection agency, which has quoted a fee of 1% of sales receipts. It is estimated that using the service will have the effect of reducing average days for credit customers to pay by 20 days and eliminating 50% of irrecoverable debts.

Required:

Calculate the change in working capital requirements and irrecoverable debts which would result from the use of the debt collection service and recommend whether the service should be adopted by FONT. Your answer should clearly show all workings. **(5 marks)**

261 LOT

LOT produces garden seats which are sold on both domestic and export markets. Sales to the export market next year are expected to be $4.8 million, and are expected to occur steadily throughout the year. An initial deposit of 15% of the sales price is paid by all export customers.

All export sales are on 60 days' credit with an average collection period for credit sales of 75 days. Irrecoverable debts are currently 1.25% of export sales (net of the deposit).

LOT wishes to investigate the effects of extra advertising that could be undertaken to stimulate export sales. LOT has been approached by a European satellite TV company which believes that $300,000 of advertising could increase export sales in the coming year by up to 30%. There is a 0.2 chance of a 20% increase in export sales, a 0.5 chance of a 25% increase and a 0.3 chance of a 30% increase. Direct costs of production are 65% of the sales price. Administration costs would increase by $30,000, $40,000 and $50,000 for the 20%, 25% and 30% increases in export sales respectively. Increased export sales are likely to result in lengthening the average collection period of the credit element of all exports by five days, and irrecoverable debts will increase to 1.5% of all export credit sales.

LOT can borrow overdraft finance at 10% per year. These rates are not expected to change in the near future.

Taxation may be ignored.

Required:

Calculate the expected effect of the advertising campaign on the entity's annual profit.

(5 marks)

262 SCL

SCL is a wholesale supplier of building materials. It is experiencing severe short-term cash flow difficulties. Sales invoices are about $2 million per month. The usual credit period extended to customers is 60 days, but the average period being taken is 90 days. The overdraft rate is 9% per annum.

A factoring company has offered a full factoring agreement without recourse on a permanent basis. The factor will charge a fee of 2.5% on total invoicing and will provide an immediate advance of 80% of invoiced amounts at an annual interest rate of 10%. Settlement of the remaining 20% will be after 60 days. SCL should avoid $300,000 a year in the administration costs of running the receivables ledger if the factoring arrangement is taken up.

Required:

Calculate the annual net cost, in cash terms, of the proposed factoring agreement assuming that there are 360 days in a year. State any other assumptions you have made. (Ignore taxation.) **(5 marks)**

263 CREDITWORTHY

Summarise the customary methods of establishing the creditworthiness of potential new customers. **(5 marks)**

264 EXCESSIVE CREDIT

Write a memo to the financial controller, suggesting how your organisation, a supplier of water purifying equipment, could most effectively prevent customers from taking excessive credit. **(5 marks)**

265 BF (NOV 05 EXAM)

BF manufactures a range of domestic appliances. Due to past delays in suppliers providing goods, BF has had to hold an inventory of raw materials, in order that the production could continue to operate smoothly. Due to recent improvements in supplier reliability, BF is re-examining its inventory holding policies and recalculating economic order quantities (EOQ).

- Item 'Z' costs BF $10.00 per unit.

- Expected annual production usage is 65,000 units.

- Procurement costs (cost of placing and processing one order) are $25.00.

- The cost of holding one unit for one year has been calculated as $3.00.

The supplier of item 'Z' has informed BF that if the order were 2,000 units or more at one time, a 2% discount would be given on the price of the goods.

Required:

(a) Calculate the EOQ for item 'Z' before the quantity discount. **(2 marks)**

(b) Advise BF if it should increase the order size of item 'Z' so as to qualify for the 2% discount. **(3 marks)**

(Total: 5 marks)

266 PRINCIPLES OF SHORT-TERM INVESTMENT

You are working as assistant to the Treasurer of GIL, a company that currently has a large cash surplus of about $250 million. The directors of GIL have not yet decided what to do with this money. They might use it to finance a takeover, or they might use it to pay a special dividend to the shareholders at the end of the year. The board have decided to defer a decision, and expect to hold the cash for at least another nine months, possibly longer.

The money is currently held in a bank deposit account, but the return is quite low, and the directors are hoping that the money can be invested elsewhere to earn more money. One director believes that GIL should invest in Treasury bills, and another has argued that corporate bonds would be more appropriate. In order to provide a focus for a board discussion, they have asked you to prepare a memo.

Required:

Prepare a brief memo setting out the principles that are applied when deciding how to invest large but short-term cash surpluses, and suggest how investing in Treasury bills or investing in corporate bonds would relate to these principles. **(5 marks)**

267 AD (MAY 05 EXAM)

AD, a manufacturing entity, has the following balances at 30 April 20X5:

Extract from financial statements:	$000
Trade receivables	216
Trade payables	97
Revenue (all credit sales)	992
Cost of sales	898
Purchases in year	641
Inventories at 30 April 20X5:	
Raw materials	111
Work in progress	63
Finished goods	102

Required:

Calculate AD's working capital cycle. **(5 marks)**

268 BH (NOV 05 EXAM)

BH purchased a bond with a face value of $1,000 on 1 June 20X3 for $850. The bond has a coupon rate of 7%. BH intends holding the bond to its maturity on 31 May 20X8 when it will repay its face value.

Required:

(a)   Explain the difference between the coupon rate of a security and its yield to maturity.

(2 marks)

(b)   Calculate the bond's yield to maturity.

(3 marks)

(Total: 5 marks)

269 RISK AND YIELD (NOV 06 EXAM)

DH raised cash through an equity share issue to pay for a new factory it planned to construct. However, the factory contract has been delayed and payments are not expected to be required for three or four months. DH is going to invest its surplus funds until they are required.

One of the directors of DH has identified three possible investment opportunities:

(i)   Treasury bills issued by the central bank of DH's country. They could be purchased on 1 December 20X6 for a period of 91 days. The likely purchase price is $990 per $1,000.

(ii)   Equities quoted on DH's local stock exchange. The stock exchange has had a good record in recent months with the equity index increasing in value for 14 consecutive months. The director recommends that DH invests in three large multinational entities, each paying an annual dividend that provides an annual yield of 10% on the current share price.

(iii) DH's bank would pay 3.5% per year on money placed in a deposit account with 30 days' notice.

Required:

As Assistant Management Accountant, you have been asked to prepare notes on the risk and effective yield of each of the above investment opportunities for use by the Management Accountant at the next board meeting.   **(5 marks)**

Section 3

SECTION C-TYPE QUESTIONS

Tutorial note

Since May 2007 there is only one question in Section C. It is worth 30 marks and requires the production of at least two out of three of the following: income statement, balance sheet and cash flow statement.

SINGLE COMPANY FINANCIAL ACCOUNTS

270   UJM

(a)   The following trial balance was extracted from the books of UJM at 31 March 20X7:

	$000	$000
5% loan notes		10,000
Administration expenses	5,900	
Bank	4,200	
Buildings at valuation (at 31 March 20X6)	50,000	
Cost of goods sold	66,200	
Distribution expenses	1,600	
Dividend paid	1,500	
Inventories (at 31 March 20X7)	6,100	
Land at valuation (at 31 March 20X6)	6,000	
Loan note interest (six months to 30 September 20X6)	250	
Ordinary shares $1 each		25,000
Payables		9,539
Plant and machinery at cost	30,000	
Provision for depreciation – buildings (at 31 March 20X6)		5,000
Provision for depreciation – plant and machinery (at 31 March 20X6)		10,000
Allowance for receivables (at 31 March 20X6)		400
Receivables	14,300	
Accumulated profits (at 31 March 20X6)		4,411
Revaluation reserve – land and buildings		3,000
Revenue		101,050
Share premium account		17,650
	186,050	186,050

Additional information available was as follows:

(i)   The directors had a valuation carried out on the land and buildings by an independent valuer and were informed that at 31 March 20X7 the buildings value was $39,000,000. The directors decided to adjust the valuation of the buildings in the financial statements for the year ended 31 March 20X7. The land was revalued at $6,000,000 at 31 March 20X6 and had not changed at 31 March 20X7. The land had originally cost $4,000,000. The buildings had originally cost $53,260,000 ten years ago and were revalued on 31 March 20X1.

     (ii)   Depreciation on buildings is regarded as an administrative expense and is 2% of gross valuation per annum. Depreciation on plant and machinery is regarded as a 'cost of sales' expense and is at 20% per annum on cost.

     (iii)   On 15 April 20X7, UJM was advised that one of its major customers had gone into liquidation. The outstanding balance on their account at 31 March 20X7 was $3,059,000. It is very unlikely that any money will be received from the liquidator.

     (iv)   Because of the recent increase in bankruptcies, the directors of UJM have decided that it would be prudent to increase the allowance for receivables to the equivalent of 5% of the receivables balance.

     (v)   Income tax due for the year is estimated at $5,660,000.

     (vi)   During the year, the directors made a bonus issue; all existing shareholders received one new share free for every four shares held.

Required:

Prepare UJM's income statement for the year ended 31 March 20X7 and its balance sheet at that date, in a form suitable for presentation to the shareholders, in accordance with all current regulations. **(15 marks)**

(b)   Y's income statement for the year ended 31 December 20X4 and balance sheets at 31 December 20X3 and 31 December 20X4 were as follows:

Income statement for the year ended 31 December 20X4

	$000	$000
Sales		360
Raw materials consumed	35	
Staff costs	47	
Depreciation	59	
Loss on disposal	9	
		150
Profit from operations		210
Finance costs		14
Profit before tax		196
Income tax expense		62
Profit after tax		134

Summary balance sheets as at

	31 December 20X4		31 December 20X3	
	$000	$000	$000	$000
Non-current assets				
Cost		798		780
Depreciation		159		112
		639		668
Current assets				
Inventory	12		10	
Trade receivables	34		26	
Bank	24	70	28	64
		709		732

Share capital		180		170
Share premium		18		12
Accumulated profits		343		245
		541		427
Non-current liabilities				
Long term loans	100		250	
Deferred tax	20		16	
		120		266
Current liabilities				
Trade payables	21		15	
Income tax	27		24	
		48		39
		709		732

Additional information:

(1)   During the year, the company paid $45,000 for a new piece of machinery.

(2)   There were no revaluations of non-current assets during the year.

(3)   During the year, the company paid a dividend of $36,000.

Required:

Prepare a cash flow statement for Y for the year ended 31 December 20X4 in accordance with the requirements of IAS 7, using the indirect method.   **(15 marks)**

(Total: 30 marks)

271   MOP

MOP manufactures components for sale to the electronics industry. The following trial balance has been extracted from its financial records:

MOP – Trial balance at 30 September 20X5

	$ million	$ million
Administrative expenses	64	
Cash and cash equivalents	98	
Cost of sales	842	
Deferred tax		291
Disposal of plant and equipment	11	
Distribution costs	148	
Dividend – interim paid	300	
Income tax expense		37
Interest	72	
Interest-bearing borrowings (repayable 20Y8)		1,618
Inventories at 30 September 20X5	45	
Plant and equipment – cost	794	
Plant and equipment – accumulated depreciation		324
Property – cost	4,456	
Property – accumulated depreciation		811
Retained profit brought forward		1,132
Revenue		2,970
Issued share capital		600
Trade payables		27
Trade receivables	980	
	7,810	7,810

Notes:

(i)   Seller is an enterprise which is one of MOP's largest suppliers. G, one of MOP's Directors, owns 98% of Seller. MOP purchased $43 million of goods from Seller during the year ended 30 September 20X5, all under Seller's normal terms and conditions. MOP owed Seller $3 million at 30 September 20X5.

(ii) Plant and equipment which had cost $125 million, and had been depreciated by $78 million, was sold during the year. New plant and equipment was purchased for $160 million. These transactions have been included in the above figures. There were no other transactions involving non-current assets.

(iii) Depreciation for the year has still to be charged (to cost of sales) as follows:

Property   2% of cost

Plant and equipment   25% reducing balance

A whole year's depreciation is charged in the year of acquisition and none in the year of disposal.

(iv) The trial balance figure for inventories is calculated on the following basis:

	Purchase price $ million	*Attributable manufact- uring overheads* $ million	*Attributable non-manu- facturing overheads* $ million	*Total cost* $ million	*Net realisable value* $ million
Current inventory	26	7	3	36	51
Obsolete inventory	6	2	1	9	5
Total				45	56

Total cost is lower than total net realisable value and so the Directors have valued the inventory at $45 million. The external auditors have refused to accept this valuation, arguing that it is inconsistent with the requirements of IAS 2 *Inventories*. MOP's Directors have agreed to correct the inventory figure to bring it into line with IAS 2.

(v)   The Directors have estimated the tax charge for the year at $120 million. The balance on the income tax expense account is the amount remaining after settling the liability for the year ended 30 September 20X4.

(vi) The provision for deferred tax has arisen from the temporary differences arising from accelerated capital allowances on the enterprise's non-current assets. The tax written-down value of non-current assets at 30 September 20X5 was $2,985 million. It is estimated that tax will be paid at a rate of 30% when these temporary differences reverse.

(vii) The Directors have proposed a final dividend of $150 million.

Required:

Prepare MOP's income statement for the year ended 30 September 20X5 and its balance sheet at that date. These should be in a form suitable for publication and should be accompanied by notes as far as you are able to prepare these from the information provided.

Do NOT prepare a statement of accounting policies or a statement of changes in equity.

(20 marks)

272   HI RETAIL

Hi, listed on its local stock exchange, is a retail organisation operating several retail outlets. A reorganisation of the enterprise was started in 20X1 because of a significant reduction in profits. This reorganisation was completed during the current financial year, to 30 September 20X2.

The trial balance for Hi at 30 September 20X2 was as follows:

	$000	$000
10% loan notes (redeemable 20X9)		1,000
Accumulated profits at 30 September 20X1		2,400
Administrative expenses	615	
Bank and cash	959	
Buildings	11,200	
Cash received on disposal of equipment		11
Cost of goods sold	4,491	
Distribution costs	314	
Equipment and fixtures	2,625	
Interest paid on loan notes – half year to 31 March 20X2	50	
Interim dividend paid	800	
Inventory at 30 September 20X2	822	
Investment income received		37
Non-current asset investments at market value 30 September 20X1	492	
Ordinary shares of $1 each, fully paid		4,000
Provision for deferred tax		256
Provisions for depreciation at 30 September 20X1:		
Buildings		1,404
Equipment and fixtures		1,741
Revaluation reserve		172
Sales revenue		9,415
Share premium		2,388
Trade payables		396
Trade receivables	852	
	23,220	23,220

Additional information provided:

(i)   Non-current asset investments are carried in the financial statements at market value. The market value of the non-current asset investments at 30 September 20X2 was $522,000. There were no movements in the investments held during the year.

(ii)   On 1 November 20X2, Hi was informed that one of its customers, X, had ceased trading. The liquidators advised Hi that it was very unlikely to receive payment of any of the $45,000 due from X at 30 September 20X2.

(iii)   Another customer is suing for damages as a consequence of a faulty product. Legal advisers are currently advising that the probability of Hi being found liable is 75%. The amount payable is estimated to be the full amount claimed of $100,000.

(iv)   The income tax due for the year ended 30 September 20X2 is estimated at $1,180,000 and the deferred tax provision needs to be increased to $281,000.

(v)   During the year, Hi disposed of old equipment for $11,000. The original cost of this equipment was $210,000 and accumulated depreciation at 30 September 20X1 was $205,000.

(vi)   Depreciation is charged using the straight-line basis on non-current assets as follows:

   Buildings: 3%   Equipment and fixtures: 20%

Depreciation is regarded as a cost of sales. A full year's charge for depreciation is made in the year of acquisition, and no depreciation is charged in the year of disposal.

(vii) On 1 April 20X2, Hi made a rights issue of one new share for four existing shares, at a price of $3. All the rights were taken up and all money paid by 30 September 20X2.

Required:

Prepare the income statement and a statement of changes in equity for Hi for the year to 30 September 20X2 and a balance sheet at that date, in a form suitable for presentation to the shareholders, in accordance with the requirements of International Financial Reporting Standards. **(20 marks)**

273 AZ FINANCIAL STATEMENTS (PILOT PAPER)

AZ is a quoted manufacturing enterprise. Its finished products are stored in a nearby warehouse until ordered by customers. AZ has been re-organising the business to improve performance.

The trial balance for AZ at 31 March 20X3 was as follows:

	$000	$000
7% loan notes (redeemable 20X7)		18,250
Accumulated profits at 31 March 20X2		14,677
Administrative expenses	16,020	
Bank and cash	26,250	
Cost of goods manufactured in the year to 31 March 20X3 (excluding depreciation)	94,000	
Distribution costs	9,060	
Dividends paid	1,000	
Dividends received		1,200
Equity shares: $1 each fully paid		20,000
Interest paid	639	
Inventory at 31 March 20X2	4,852	
Plant and equipment	30,315	
Provision for depreciation at 31 March 20X2:		
Plant and equipment		6,060
Vehicles		1,670
Allowance for trade receivables		600
Restructuring costs	121	
Sales revenue		124,900
Share issue expenses	70	
Share premium		500
Trade payables		8,120
Trade receivables	9,930	
Vehicles	3,720	
	195,977	195,977

Additional information provided:

(i) Non-current assets are being depreciated as follows:

• Plant and equipment 20% per annum straight line

• Vehicles 25% per annum reducing balance.

Depreciation of plant and equipment is considered to be part of cost of sales, while depreciation of vehicles should be included under distribution costs.

(ii) Tax due for the year to 31 March 20X3 is estimated at $15,000.

(iii) The closing inventory at 31 March 20X3 was $5,180,000.

(iv)   A dividend of 5 cents per ordinary share was paid in February 20X3.

(v)   The 7% loan notes are 10-year loans due for repayment by 31 March 20X7. AZ incurred no other interest charges in the year to 31 March 20X3.

(vi)   The restructuring costs in the trial balance represent the cost of the final phase of a major fundamental restructuring of the enterprise to improve competitiveness and future profitability.

(vii) At 31 March 20X3, AZ was engaged in defending a legal action against the enterprise. Legal advisers have indicated that it is reasonably certain that the outcome of the case will be against the enterprise. The amount of compensation is currently estimated at $25,000 and has not been included in the trial balance.

(viii) On 1 October 20X2, AZ issued 1,000,000 equity shares at $1.50 each. All money had been received and correctly accounted for by the year end.

Required:

Prepare AZ's income statement for the year to 31 March 20X3, a balance sheet at that date, and a statement of changes in equity for the year. These should be in a form suitable for presentation to the shareholders, in accordance with the requirements of International Accounting Standards.

Notes to the financial statements are NOT required, but all workings must be clearly shown.

(20 marks)

274   AF (MAY 05 EXAM)

AF is a furniture manufacturing entity. The trial balance for AF at 31 March 20X5 was as follows:

	$000	$000
6% loan notes (redeemable 20Y0)		1,500
Accumulated profits at 31 March 20X4		388
Administrative expenses	1,540	
Available for sale investments at market value 31 March 20X4	1,640	
Bank and cash	822	
Cost of sales	3,463	
Distribution costs	1,590	
Dividend paid 1 December 20X4	275	
Interest paid on loan notes – half year to 30 September 20X4	45	
Inventory at 31 March 20X5	1,320	
Investment income received		68
Land and buildings at cost	5,190	
Ordinary shares of $1 each, fully paid		4,500
Plant and equipment at cost	3,400	
Provision for deferred tax		710
Provisions for depreciation at 31 March 20X4: Buildings		1,500
Provisions for depreciation at 31 March 20X4: Plant and equipment		1,659
Revaluation reserve		330
Sales revenue		8,210
Share premium		1,380
Trade payables		520
Trade receivables	1,480	
	20,765	20,765

Additional information provided:

(i) Available for sale investments are carried in the financial statements at market value. The market value of the available for sale investments at 31 March 20X5 was $1,750,000.

(ii) There were no sales or purchases of non-current assets or available for sale investments during the year ended 31 March 20X5.

(iii) Income tax due for the year ended 31 March 20X5 is estimated at $250,000. There is no balance outstanding in relation to previous years' corporate income tax. The deferred tax provision needs to be increased by $100,000.

(iv) Depreciation is charged on buildings using the straight-line basis at 3% each year. The cost of land included in land and buildings is $2,000,000. Plant and equipment is depreciated using the reducing balance method at 20%. Depreciation is regarded as a cost of sales.

(v) AF entered into a non-cancellable five year operating lease on 1 April 20X4 to acquire machinery to manufacture a new range of kitchen units. Under the terms of the lease, AF will receive the first year rent free, then $62,500 is payable for four years commencing in year two of the lease. The machine is estimated to have a useful economic life of 20 years.

(vi) The 6% loan notes are 10 year loans due for repayment March 20Y0. AF incurred no other finance costs in the year to 31 March 20X5.

Required:

Prepare the income statement for AF for the year to 31 March 20X5 and a balance sheet at that date, in a form suitable for presentation to the shareholders and in accordance with the requirements of International Financial Reporting Standards.

Notes to the financial statements are NOT required, but all workings must be clearly shown. Do NOT prepare a statement of accounting policies or a statement of changes in equity.

(20 marks)

275 BG (NOV 05 EXAM)

BG provides office cleaning services to a range of organisations in its local area. BG operates through a small network of depots that are rented spaces situated in out-of-town industrial developments. BG has a policy to lease all vehicles on operating leases.

The trial balance for BG at 30 September 20X5 was as follows:

	$000	$000
10% bonds (redeemable 2010)		150
Administrative expenses	239	
Available for sale investments at market value 30 September 20X4	205	
Bank and cash	147	
Bond interest paid – half year to 31 March 20X5	8	
Cost of cleaning materials consumed	101	
Direct operating expenses (including cleaning stuff)	548	
Dividend paid	60	
Equipment and fixtures, cost at 30 September 20X5	752	
Equity shares $1 each, fully paid		200
Income tax	9	
Inventory of cleaning materials at 30 September 20X5	37	
Investment income received		11
Provision for deferred tax		50

	$000	$000
Provision for depreciation at 30 September 20X4:		
Equipment and fixtures		370
Provision for legal claim balance at 30 September 20X4		190
Retained earnings at 30 September 20X4		226
Revaluation reserve at 30 September 20X4		30
Revenue		1,017
Share premium		40
Trade payables		24
Trade receivables	141	
Vehicle operating lease rentals paid	61	
	2,308	2,308

Additional information:

(i) Available for sale investments are carried in the financial statements at market value. The market value of the available for sale investments at 30 September 20X5 was $225,000. There were no purchases or sales of available for sale investments held during the year.

(ii) The income tax balance in the trial balance is a result of the underprovision of tax for the year ended 30 September 20X4.

(iii) The taxation due for the year ended 30 September 20X5 is estimated at $64,000 and the deferred tax provision needs to be increased by $15,000.

(iv) Equipment and fixtures are depreciated at 20% per annum straight line. Depreciation of equipment and fixtures is considered to be part of direct cost of sales. BG's policy is to charge a full year's depreciation in the year of acquisition and no depreciation in the year of disposal.

(v) The 10% bonds were issued in 20X0.

(vi) BG paid an interim dividend during the year, but does not propose to pay a final dividend as profit for the year is well below expectations.

(vii) At 30 September 20X4, BG had an outstanding legal claim from a customer alleging that BG had caused a major fire in the customer's premises. BG was advised that it would very probably lose the case, so a provision of $190,000 was set up at 30 September 20X4. During 20X5, new evidence was discovered and the case against BG was dropped. As there is no further liability, the directors have decided that the provision is no longer required.

Required:

Prepare the income statement and a statement of changes in equity for BG for the year to 30 September 20X5 and a balance sheet at that date, in a form suitable for presentation to the shareholders and in accordance with the requirements of International Financial Reporting Standards.

Notes to the financial statements are NOT required, but all workings must be clearly shown. All workings should be to the nearest $000. Do NOT prepare a statement of accounting policies. **(20 marks)**

276   V

V imports electronic goods and resells these to large retail organisations. It specialises in luxury products such as electronic games and portable audio equipment. Almost half of the entity's sales occur during the months of October and November.

V faces intense competition and attempts to compete by anticipating consumer trends and offering products which are new to the market.

V's trial balance at 30 September 20X4 is as follows:

	$000	$000
Sales revenue		9,800
Purchases	1,660	
Inventory at 30 September 20X3	480	
Warehouse and delivery wages	350	
Sales commissions	180	
Sundry distribution costs	310	
Sundry administration expenses	85	
Administration staff salaries	240	
Legal fees and damages	270	
Income tax	45	
Interim dividend paid	600	
Warehouse premises – valuation	8,500	
Warehouse premises – depreciation		400
Computer network – cost	900	
Computer network – depreciation		200
Delivery vehicles – cost	700	
Delivery vehicles – depreciation		280
Trade receivables	910	
Trade payables		470
Bank	90	
Loan – repayable 20X9		500
Loan interest	5	
Deferred tax		540
Application and allotment		110
Share capital		1,000
Revaluation reserve		760
Accumulated profits		1,265
	15,325	15,325

Notes:

(i)   The closing inventory was counted on 30 September 20X4 and was valued at $520,000.

(ii)   The legal fees and damages were paid in settlement of a claim against V. A wiring fault in a compact disc player had caused a fire in a customer's store. This is the first time that such an event has occurred. V has introduced safety checks on new products which will help to prevent any recurrence of this type of accident.

(iii) Depreciation on non-tangible current assets has still to be charged for the year on the following bases:

Warehouse buildings	2% of cost
Computer network	25% of net book value (reducing balance method)
Vehicles	25% of net book value (reducing balance method)

The valuation of the warehouse premises consists of land valued at $2 million and buildings valued at $6,500,000. A valuation of the properties has just been carried out by independent external surveyors, who put the value of the land at $2,500,000 and the buildings at $7 million, as at 30 September 20X4. The revaluation has not yet been recorded in the accounts.

(iv)   The current tax charge for the year has been estimated at $1,750,000, and the deferred tax liability will be increased to $690,000.

(v)   In October 20X4 the directors proposed a final dividend of $1,000,000.

(vi)   V is in the process of issuing 200,000 new shares. Its shares have a nominal value of $1.00 each. At the year end the company had received $110,000 from applicants for the new issue. This balance should be treated as a current liability in the balance sheet at 30 September 20X4.

Required:

Prepare an income statement for V for the year ended 30 September 20X7, and a balance sheet at that date. These should be in a form suitable for publication insofar as is possible given the information provided. *Notes to the financial statements are NOT required, but all workings must be clearly shown. Do NOT prepare a statement of accounting policies or a statement of changes in equity.*   **(20 marks)**

277   DM (NOV 06 EXAM)

The trial balance for DM, a trading entity, at 30 September 20X6 was as follows:

	$000	$000
6% Loan (repayable 20Z5)		140
Administrative expenses	91	
Cash and cash equivalents	43	
Distribution costs	46	
Dividend paid 1 June 20X6	25	
Inventory at 30 September 20X5	84	
Inventory purchases	285	
Land and buildings at cost	500	
Equity shares $1 each, fully paid		300
Plant and equipment at cost	211	
Provision for deferred tax at 30 September 20X5		40
Provision for depreciation at 30 September 20X5 – Buildings		45
Provision for depreciation at 30 September 20X5 – Plant and equipment		80
Retained earnings at 30 September 20X5		32
Sales revenue		602
Share premium		50
Trade payables		29
Trade receivables	6	
Vehicle lease rental paid	27	
	1,318	1,318

Additional information:

(i)   Inventory at 30 September 20X6 was $93,000.

(ii)   There were no sales of non-current assets during the year ended 30 September 20X6.

(iii)   The income tax due for the year ended 30 September 20X6 is estimated at $24,000. The deferred tax provision needs to be increased by $15,000.

(iv)   Depreciation is charged on buildings using the straight line method at 3% per annum. The cost of land included in land and buildings is $200,000. Buildings depreciation is treated as an administration expense.

(v)   Plant and equipment is depreciated using the reducing balance method at 20%. Plant and equipment depreciation is regarded as a cost of sales.

(vi)   Vehicles are depreciated using the straight line method at 20% per year. Vehicles depreciation is regarded as a distribution cost.

(vii)   During the year DM issued 100,000 new $1 equity shares at a premium of 50%. The proceeds were all received before 30 September 20X6 and are included in the trial balance figures.

(viii)   DM entered into a non-cancellable five-year finance lease on 1 October 20X5 to acquire a number of vehicles for use in the entity. The vehicles had a fair value of $100,000 and the annual lease payment is $27,000 per year in arrears. The finance charge is to be allocated using the actuarial method. The interest rate implicit in the lease is 10.92%. All the vehicles have economic useful lives of five years. The only entry in the accounting system is the lease payments made to date of $27,000.

(ix)   The 6% loan was taken out on 1 December 20X5.

Required:

Prepare the income statement and a statement of changes in equity for the year ended 30 September 20X6 and a balance sheet at that date, in a form suitable for presentation to the shareholders and in accordance with the requirements of International Financial Reporting Standards.

Notes to the financial statements are NOT required, but all workings must be clearly shown and should be to the nearest $000. Do NOT prepare a statement of accounting policies.

(20 marks)

278   C CASH FLOW

The financial statements of C for the year to 31 March 20X4 were as follows:

Balance sheets at	*31 March 20X4*		*31 March 20X3*	
	$000	$000	$000	$000
Non-current assets:				
Intangible assets	111		90	
Tangible assets	7,724		4,923	
		7,835		5,013
Current assets:				
Inventories	1,337		864	
Trade receivables	743		435	
Investment	0		730	
Bank	489		7	
Cash	27		22	
		2,596		2,058
Total assets		10,431		7,071

	31 March 20X4		31 March 20X3	
	$000	$000	$000	$000
Capital and reserves:				
Ordinary shares $1 each		2,000		1,500
Share premium account		1,500		500
Revaluation reserve		1,080		630
Accumulated profits		3,311		2,876
		7,891		5,506
Non-current liabilities:				
Loans	1,006		410	
Deferred tax	254		291	
		1,260		701
Current liabilities:				
Trade payables	626		552	
Tax	234		188	
Interest payable	20		4	
Other provisions	400		120	
		1,280		864
Total equity and liabilities		10,431		7,071

Income statement for the year to 31 March 20X4

	$000	$000
Revenue		14,780
Cost of sales		(9,607)
Gross profit		5,173
Distribution costs	(1,222)	
Administrative expenses (including provisions)	(2,924)	
		(4,146)
Profit from operations		1,027
Finance cost	(45)	
Income from investments	0	
		(45)
Profit before tax		982
Income tax expense		(197)
Net profit for the period		785

Additional information:

(i)   Tangible non-current assets balances were as follows:

	31 March 20X4	31 March 20X3	
	Cost or valuation	Cost or valuation	Accumulated depreciation/ amortisation
	$000	$000	$000
Land	3,636	3,186	0
Buildings	3,063	1,663	416
Plant, machinery and equipment	2,188	1,161	671

(ii) Intangible non-current assets comprise development expenditure incurred in previous years and in the current year, and being carried forward to future periods. Development expenditure amortised during the year was $18,000.

(iii) Tangible non-current assets include land which was revalued by $450,000 on 31 March 20X4.

(iv) Machinery disposed of in the year had originally cost $400,000; accumulated depreciation at 31 March 20X3 was $380,000. The agreed selling price of $31,000 had not been received by the year-end and is included in receivables.

In addition to this contract, other new plant and machinery had been purchased during the year.

(v) Depreciation charged for the year was:

• buildings 2.5% straight line

• plant, machinery and equipment 20% reducing balance.

(vi) C's accounting policy is to charge a full year's depreciation in the year of acquisition and no depreciation in the year of disposal.

(vii) Receivables consist of:

	31 March 20X4 $000	31 March 20X3 $000
Trade receivables	712	401
Receivable arising from sale of non-current assets	31	0
Interest receivable on current asset investments	0	34

(viii) The current asset investment was a government bond, which matured on 31 March 20X3 and was redeemed in April 20X3 for $750,000.

(ix) C did not repurchase any of its shares during the year.

(x) An interim dividend of $350,000 was paid during the year.

Required:

Prepare the following for C for the year ended 31 March 20X4, in the form prescribed by IAS 7 *Cash Flow Statements:*

(a) a cash flow statement, using the indirect method **(18 marks)**

(b) an analysis of cash and cash equivalents. **(2 marks)**

Note: Do NOT prepare a reconciliation of net cash flows to the movement in net debt or an analysis of changes in net debt. All workings must be clearly shown.

(Total: 20 marks)

279   TEX CASH FLOW STATEMENT (PILOT PAPER)

The following information has been extracted from the draft financial statements of TEX, a manufacturing enterprise:

TEX – Income statement for the year ended 30 September 20X3

	$000
Revenue	15,000
Cost of sales	(9,000)
Gross profit	6,000
Other operating expenses	(2,300)
	3,700
Finance cost	(124)
Profit before tax	3,576
Income tax expense	(1,040)
Dividends	(1,100)
	1,436

TEX – Balance sheets at 30 September

	20X3		20X2	
	$000	$000	$000	$000
Assets				
Non-current assets		18,160		14,500
Current assets				
Inventories	1,600		1,100	
Trade receivables	1,500		800	
Bank	150		1,200	
		3,250		3,100
Total assets		21,410		17,600
Equity and liabilities				
Capital and reserves:				
Issued capital		10,834		7,815
Accumulated profits		5,836		4,400
		16,670		12,215
Non-current liabilities:				
Interest-bearing borrowings	1,700		2,900	
Deferred tax	600		400	
		2,300		3,300
Current liabilities				
Trade payables	700		800	
Proposed dividend	700		600	
Tax	1,040		685	
		2,440		2,085
		21,410		17,600

Non-current assets

	Property $000	Plant $000	Total $000
At 30 September 20X2			
Cost	8,400	10,800	19,200
Depreciation	1,300	3,400	4,700
Net book value	7,100	7,400	14,500
At 30 September 20X2			
Cost	11,200	13,400	24,600
Depreciation	1,540	4,900	6,440
Net book value	9,660	8,500	18,160

(i) Plant disposed of during the year had an original cost of $2,600,000 and accumulated depreciation of $900,000; cash received on disposal was $730,000.

(ii) All additions to non-current assets were purchased for cash.

(iii) Dividends were declared before the balance sheet dates.

Required:

Prepare TEX's cash flow statement and associated notes for the year ended 30 September 20X3, in accordance with IAS 7 *Cash Flow Statements*. **(20 marks)**

280 DIRECT AND INDIRECT

The following information has been extracted from the draft financial information of B.

Income statement for the year ended 31 December 20X4

	$000	$000
Sales revenue		490
Raw materials consumed	(49)	
Staff costs	(37)	
Depreciation	(74)	
Loss on disposal of non-current asset	(4)	
		(164)
Profit from operations		326
Interest payable		(23)
Profit before tax		303
Income tax expense		(87)
Profit after tax		216

Balance sheets

	31 December 20X4		31 December 20X3	
Assets	$000	$000	$000	$000
Non-current assets (see below)		1,145		957
Current assets:				
Inventory	19		16	
Trade receivables	40		30	
Bank	19		32	
	———	78	———	78
Total assets		1,223		1,035
Equity and liabilities				
Equity				
Share capital		182		152
Share premium		141		80
Revaluation reserve		170		0
Accumulated profits		553		389
		1,046		621
	$000	$000	$000	$000
Non-current liabilities				
Long-term loans	70		320	
Deferred tax	16		7	
		86		327
Current liabilities:				
Payables	33		32	
Income tax	58	91	55	87
Total equity and liabilities		1,223		1,035

Non-current assets:
Cost or valuation

	20X4	20X4	20X4	Total
At 31 December 20X3	830	470	197	1,497
Additions	–	43	55	98
Disposals	–	(18)	–	(18)
Adjustment on revaluation	70	–	–	70
At 31 December 20X4	900	495	252	1,647

Depreciation

At 31 December 20X3	(90)	(270)	(180)	(540)
Charge for year	(10)	(56)	(8)	(74)
Disposals	–	12	–	12
Adjustment on revaluation	100	–	–	100
At 31 December 20X4	0	(314)	(188)	(502)

Net book value

At 31 December 20X4	900	181	64	1,145
At 31 December 20X3	740	200	17	957

Additional information:

(1) Payables in the balance sheet consisted of the following:

	At 31 December 20X4 $000	At 31 December 20X3 $000
Trade payables	31	24
Accrued interest	2	8
Total	33	32

(2) B paid dividends of $52 million during the year.

Required:

(a) Prepare a cash flow statement for B for the year ended 31 December 20X4 in accordance with the requirements of IAS 7, using the indirect method. **(15 marks)**

(b) Prepare the 'cash flows from operating activities' section of a cash flow statement for B for the year ended 31 December 20X4 in accordance with the requirements of IAS 7, using the direct method. **(5 marks)**

(Total: 20 marks)

281 AG (MAY 05 EXAM)

The financial statements of AG are given below:

Balance sheets as at	31 March 20X5 $000	$000	31 March 20X4 $000	$000
Non-current assets:				
Plant, property and equipment	4,500		4,800	
Development expenditure	370	4,870	400	5,200
Current assets:				
Inventories	685		575	
Trade receivables	515		420	
Cash and cash equivalents	552	1,752	232	1,227
Total assets		6,622		6,427
Equity and liabilities equity:				
Share capital	2,600		1,900	
Share premium account	750		400	
Revaluation reserve	425		300	
Retained earnings	1,430		1,415	
Total equity		5,205		4,015

	31 March 20X5		31 March 20X4	
	$000	$000	$000	$000
Non-current liabilities:				
10% loan notes	0		1,000	
5% loan notes	500		500	
Deferred tax	250		200	
Total non-current liabilities		750		1,700
Current liabilities:				
Trade payables	480		350	
Income tax	80		190	
Accrued expenses	107		172	
Total current liabilities:		667		712
Total equity and liabilities		6,622		6,427

Income statement for the year ended 31 March 20X5

	$000	$000
Revenue		7,500
Cost of sales		4,000
Gross profit		3,500
Distribution costs	900	
Administrative expenses	2,300	3,200
Profit from operations		300
Finance costs		45
Profit before tax		255
Income tax expense		140
Profit for the period		115

Additional information:

(i)   On 1 April 20X4, AG issued 1,400,000 $0.50 ordinary shares at a premium of 50%.

(ii)   On 1 May 20X4, AG purchased and cancelled all its 10% loan notes at par.

(iii) Non-current tangible assets include properties which were revalued upwards by $125,000 during the year.

(iv)   Non-current tangible assets disposed of in the year had a net book value of $75,000; cash received on disposal was $98,000. Any gain or loss on disposal has been included under cost of sales.

(v)   Cost of sales includes $80,000 for development expenditure amortised during the year.

(vi)   Depreciation charged for the year was $720,000.

(vii) The accrued expenses balance includes interest payable of $87,000 at 31 March 20X4 and $12,000 at 31 March 20X5.

(viii) The income tax expenses for the year to 31 March 20X5 is made up as follows:

	$000
Corporate income tax	90
Deferred tax	50
	140

(ix) Dividends paid during the year were $100,000.

Required:

Prepare a cash flow statement, using the indirect method, for AG for the year ended 31 March 20X5, in accordance with IAS 7 *Cash Flow Statements*.   **(20 marks)**

282   RED

The following financial statements relate to Red:

Income statement for the year to 31 March 20X6

	$ million	$ million
Revenue		355
Operating costs		(235)
Gross profit		120
Finance charge	(7)	
Interest income	3	
	—	4
Profit before taxation		116
Income tax expense		(32)
Profit for the period		84

Summarised balance sheets as at:

	31 March 20X6 $ million	31 March 20X5 $ million
Non-current assets		
Tangible assets	272	196
Intangible assets	3	5
	275	201
Current assets		
Inventories	120	148
Trade receivables	152	116
Interest receivable	1	2
Investments	95	0
Cash at bank	4	21
	372	287
Total assets	647	488

	31 March 20X6 $ million	31 March 20X5 $ million
Equity and liabilities		
Share capital: ordinary shares of $1 each	110	90
Share premium	64	55
Revaluation surplus	7	0
Accumulated profits	135	81
	316	226
Non-current liabilities		
6% bonds (redeemable after 7 years)	20	40
Finance leases	50	42
Deferred tax	12	8
Current liabilities	249	172
Total equity and liabilities	647	488

The following information is relevant:

(1) During the year, Red issued 10 million ordinary shares at 100% above their par value, incurring issue costs of $1 million. After this, Red made a bonus issue of 1 new share for every 10 shares held.

(2) Tangible non-current assets include property that was revalued during the year, resulting in a revaluation surplus of $7 million. Assets capitalised under finance lease agreements amounted to $28 million. Non-current assets with a net book value of $19 million were disposed of for $21 million. The depreciation charge on tangible non-current assets for the year was $37 million.

(3) There were no acquisitions or disposals of intangible non-current assets during the year.

(4) Investments purchased during the year were $80 million of loan stock redeemable in 20X9 and a loan note to a major public company which is repayable on demand. The market value of these investments at 31 March 20X6 was the same as their original purchase cost.

(5) *Analysis of current liabilities:*

	31 March 20X6 $ million	31 March 20X5 $ million
Trade payables	216	135
Finance leases	5	3
Income taxes	17	12
Interest payable	3	2
Bank overdraft	8	20
	249	172

(6) $20 million of 6% bonds were redeemed at par on 31 March 20X6.

(7) Interest on the finance leases of $3 million is included in the finance charge in the income statement.

(8) Dividends of $20 million were paid during the year.

Required:

Prepare a cash flow statement for Red for the year to 31 March 20X6 (indirect method).

(20 marks)

283   CJ (MAY 06 EXAM)

The financial statements of CJ for the year to 31 March 20X6 were as follows:

Balance sheets at	*31 March 20X6*		*31 March 20X5*	
	$000	$000	$000	$000
Non-current tangible assets				
Property	19,160		18,000	
Plant and equipment	8,500		10,000	
Available for sale investments	1,500		2,100	
		29,160		30,100
Current assets				
Inventory	2,714		2,500	
Trade receivables	2,106		1,800	
Cash at bank	6,553		0	
Cash in hand	409		320	
		11,782		4,620
Total assets		40,942		34,720
Equity and liabilities				
Ordinary shares $0.50 each	12,000		7,000	
Share premium	10,000		5,000	
Revaluation reserve	4,200		2,700	
Retained profit	3,009		1,510	
		29,209		16,210
Non-current liabilities				
Interest-bearing borrowings	7,000		13,000	
Provision for deferred tax	999	7,999	800	13,800
Current liabilities				
Bank overdraft	0		1,200	
Trade and other payables	1,820		1,700	
Corporate income tax payable	1,914		1,810	
		3,734		4,710
		40,942		34,720

Income statement for the Year to 31 March 20X6

	$000
Revenue	31,000
Cost of sale	(19,000)
Gross profit	12,000
Other income	200
Administrative expenses	(3,900)
Distribution costs	(2,600)
	5,700
Finance cost	(1,302)
Profit before tax	4,398
Income tax expense	(2,099)
Profit for the period	2,299

Additional information:

(1)   On 1 April 20X5, CJ issued 10,000,000 $0.50 ordinary shares at a premium of 100%.

(2)   No additional available for sale investments were acquired during the year.

(3)   On 1 July 20X5, CJ repaid $6,000,000 of its interest-bearing borrowings.

(4)   Properties were revalued by $1,500,000 during the year.

(5)   Plant disposed of in the year had a net book value of $95,000; cash received on disposal was $118,000.

(6)   Depreciation charged for the year was properties $2,070,000 and plant and equipment $1,985,000.

(7)   The trade and other payables balance includes interest payable of $650,000 at 31 March 20X5 and $350,000 at 31 March 20X6.

(8)   Dividends paid during the year, $800,000, comprised last year's final dividend plus the current year's interim dividend. CJ's accounting policy is not to accrue proposed dividends.

(9)   Other income comprises:

	$
Dividends received	180,000
Gain on disposal of available for sale investments	20,000
	200,000

Dividends receivable are not accrued.

(10) Income tax expense comprises:

	$
Corporate income tax	1,900,000
Deferred tax	199,000
	2,099,000

Required:

Prepare CJ's cash flow statement for the year ended 31 March 20X6, in accordance with IAS 7 *Cash Flow Statements*.

(20 marks)

284 **DN (NOV 06 EXAM)**

DN's draft financial statements for the year ended 31 October 20X6 are as follows:

DN Income statement for the Year to 31 October 20X6

	$000	$000
Revenue		2,600
Cost of sales		
Parts and sub-assemblies	(500)	
Labour	(400)	
Overheads	(400)	(1,300)
Gross profit		1,300
Administrative expenses	(300)	
Distribution costs	(100)	(400)
Profit from operations		900
Finance cost		(110)
Profit before tax		790
Income tax expense		(140)
Profit for the period		650

DN Balance sheet at	*31 October 20X6*		*31 October 20X5*	
	$000	$000	$000	$000
Assets				
Non-current assets				
Property, plant and equipment		4,942		4,205
Current assets				
Inventories	190		140	
Trade receivables	340		230	
Cash and cash equivalents	0	530	45	415
Total assets		5,472		4,620

Equity and liabilities

Equity

Equity shares of $0.50 each	1,300		1,000
Share premium	300		0
Revaluation reserve	400		0
Retained earnings	1,660		1,410
Total equity		3,660	2,410
Non-current liabilities			
Bank loans (various rates)		1,500	2,000
		5,160	4,410
Current liabilities		312	210
Total equity and liabilities		5,472	4,620

Additional information:

(i)   Property, plant and equipment comprises:

	20X6 $000	20X5 $000
Property	3,100	2,800
Plant and equipment	1,842	1,405

(ii)   Plant and equipment sold during the year for $15,000 had originally cost $60,000 five years ago. The plant and equipment were depreciated on the straight line basis over six years. Any gain/loss on disposal has been included in overheads.

(iii)   Properties were revalued on 31 October 20X6.

(iv)   DN made an equity share issue on 31 October 20X6. The new shares do not rank for dividend until the following accounting period.

(v)   DN's funding includes two bank loans:

- $1,500,000 6% loan commenced 30 June 20X6, due for repayment 29 June 20X9

- $2,000,000 7% loan repaid early on 1 July 20X6.

(vi)   Current liabilities:

	20X6 $000	20X5 $000
Trade payables	105	85
Interest payable	55	75
Tax payable	70	50
Bank overdraft	82	0
Total current liabilities	312	210

(vii)   A dividend of $0.20 per share was paid on 1 May 20X6.

(viii) Overheads include the annual depreciation charge of $100,000 for property and $230,000 for plant and equipment.

Required:

Prepare DN's cash flow statement for the year ended 31 October 20X6, using the indirect method, in accordance with IAS 7 *Cash Flow Statements*.

(20 marks)

Section 4

ANSWERS TO SECTION A-TYPE QUESTIONS

PRINCIPLES OF BUSINESS TAXATION

1   The competent jurisdiction is the country whose tax laws apply to the entity.

2   A taxable person is an individual, company or other organisation who is liable to pay direct taxes.

3   **A**

Taxes on property ownership and taxes on dividends received are direct taxes because the tax falls directly on the property owner or the receiver of the dividends. An excise duty on tobacco is an indirect tax: it is paid by traders in tobacco but the cost is passed on to the consumers of tobacco through the selling prices of tobacco goods.

4   In order that different tax rules can be applied to different types or sources of income.

Tutorial note

For example, different tax rules might be applied to earned income in employment, profits from a trade, interest income, dividend income and income from rented property. Each type of income can be classified according to its Schedule and taxed accordingly.

---

5   **D**

This was an unusual question from the CIMA pilot paper. Clearly, a tax on profits is not an indirect tax; therefore answers A and C cannot be correct. However, there is nothing to prevent a tax on profits from being called a profits tax or an earnings tax or an income tax (given that profits are reported in income statements). Direct tax is a general term that would include a tax on profits. CIMA's preferred answer is D. There is no clear reason why answer B cannot be correct too although, in the UK, 'income tax' is a tax on the income of individuals, not enterprises.

6   **D**

The taxes in answers A, B and C are all direct taxes.

7   A direct tax is one that is levied directly on the person who is intended to pay the tax.

---

8 **Tutorial note**

The question is not sufficiently specific, and so arguably unfair. There are five sources of tax rules in the answer below, but two have been linked into a common category, as intended by the CIMA pilot paper (and as suggested by the syllabus for this paper).

1   Domestic legislation and judicial rulings.

2   Tax authority statements of practice.

3   Directives from a supranational body.

4   International treaties (for example, double taxation treaties).

9   Deferred taxation is an adjustment to the annual tax charge for temporary differences between accounting profit and taxable profit.

10   The answer is a $24,000 reduction in the total tax charge.

	$
Tax base of asset after 3 years	307,200
($600,000 × 80% × 80% × 80%)	
Selling price	300,000
Loss on disposal for tax purposes	7,200
Decrease in current tax (40%)	2,880
Tax base of asset on disposal	307,200
Carrying amount in the accounts (600,000 – 240,000)	360,000
Deductible temporary timing difference	52,800
Deferred tax deduction (40%)	21,120

	$
Decrease in current tax	(2,880)
Deferred tax deduction	(21,120)
Net reduction in total tax charge	(24,000)

11   The answer is $10.1 million.

The revaluation creates a temporary difference. The fact that the company has no intention of disposing of the assets is irrelevant. The revaluation increases the accounting value of the assets by $7 million, but the tax base value of the assets is unchanged. The increase in the difference between the accounting value and the tax base adds to deferred tax. The amount of the increase in $7 million × tax rate of 30% = $2.1 million.

	$ million
Deferred tax liability brought forward	8.0
Deferred tax charge	2.1
Deferred tax at 30 June 20X5	10.1

12 The answer is $2,013.

	Accounting depreciation	Tax depreciation	Difference
	$	$	$
Cost	20,000	20,000	
Less: Depreciation b/fwd	5,000	12,500	
	15,000	7,500	
20X3	1,630	2,120	
20X4	1,590	1,860	
20X5	1,530	1,320	
Written down value at 31 December 20X5	10,250	2,200	8,050
Tax at 25%			2,013

13 The answer is $294,120.

	$
Deferred tax increase (759,000 – 642,000) =	117,000
Charge for year (946,000 × 22%) =	208,120
Overprovision from previous year	(31,000)
Income tax expense	294,120

14 **A**

	$
Current year charge	320,000
Over-provision for prior year	(10,000)
Charge	310,000

15 The answer is $24,100.

	$	$
Pre-tax profit in the accounts		80,000
Add back:		
Accounting depreciation	60,000	
Non-allowable expenditure	12,000	
		72,000
		152,000
Deduct:		
Tax depreciation	(70,000)	
Non-taxable income	(5,000)	
		(75,000)
Taxable profit		77,000
Current tax charge at 30%		$23,100

	$
Current tax charge	23,100
Over-provision of tax in the previous year	(2,000)
Deferred tax (30% of (70,000 – 60,000))	3,000
	24,100

16 The answer is $17,500.

(4/12 × $75,000 × 20%) + (8/12 × $75,000 × 25%)

17 **A**

The tax base of the asset is its valuation for tax purposes, which is $14,000 ($20,000 cost minus accumulated tax depreciation already allowed $6,000). The temporary difference between the tax base and the carrying value of the asset in the accounts is $4,000 ($6,000 – $2,000), and with tax at 30% the amount of deferred taxation is $1,200.

However, statement 3 is incorrect The tax base of the asset is $14,000 and the carrying value in the accounts is higher, $18,000. When the accounts value of the asset is higher, an additional deferred tax charge is required. The $1,200 is therefore added to the tax charge, not deducted from the tax charge for the period.

18 The answer is $22,500.

	$
Accounting profit	95,000
Adjustments:	
Non-taxable income	(15,000)
Non-tax allowable expenditure	10,000
Taxable profits	90,000
Tax at 25%	22,500

19 Tax avoidance is exploiting the detailed provisions of the tax laws in order to avoid paying tax. Tax avoidance is legal. Tax evasion is deliberately breaking the law to pay less tax, for example by withholding information about taxable income.

20 **B**

Double tax relief does not prevent you from paying tax twice. For example, suppose that your company is based in Country A and has a subsidiary operating in Country B, and there is a double taxation agreement between the countries. If tax on profits in Country B is 10% and in Country A is 15%, your company would pay tax at 10% in Country B and tax at 15% in Country A on the subsidiary's profits. Double tax relief therefore mitigates tax – you don't have to pay 35% in tax (10% + 25%) – but you might still have to pay tax on the profits twice, once in each country.

21 **C**

Withholding tax is a tax deducted at source before payment of interest or dividends.

22   The answer is $44,800.

The dividend per share is $560,000/4 million = $0.14 per share.

The gross dividend income is 240,000 shares × $0.14 × (100/75) = $44,800.

Of this gross income, the shareholder is assumed to have already paid 25% ($11,200) in tax at source, and received cash of $33,600.

23   The answer is $390,000.

	$	$
Company's liability for tax (40% × $870,000)		348,000
Gross dividend income for shareholders ($630,000 × 100/75)	840,000	
Tax on gross dividend (30% × $840,000)	252,000	
Tax credit (25% × $840,000)	210,000	
Tax payable by shareholders		42,000
Total tax revenue for the government		390,000

24   **B**

Under a full imputation system, the entire tax paid by a company on its dividends is credited against the personal income tax liabilities of the shareholders.

25   **A**

Company tax @ 25% = $100,000

If the total tax paid is $175,000, then $75,000 must have been paid by the shareholder.

As the tax rate payable by the shareholder is 30%, the income recognised by the shareholder. must have been:

75,000/0.3 = 250,000

As this is the amount that was actually paid as a dividend and no tax credit has been given, then this is a classical tax system.

26   Thin capitalisation rules are often applied where a subsidiary in a multinational group is financed largely by inter-company borrowings. Interest on 'excessive debt' is re-characterised as dividends, and so is not a deductible expense for tax purposes.

27   A rule requiring that all transfers between group members should be at arm's length prices (fair price or market price).

28   **Year 1: Taxable capital gains of $6,000.** $50,000 of the trading losses in Year 2 can be carried back and set off against the profit in Year 1, reducing the taxable trading profit to 0. The capital loss in Year 2 cannot be carried back to Year 1.

Year 2: No taxable trading profits or gains. Trading loss and capital loss in the year. Unrelieved trading losses of $40,000 and the unrelieved capital losses of $8,000 are carried forward to Year 3.

Year 3: No taxable trading profits or gains. Unrelieved trading losses of $40,000 are set against the trading profits of $30,000. The unrelieved trading loss is now $10,000 and is carried forward to Year 4. The unrelieved capital loss brought forward is set off against the capital gain in Year 3, leaving $3,000 of unrelieved capital losses to carry forward to Year 4.

Year 4: Taxable trading profits of $60,000 and taxable capital gains of $3,000. Taxable trading profits = $70,000 – $10,000 unrelieved losses brought forward. Taxable capital gains = $6,000 – $3,000 unrelieved losses brought forward.

29   C

Group loss relief allows members of the group to surrender their losses to any other member of the group. Consolidation of profits and losses does not apply to tax computations and so answer A is incorrect. Group loss relief is an option that can be taken by the group, and is not compulsory. Therefore answers B and D are incorrect.

30   B

	$
Gross dividend taken into DP's taxable income	50,000
Tax @ 12%	6,000
Less tax credit	(5,000)
Remaining tax liability	1,000

31   B

The term 'effective incidence' is sometimes used to refer to the person who bears the cost of a tax. For example, sales tax is generally collected and paid over to the tax authorities by the trader who supplies the goods or services. However, it is the final consumer of those goods or services who suffers the effective incidence (or bears the burden) of the sales tax. So answer B is correct.

32   The answer is $4,000.

A business is only allowed to deduct revenue expenditure in calculating its taxable profits. Therefore the capital repayments of the loan are not an allowable expense. However, the interest payments on the loan (the finance costs) are deductible.

The cost of the new computer equipment is a capital expense and therefore not deductible. However, the business may claim tax allowances.

	$
Revenue	45,000
Deduct – operating costs	(23,000)
– finance costs	(4,000)
– tax allowances ($20,000 × 10%)	(2,000)
Taxable profit	16,000
Tax liability $16,000 × 25% =	4,000

33   **A**

200 items × $50 × 15% = $1,500 VAT payable (output tax).

200 items × ($30 + $5) × 15% = $1,050 VAT reclaimable (input tax).

The net amount payable is therefore $450 ($1,500 – $1,050).

34   **A**

A tax authority is unlikely to have the power of arrest. This power will usually be restricted to the police or other law enforcement officers.

35   **B**

The OECD's list of permanent establishments includes a place of management, a workshop and a quarry. A building site is only included if it lasts more than 12 months. Specifically excluded from the definition of permanent establishment are facilities used only for the purpose of storage, display or delivery of goods.

36   A tax base is the amount attributed to that asset or liability for tax purposes.

37   The answer is $90,000.

The OECD Model Convention states that the maximum withholding tax on dividends should be 15% (15% × $600,000 = $90,000) when the shareholder receiving the dividend owns less than 25% of the shares. (The maximum withholding tax is 5% when the shareholder owns at least 25% of the shares. The maximum rate of withholding tax on interest payments permitted under the OECD Model Convention is 10%.)

38   **B**

	$
Purchase cost	200,000
Tax allowance in year to 31 March 20X2	(50,000)
	150,000
Tax allowance in year to 31 March 20X3	(37,500)
	112,500
Tax allowance in year to 31 March 20X4	(28,125)
Tax written down value at 31 March Year 4	84,375
Carrying value in the accounts	140,000
($200,000 minus (3 × 10% × $200,000)	
Timing difference	55,625
Tax rate	30%
Deferred tax balance	$16,688

39   The place where management is exercised (which might not be the country of incorporation).

The OECD Model Convention states that, if a company can be defined as 'resident' of two countries that have a double taxation agreement, 'it shall be deemed to be resident only of the State in which its place of effective management is situated'.

40 D

An indirect tax per unit of an item, such as a tax per litre of gasoline, is a unit tax. An ad valorem tax is a tax whose amount is dependent on the value of the taxed item. A sales tax (value added tax) is an ad valorem indirect tax because the tax is 20% of the selling price excluding tax. A tax of 3% on the value of property purchased is also an ad valorem tax, but it is a direct tax, not an indirect tax.

41 The answer is $66,750.

	Tax allowances $		Depreciation charge $
Y/e 30/9/X4		*Y/e 30/9/X4*	
Cost	900,000	Cost	900,000
Allowance (900,000 × 50%)	(450,000)	Depreciation (900,000 – 50,000)/5 years	(170,000)
C/f	450,000	C/f	730,000
Y/e 30/9/X5		*Y/e 30/9/X5*	
Allowance (450,000 × 25%)	(112,500)	Depreciation	(170,000)
C/f	337,500	C/f	560,000

Deferred tax provision at 30 September 20X5

	$
Accounting book value	560,000
Tax written down value	337,500
	222,500
Tax at 30% =	66,750

42 *30/9/X3* Trading profit $200 × 20% = **$40**

Capital loss c/f $100

30/9/X4 Trading loss c/f $120

Capital loss of $100 b/f is c/f

30/9/X5 Trading profit $150 – $120 = $30

Capital gain $130 – $100 = $30

Total $30 + $30 = $60 × 20% = **$12**

43 The answer is $14,000.

BZ paid VAT on its sales of luxury goods of $120,000 × 20% = $24,000. Against this sum it could deduct VAT of $100,000 × 10% = $10,000 suffered on its purchases.

44   C

The incidence of tax refers to the distribution of the tax burden. Formal incidence is on the person who has direct contact with the tax authorities. In the case of sales tax, the seller must account for the tax and pay it to the tax authorities. The customer, however, has the effective incidence because it is he who ends up bearing the cost of the tax as he cannot pass it on to anyone else. Sales tax is an example of an indirect tax, whereas income tax is an example of a direct tax as the formal and effective incidence of the tax are the same.

45   A

BM is paying tax at the rate of 10% (3,000/30,000) on profits of $30,000. BV is paying tax at the rate of 12.5% (7,500/60,000) on profits of $60,000. This is an example of a progressive tax as it takes an increasing proportion of income as income rises.

A proportional tax is one that takes the same proportion of income as income rises. Using the figures in the question, BY would pay $6,000 ($60,000 × 10%) if the tax were proportional.

A regressive tax is one which takes a decreasing proportion of income as income rises. This would be the case if BM (with the lower income) paid tax at the rate of 12.5%, whilst BV (with the higher income) paid tax at the rate of 10%.

It is arguable that answer C is also correct. This would appear to be a direct tax as it is assessed on and collected from the person who ultimately bears the burden of the tax.

46   Government sets deadlines for filing returns and paying tax so that:

- taxpayers know when payment is required
- the tax authorities can forecast their cash flows
- they can impose penalties for late payment/late filing.

47   CU (250 – 100) × 15%= $22,500

CZ (600 – 250) × 15%= $52,500

48   D

Each of the other three factors can be taken into account in determining tax residence

49   C

Equity

50   Sales tax payable:

DA   (500 – 200) @ 15% = 45

DB   (1,000 – 500) @ 15% = 75

51		$
Sales tax on manufacturing costs	200 @ 7%	14
Sales tax to DB	500 @ 7%	35
Sales tax to customer	1,000 @ 7%	70
		119

Tutorial note

CIMA's official answer ignores the initial sale of the goods from the manufacture to DA and instead shows the answer as $105 (35 + 70).

PRINCIPLES OF REGULATION OF FINANCIAL REPORTING

52   D

The IFRIC interprets International Financial Reporting Standards and, after public consultation and reporting to the IASB, it issues an interpretation.

53   A

The IASC Foundation is the supervisory body, and consists of trustees whose main responsibilities are governance issues and ensuring that sufficient funding is available.

54   D

The objectives of financial statements are set out in the IASB *Framework*. Note that providing information about 'changes in the financial position', as well as information about financial position and financial performance, is included in these objectives.

55   B

You should learn the IASB definitions of both assets and liabilities. The definition in the question is in two parts: (1) a liability is a present obligation that has arisen out of a past event, and (2) it is certain or probable that settlement of this obligation will result in an outflow of economic benefits, such as a payment of money. It is also necessary for the amount of the liability to be measured reliably.

56   C

The IASB *Framework* states that materiality is a threshold or cut-off point for reporting information, but is not a qualitative characteristic that financial information must have to be useful.

57   Decreases in economic benefits during the accounting period in the form of outflows or depletions of assets that result in decreases in equity, other than those relating to distributions to equity participants.

58   **The need for timeliness.** Information must be provided in a timely manner, so that it is not out-of-date.

Balance between benefit and cost. The need for the benefits from the provision of information to exceed the costs of providing it.

59   **C**

The beginning of IAS 1 has elements in common with the IASB *Framework*. It mentions the going concern, accruals and consistency concepts, plus the three concepts in Answer C.

'Materiality and aggregation' is the requirement that each material class of similar items should be presented separately in the financial statements, and items of a dissimilar nature should be presented separately unless they are immaterial.

'Offsetting' means that assets and liabilities cannot be offset against each other (shown as a net amount) and income and expenditure cannot be offset against each other. However, this requirement does not apply where an IFRS/IAS permits offsetting.

'Comparative information' is the requirement to present in the financial statements comparative information for the previous accounting period (unless an IFRS states that this is not necessary).

60   **C**

The IASB *Framework* defines equity as the residual interest in the assets of the enterprise after all the liabilities have been deducted from total assets. It is important to recognise this idea that equity is a balancing figure: Assets – Liabilities. Balance sheets should be prepared with a view to measuring assets and liabilities in the best manner, and equity is the amount left over when liabilities are subtracted from assets.

61   **B**

Consistency is one of the four main characteristics of financial information identified by the IASB *Framework*. Sub-characteristics of reliability (another of the four main characteristics) are faithful representation, substance over form, neutrality, prudence and completeness.

62   An asset is a resource controlled by the enterprise as a result of past events and from which future economic benefits are expected to flow to the enterprise.

63   **A**

IAS 1 states that the accounting policies adopted by an entity should ensure that the information in the financial statements is reliable and relevant. These are two of the four qualitative characteristics of information identified by the IASB *Framework*. Presumably, the other two main qualities (understandability and comparability) are not directly related to the selection of accounting policies.

64   **B**

The auditor expresses an *opinion* on the truth and fairness of the financial statements; the auditor does *not certify* that the financial statements give a true and fair view – statement (i) is therefore false. All the other statements are correct.

65 C

The disagreement is material and it affects the auditor's opinion. However, as the financial statements are not seriously misleading, the auditor should issue an 'except for' qualification. (If the financial statements were seriously misleading, he would issue an adverse opinion.)

66 D

The term GAAP means generally accepted accounting practice.

67 C

The IASC Foundation trustees have responsibility for governance issues and for ensuring that funds are available for the various bodies (IASB etc) to carry on their work.

68 D

The two assumptions underlying the conceptual framework are the accruals basis and the going concern basis.

69 C

The four main characteristics or qualities of financial information are understandability, relevance, reliability and comparability. It is worth noting that, although the accruals basis is recognised in International Accounting Standards, the term 'matching concept' is not used.

70 B

When there is a material qualification by the external auditors (as distinct from a pervasive qualification) the audit report should give an 'except for' opinion. The auditors will state that, in their opinion, the financial statements give a true and fair view, except for ....

71 C

The IASC Foundation appoints the members of the IASB. The SAC advises the IASB. IFRIC reports to the IASB.

72 D

If the auditors disagree with the treatment of a material item, they should firstly try to persuade the directors to change the item's treatment. They cannot force the directors to change the treatment, therefore answer C is incorrect. If the directors do not change the item's treatment, the auditors may give a qualified opinion.

73 Auditors usually have the power to:

- access the books, records, documents and accounts

- attend and speak at meetings of equity holders

- require officers of the entity to provide them with information and explanations.

74 1 Advisory group appointed to advise on the project/topic.

2 Discussion document issued for public comment.

3 Exposure Draft published, as long as it has support from eight IASB members, together with details of any dissenting opinions from IASB members.

75 Expenses and equity.

SINGLE COMPANY FINANCIAL ACCOUNTS

76 B

Expenses are analysed into cost of sales, distribution costs and administrative expenses.

77 The following items are mentioned in IAS 1 as the sub-classifications of receivables:

(a) amounts receivable from trade customers

(b) amounts receivable from related parties

(c) prepayments

(d) other items.

78 C

Both items must be shown on the face of the income statement. Other items to include in the income statement include revenue, the tax expense and the profit or loss for the period (IAS 1).

79 A

IAS 1 states that the financial statements must be prepared on a going concern basis, unless management intends to liquidate the entity or to cease trading, or has no realistic alternative but to do so. When the financial statements are not prepared on a going concern basis, this fact must be disclosed. It is not therefore a requirement of IAS 1 that a note should state that the accounts are prepared on a going concern basis. (However, there might be a similar requirement, for example in a corporate governance code, that the directors should state in the annual report and accounts that the entity is a going concern.)

80 D

Revenue and finance costs must be shown on the face of the income statement.

81 C

Current assets are cash and other assets consumed or held primarily for the purpose of being traded.

The current portion of an amortising loan repayable within the next 12 months (= the loan principal repayable in the next 12 months) is also 'current', but in this case the company is presumably the borrower and not the lender, therefore the item is a current liability, not a current asset.

82 A

A revaluation of a non-current asset is not reported through the income statement, but as an adjustment to the equity reserves (revaluation reserve account). The revaluation will therefore affect the balance sheet and the statement of changes in equity, but not the income statement. A revaluation is not a cash flow transaction, and so would not appear in the cash flow statement.

83 The answer is (in $000) 13,778.

The calculation is as follows:

	$000
Profit before tax	12,044
Add Depreciation	1,796
Loss on sale of tangible non-current assets	12
	13,852
Increase in inventories	(398)
Increase in receivables	(144)
Increase in payables	468
Cash generated from operations	13,778

84 The answer is £105,000.

	$
Balance at 30 September 20X4	180
Revaluation (30 – 10)	20
Disposal at NBV (90 – 85)	(5)
Depreciation	(40)
	155
Balance at 30 September 20X5	(260)
Purchases	105

Disposal

	$		$
Cost	90	Bank	15
Profit	10	Dep'n (balance)	85
	100		100

85 **A**

	$
Accrued interest b/f	12,000
Interest payable per income statement	41,000
Accrued interest c/f	(15,000)
Paid	38,000

86 The answer (in $000) is 350.

	$000
Total opening balances (380 + 80)	460
Add: Tax charge for the year	450
	910
Less: Total closing balances (460 + 100)	560
Tax paid during the period	350

87   D

Repayment of borrowings will be included in financing cash flows. Cash paid for the purchase of non-current assets and cash received from the sale of non-current assets are cash flows from investing activities. Dividends **received** are also a cash flow from investing activities.

88   D

All four items are included in the required disclosures for each reportable segment (IAS 14). Note that the carrying amount (balance sheet value) of the segment assets must be shown, and revenue should be shown as revenue from external customers and revenue from other segments. IAS 14 refers to the profit or loss of a segment as the 'segment result'.

89   A

IAS 14 requires an entity to identify its primary basis of segment reporting (between business segments and geographical segments) and its secondary basis. Extensive disclosures are required for the primary basis, including segment revenue and result. Less extensive disclosures are required for the secondary reporting basis, but this includes revenue.

Segment revenue must therefore always be analysed by both business segment and geographical segment.

90   B

External revenue and segment profit need separate disclosure under IAS 14 in respect of segments reported as primary segments.

91   D

CL should select business segments as its primary reporting format as its risks and returns are governed mainly by differences in the products that it sells.

CQ should select geographical segments as its primary reporting format as its risks and returns are governed mainly by the fact that it operates in different countries.

92   • It must be a distinguishable component of the entity.

• The risks and returns are different from those for other parts of the business.

• It contributes at least 10% of total sales revenue, profits or assets.

93   IAS 18 states that revenue from the sale of goods should be recognised when the following five conditions have been met:

• The significant risks and rewards of ownership have been transferred to the buyer.

• The seller does not retain any continuing influence or control over the goods.

• Revenue can be measured reliably.

• It is reasonably certain that the buyer will pay for the goods.

• The seller's costs can be measured reliably.

Note: Only FOUR of the above were required.

94 C

The prior period error is corrected by restating the comparative amounts for the previous period at their correct value. A note to the accounts should disclose the nature of the error, together with other details.

95 B

A change from writing off borrowing costs to capitalising them is regarded as a change in accounting policy. So answer B is correct. A change in the method used to calculate depreciation or provisions is regarded as a change in accounting estimate. Therefore answers A and C are incorrect. Making a provision for a previously disclosed contingent liability is also not a change in accounting policy. So answer D is incorrect.

96 (1) When a change in accounting policy is required by a new or revised accounting standard.

(2) If the change in policy results in financial statements providing reliable and more relevant information.

97 The answer is $3,700,000.

The division is presumably a cash-generating unit that will be classified as a discontinued operation within the meaning of IFRS 5. A discontinued operation is one that has been disposed of or is classified as 'held for sale'.

IFRS 5 requires that assets (or a group of assets) classified as held for sale should be measured at the lower of carrying amount and fair value less costs to sell. This means that any future profits on disposal cannot be recognised (since carrying amount is lower).

IFRS 5 also requires that on the face of the income statement there should be a total figure for:

(a) the post-tax profit or loss of the discontinued operation, and

(b) the post-tax gain or loss recognised on the measurement to fair value less costs to sell of the assets constituting the discontinued operation.

This total figure should also be analysed into its component elements (either in a note to the accounts or on the face of the income statement).

The total figure to be shown for the year is therefore:

	$
Profit from discontinued operation	300,000
Lower of carrying amount and fair value less costs to sell:	
Item (i): Provision for closure costs	(3,000,000)
Item (iii): Impairment of plant	(1,000,000)
Amount to disclose for the discontinued operation	(3,700,000)

Notes:

(1) The closure costs should not include any apportionment of head office costs.

(2) It is assumed that the loss on the sale of the plant in January gives evidence of an impairment in value, which is therefore included as an adjusting event after the balance sheet date.

98 The answer is $580,000.

	Land $000	Buildings $000	Total $000
Cost	120	200	
Accumulated depreciation to the revaluation date	-	(100)	
Carrying value at the revaluation date	120	100	220
Revalued amount	200	600	800
Credit to revaluation reserve			580

99 The answer is $60,000.

The building will be depreciated over its remaining expected useful economic life, which is 10 years. The annual depreciation charge for the building will therefore be $600,000/10 years = $60,000 each year.

100 C

The four definitions might all seem similar, but property, plant and equipment are **tangible** assets, not any assets. IAS 16 states that a tangible asset should be held for **more than one accounting period** (rather than for more than 12 months) to qualify as property, plant and equipment.

101 A

The cost of servicing and maintenance (including the cost of an 'overhaul') must be treated as an expense and charged against profit in the period in which it occurs.

102 A

This issue is dealt with in IAS 16 and IAS 8. IAS 16 states that, if there is a change in the expected pattern of consumption of the future economic benefits from an item of property, plant and equipment, the method of depreciation should be changed to reflect the future pattern. This should be treated as a change in accounting estimate in accordance with IAS 8. IAS 8 states that the effect of the change relating to the current period should be reflected as an expense for the current period, and the effect on future periods should be reflected as an expense in those future periods. There is no retrospective adjustment to the accumulated depreciation.

103 The carrying value is the revalued amount of the asset less any subsequent accumulated depreciation and subsequent accumulated impairment losses.

104 A

IAS 16 states that when the revaluation model is used, revaluations should be made with sufficient regularity to ensure that the carrying value of the assets remain close to fair value. IAS 16 also states that, if one item in a class of assets is revalued, all the assets in that class must be revalued.

105 A

		$
1 July 20X2	Cost	50,000
30 June 20X3	Carrying amount $80\% \times 50,000$	40,000
30 June 20X4	Carrying amount $60\% \times 50,000$	30,000

On 1 July 20X4 the asset is revalued from a carrying amount (net book value) of $30,000 to a fair value of $60,000, establishing a revaluation reserve of $30,000. There are three years of useful life remaining.

	$
30 June 20X5 Carrying amount = ⅔ × 60,000	40,000
1 July 20X5 Disposal proceeds	35,000
Loss on disposal	(5,000)

There is a loss on disposal of $5,000, and the $30,000 revaluation reserve is transferred to accumulated profits as a movement on reserves.

106   A

As the lining of the furnace was identified as a separate item in the accounting records, its replacement will be viewed as capital expenditure. The other three options all involve either replacing part of an asset or restoring it to its original condition.

107   The answer is $5,250 pa.

	$
1.10.X2 purchase	21,000
Depreciation to 30.9.X5	
21,000/6 × 3	(10,500)
Balance 30.9.X5	10,500

The machine will be used for two more years, at which point it will be worthless. Assuming that production is still profitable with the increased depreciation charge, it should be written off over its remaining useful life, such that the charge recognised in the year to 30 September 20X6 should be $5,250 ($10,500 × ½).

108   Valuation $95,000.

Provision for accumulated depreciation at 31 March 20X5 $28,500.

Workings	$
Cost (1/4/X1)	100,000
$100,000 × 10% × 2 years	20,000
	80,000
To revaluation reserve	15,000
Revaluation (1/4/X3)	95,000
Depreciation $95,000/8 years	11,875
B/f 1/4/X4	83,125
Depreciation $83,125/5 years	16,625
Net book value at 31/3/X5	66,500

109   Depreciable amount is … the asset's cost or valuation less its residual value.

110 B

The cost of the decommissioning is assumed to be an obligation for the company. If so, an amount should be included in the cost of the asset when it is first recognised (on 1 July 20X4).

The amount to include in the cost of the asset for decommissioning costs is the present value of the expected future decommissioning costs. The present value is calculated by multiplying the expected future cost by a discount factor, which in this case is the discount factor for Year 5 (20X9) at 12%. $4,000,000 × 0.567 = $2.268 million.

Therefore:

Debit:	Cost of asset	$2.268 million
Credit:	Provision for decommissioning costs	$2.268 million

The asset is depreciated in the normal way, which in this example is on a straight-line basis over five years.

In addition, the decommissioning cost should be increased to $4 million by the end of Year 5. This is done by making a finance charge each year. This is charged at the cost of capital (12%) and applied to the balance on the provision account. The finance charge for the year to 30 June 20X5 is 12% × $2.268 million = $272,160.

Debit:	Finance charge (expense)	$272,160
Credit:	Provision for decommissioning costs	$272,160

	$
Depreciation charge ($2.268 million/5 years)	453,600
Finance charge	272,160
	————
Impairment loss	725,760
	————

111 C

IAS 2 states that:

(a)   selling costs cannot be included in inventory cost, therefore item (i) cannot be included

(b)   general overheads cannot be included (item (iii))

(c)   overhead costs should be added to inventory cost on the basis of normal capacity of the production facilities, therefore item (vi) cannot be included in cost

(d)   the cost of **factory** management and administration can be included, so that item (iv) can be included in inventory values.

112   Standard cost or the retail method of inventory costing may be used for convenience if the results approximate to cost. LIFO cannot be used.

113   The answer is $55,800.

	Cost	Recoverable amount (Net Realisable Value)	Lower of cost and recoverable amount
Item 1	$24,000	See *note 1*	$24,000
Item 2	$33,600	$31,800 *(note 2)*	$31,800
			————
			$55,800
			————

Notes:

(1) The recoverable amount is not known, but it must be above cost because the contract is expected to produce a high profit margin. The subsequent fall in the cost price to $20,000 is irrelevant for the inventory valuation.

(2) The recoverable amount is $36,000 minus 50% of $8,400.

114 A

	Land $ million	Buildings $ million	Total $ million
At 30 June 20X5			
Carrying amount	1.00	4.80	5.80
Building depreciation = $5 million/50 years = $100,000 per year			
Revalued amount	1.24	5.76	7.00
Transfer to revaluation reserve			1.20
At 30 June 20X7			
Carrying amount	1.24	5.52	6.76
Building depreciation = $5.76 million/48 years = $120,000 per year			
Disposal value			6.80
Gain on disposal			0.04

The gain on disposal is $40,000. The $1.2 million balance on the revaluation reserve is transferred from the revaluation reserve to another reserve account (probably accumulated profits) but is not reported through the income statement for the year.

115 The rights do not meet the definition of an asset. As a gift, they do not have a cost, and there is no reliable measurement of probable future benefit.

116 The answer is $130,000.

Goodwill is the remaining balance after the fair value of the net tangible assets acquired and the other intangible assets acquired have been subtracted from the total purchase consideration.

	$	$
Purchase price		
Shares (10,000 × $20)		200,000
Cash		20,000
		220,000
Assets acquired		
Net tangible non-current assets	25,000	
Patents	15,000	
Brand name	50,000	
		90,000
Value of goodwill		130,000

117   Any FOUR of the following:

   (i)   the technical feasibility of completing the project

   (ii)   the intention to complete the project and use or sell the developed item

   (iii) an ability to use or sell the item

   (iv)   the generation of probable future economic benefits from the developed item

   (v)   availability of adequate technical, financial and other resources to complete the project

   (vi)   ability to measure the expenditure reliably.

118   **A**

   When purchased goodwill is reduced in value due to impairment, the impairment loss should be reported through the income statement as a loss for the period, and should not be taken directly to reserves.

119   The answer is $80,000.

   An asset should be valued at the lower of carrying amount and recoverable amount. Recoverable amount is the higher of (a) fair value less costs to sell and (b) value in use.

	A	*B*	*C*
Carrying amount	200	300	240
Recoverable amount	240	260	200
Impairment loss	nil	40	40

                                    80

120   The answer is $3,640.

	$
Cost	100,000
Depreciation 31/3/X3	(25,000)
	75,000
Depreciation 31/3/X4	(18,750)
	56,250
Depreciation 31/3/X5	(14,063)
	42,187
Depreciation 31/3/X6	(10,547)
	31,640
Recoverable amount	(28,000)
Impairment loss	3,640

121 C

The recoverable amount of an asset is the higher of (a) fair value less costs to sell ($18,000) and (b) value in use ($22,000).

122 The answer is $8,912.

	$
Carrying amount at the time of the impairment review	38,912
($76,000 × 80% × 80% × 80%)	
Revised carrying amount after impairment review	30,000
Impairment (charge in the income statement)	8,912

123 The answer is $200,000.

Expenditures on the project during the year to 31 December 20X1 are research costs, which are charged as an expense in the income statement for the year.

Expenditure in the year to 31 December 20X2 ($1,000,000) should be capitalised and reported in the balance sheet at the year end. All the expenditure should be capitalised, because the recoverable amount of the expected future benefits exceeds the costs incurred.

In the year to 31 December 20X3, the expenditures should again be included in development costs as a non-tangible asset. However, at the end of the year, the accumulated expenditures capitalised are $2,200,000 ($1,000,000 + $1,200,000). This exceeds the recoverable amount of $2,000,000.

For the year to 31 December 20X3, an impairment cost of $200,000 should therefore be charged in the income statement.

The value of the development costs in the balance sheet at 31 December 20X3 is $2,000,000.

124 A

IAS 38 states that internally generated brands, mastheads, publishing titles and customer lists should not be recognised as intangible assets. This is because the costs incurred on these items cannot be distinguished from the costs of developing the business as a whole.

125 The answer is $375,000.

Number of shares before rights issue	2,000,000
Number of shares issued in rights issue $\frac{1}{5} \times 2,000,000$	400,000

	$
Premium on new shares issued 400,000 × $(2 − 1)	400,000
Less: Issue costs	25,000
Net credit to share premium account	375,000

126   C

	Issued share capital $	Share premium $	Retained profits $
Opening	500,000	nil	500,000
Bonus issue			
$(2,000,000/2 \times 25c)$	250,000		(250,000)
	750,000		
Rights issue			
$(3,000,000/3 \times 25c)$	250,000		
$(3,000,000/3 \times 15c)$		150,000	
	1,000,000	150,000	250,000

When a company makes a bonus issue of shares, the nominal value of the new shares issued can be deducted from the share premium reserve. However, in May when the bonus issue was made, the share premium was zero; therefore the nominal value of the new shares issued must be deducted from accumulated profits. A share premium is created in September when the rights issue occurs, but it cannot be used for the bonus issue.

127   The answer is $9,725,000.

The share premium can be reduced, but in this example the maximum reduction permitted is the amount of the share premium created when the shares were issued. This is 100,000 shares $\times$ $1.25 = $125,000.

The effect of the share purchase transaction is therefore as follows:

Credit	Bank (100,000 shares $\times$ $4)	$400,000
Credit	Capital reserve (100,000 shares $\times$ $1)	$100,000
Debit	Share capital (100,000 shares $\times$ $1)	$100,000
Debit	Share premium	$125,000
Debit	Accumulated profits (balance)	$275,000

The accumulated profits reserve falls from $10,000,000 by $275,000 to $9,725,000.

128   A

The accounting entries to record all the transactions are shown below:

Bank				**Application and Allotment (A and A)**			
	$		$		$		$
Applic.	100,000			Share cap.	100,000	Bank	100,000
Allot.	400,000			Share cap.	400,000	Bank	400,000
Call	247,500						
Reissue	5,000				500,000		500,000

Share capital				Call			
	$		$		$		$
		A and A	100,000	Share premium	250,000	Bank	247,500
		A and A	400,000			Own shares	2,500
					250,000		250,000

Investment in own shares				Share premium			
	$		$		$		$
Call (own shares)	2,500	Bank	5,000			Call	250,000
Share premium	2,500					Own shares	2,500
	5,000		5,000				

129 C

Preference shares are classified as financial liabilities if the company will be required to redeem the shares or if they are cumulative.

130 B

IAS 32 *Financial Instruments: Disclosure and Presentation* states that treasury shares should be shown as a deduction from equity, either on the face of the balance sheet or in the notes.

131 B

IAS 24 states that its objective is to draw attention to the possibility that the financial statements may have been affected by material transactions with related parties.

132 B

Under IAS 24 a party is related to an entity if the party is controlled or significantly influenced by an individual who is a member of the key management personnel of the entity. Customers, suppliers and providers of finance are not normally related parties.

133 B

IAS 24 states that the following are not necessarily related parties:

(a)   providers of finance (such as a bank) simply by virtue of their normal business dealings with the entity

(b)   a customer or supplier or general agent with whom the entity transacts a considerable volume of business, merely by virtue of the resulting economic dependence.

A shareholder holding 25% of the shares can presumably exercise significant influence, and so is a related party. IAS 24 states that 'significant influence is the power to participate in the financial and operating policy decisions of an entity, but is not control over those policies. Significant influence may be gained by share ownership, statute or agreement.'

134

	$m
Total cost incurred to date	16
Estimated further costs to completion	18
	34
Contract value	40
Expected profit	6
Percentage of work completed	45%
Profit recognised in year to 31 October 20X5 (6 × 45%)	2.7
Revenue recognised in year to 31 October 20X5 (40 × 45%)	18

135   The answer is $350,000.

	$000
Cost of work certified as complete	1,650
Cost of WIP not included in completed work	550
Estimated cost to complete the contract	2,750
Total expected costs	4,950
Contract value	6,000
Expected profit	1,050

Profit to recognise in the first year = (1,650/4,950) × $1,050,000 = $350,000.

136   **B**

	$000
Costs incurred to date (1,650 + 550)	2,200
Plus: Recognised profits	350
	2,550
Progress billings	(1,600)
Gross amount due from customers	950
Costs incurred to date (1,650 + 550)	2,200
Less: Cash paid to suppliers	(1,300)
Current liability still due to suppliers	900

137   The answer is $63m.

	$m
Revenue	90
Total cost – incurred to date	(77)
– estimated future	(33)
Overall loss	(20)
Revenue for year = 90 × 70% =	63

138 The answer is $(20)m.

	$m
Cost of sales = 110 × 70% =	(77)
Loss	(14)
Provision for future loss	(6)
Total loss	(20)

139 C

Events after the balance sheet date might be favourable or unfavourable. The key point to note is that an event comes within the scope of IAS 10 if it occurs between the balance sheet date and the date that the financial statements are authorised for issue by the board of directors.

140 A

Events after the balance sheet date are 'adjusting' when they reflect a condition or situation that existed at the balance sheet date. The financial statements for the period just ended should therefore be adjusted to include the effects of this 'event'. A write-down of inventory after the balance sheet is an adjusting event when it reflects the condition of the inventory as at the balance sheet date. The settlement of an insurance claim is also an adjusting event. A liability existed at the balance sheet date, but was of an unknown amount. After the balance sheet date, the amount has been agreed and settled, and so can be included in the balance sheet as a current liability (or current provision).

The issue of new shares and the acquisition of a business after the balance sheet date should be disclosed in a note to the statements as non-adjusting events.

141 B

Provisions for future operating losses should not be recognised. If a contingent asset is probable, it should be disclosed in a note. If a contingent liability is probable, it should be treated as a provision and included in the financial statements.

142 The three conditions set out in IAS 37 *Provisions, Contingent Liabilities and Contingent Assets* for the recognition of a provision are:

- There must be a present obligation (legal or constructive) arising from a past event.

- It must be probable that an outflow of resources embodying economic benefits will be required to settle the obligation.

- There should be a reliable estimate of the amount of the obligation.

143 C

The legal action against AP is a contingent liability. As it is probable, AP should make a provision. The legal action taken by AP is a contingent asset. As it is probable, it should be disclosed in a note.

144 D

The fire is an example of a non-adjusting event as it arose after the balance sheet date and does not provide evidence of a condition that existed at the balance sheet date.

145 C

The warehouse fire is an adjusting event as it occurred before the balance sheet date. Settlement of the insurance claim should therefore be included in the financial statements. The other events are non-adjusting as they occurred after the balance sheet date and do not provide evidence of conditions existing at the balance sheet date.

146 C

A provision is only required when (i) there is a present obligation arising as a result of a past event, (ii) it is probable that an outflow of resources embodying economic benefits will be required to settle the obligation, and (iii) a reliable estimate can be made of the amount. Only answer C meets all these criteria. Answer A is incorrect because the obligation does not exist at the balance sheet date and also cannot be reliably measured at present. Answer B is an example of an adjusting event after the balance sheet date as it provides evidence of conditions existing at the balance sheet date. Answer D is a contingent liability. However, as it is remote, no provision is necessary.

147 D

Dividends declared after the balance sheet date but before the accounts are signed are not provided for but should be disclosed by way of note.

The dividend is shown as a deduction in the statement of changes in equity for the year in which it is actually paid.

148 The answer is $2,160.

	$
Total lease payments (5 × $12,000)	60,000
Less: Fair value at beginning of lease	51,900
Total finance charge	8,100

Sum of the digits from 1 to 5 = 1 + 2 + 3 + 4 + 5 = 15

The year ended 30 September 20X5 is the second year of the lease, therefore:

Finance charge in year 2 = 4/15 × $8,100 = $2,160

149 B

	Balance	Interest at 7.00%	Instalment	Balance
	$	$	$	$
31/10/X3	45,000	3,150	10,975	37,175
31/10/X4	37,175	2,602	10,975	**28,802**

150 D

A finance lease is a lease that transfers substantially all the risks and rewards incident to ownership of an asset.

151   Non-current liability = $35,697

Current liability (51,605 – 35,697) = $15,908

Interest rate 7.93%

	Bal b/fwd	*Interest*	*Payment*	*Balance c/fwd*
20X4	80,000	6,344	– 20,000	66,344
20X5	66,344	5,261	– 20,000	51,605
20X6	51,605	4,092	– 20,000	35,697

152   The answer is $33,000.

$$\text{Depreciation } \frac{(2,600 + 2,350) \times 80,000}{12,000} = \$33,000$$

MANAGING SHORT-TERM FINANCE

153   **C**

Businesses that regularly fail to pay their suppliers on time may find it difficult to obtain future credit.

154   **D**

A conservative working capital policy is one which only uses short-term financing for part of the fluctuating current assets.

155   The answer is $755,760.

		Cash received $
April sales	20% × $780,000	156,000
March sales	80% × 0.98 × $770,000 × 60%	362,208
February sales	80% × 0.98 × $760,000 × 30%	178,752
January sales	80% × 0.98 × $750,000 × 10%	58,800
		755,760

156   **B**

The current ratio is all current assets including inventory divided by current liabilities, while the acid test is the current asset figure *less inventory* divided by current liabilities. These can only be equal if a firm carries no inventory.

157   The answer is $4,800.

	Current assets $	Current liabilities $
Credit purchase:		
Inventory	+ 18,000	
Trade payables		+ 18,000
Credit sale:		
Trade receivables	+ 24,000	
Inventory (24,000 × 100/125)	– 19,200	

Working capital will increase by $4,800, as a result of the credit sale.

158   The answer is $252,000.

	$
Budgeted sales	240,000
Expected decrease in receivables	12,000
	252,000

The reduction in receivables means that the company will expect to receive more cash next month than the total of its credit sales for the month. Changes in inventory levels have no effect on expected cash receipts.

159   The answer is 44.24 days.

Receivables

	$		$
B/f	68,000	Returns	2,500
Sales	250,000	Cash	252,100
		Irrecoverable debts	
		(68,000 × 0.05)	3,400
		C/f	60,000
	318,000		318,000

Receivable days = 60/495 × 365 = 44.24 days

(***Note:*** That the estimated sales cover a period of only six months, so the annual sales figure is $495,000 (2 × 250,000 – 2,500.)

160   **B**

Turnover cycle		Days
Inventory	(8/30) × 365	97.3
Trade receivables	(4/40) × 365	36.5
Trade payables	(3/15) × 365	(73.0)
Cash conversion cycle		60.8

Note: The annual cost of purchases would be useful for measuring the inventory turnover period for raw materials. Since the question does not state whether inventory is mainly raw materials, work-in-progress or finished goods, it is probably appropriate to use the annual cost of sales to measure the average inventory turnover time. However, it is probably reasonable to assume that most trade payables relate to purchases of raw materials, and the annual purchases figure has therefore been used to calculate the payment cycle for trade payables.

161 C

Average receivables = ($10 million + $12 million)/2 = $11 million

Average trade-related receivables = 90% × $11 million = $9.9 million

Annual sales on credit = $95 million

Average collection period = (9.9 million/95 million) × 365 days = 38 days

162 The answer is $273,600.

Capital employed = $760,000 ÷ 2.5 = $304,000

Fixed assets = 70% × $304,000 = $212,800

Therefore net current assets = $304,000 – $212,800 = $91,200

Let   CA = current assets

         CL = current liabilities

(1)   CA – CL = 91,200

(2)   CA ÷ CL = 1.5

Substituting (2) in (1):

1.5 CL – CL = 91,200

0.5 CL = 91,200

CL = $182,400

CA = $182,400 × 1.5 = $273,600

163 B

	$
Purchases on credit	360,000
Increase in trade payables	15,000
Therefore payments to suppliers	345,000

164 The answer is $271,428.

Opening inventory	100,000	(2/12 × 600,000)
Purchases	600,000	
	700,000	
Closing inventory	150,000	(1.5 × 100,000)
Cost of goods sold	550,000	
Gross profit	235,714	(3/7 × 550,000)
Sales	785,714	
Working capital is:		
Inventory	150,000	
Trade receivables	196,428	(3/12 × 785,714)
	346,428	
Trade payables	75,000	(1.5/12 × 600,000)
	271,428	

165 A

If the ratio of current assets: current liabilities is 2:1, and both current assets and current liabilities are reduced by the same amount, the ratio will increase because the proportionate decrease is smaller for current assets.

Making payment to suppliers earlier increases the length of the cash cycle, which is measured as the average inventory turnover period, plus the average time for customers to pay, minus the average time to pay suppliers.

166 The answer is 88.4 days.

Trade receivable days = 290/2,400 × 365 = 44.1 days

Inventory days (assuming that inventories are finished goods) = 360/1,400 × 365 = 93.9 days

Trade payable days = 190/1,400 × 365 = 49.6 days

Working capital cycle = Inventory days + Receivable days – Payable days

= 93.9 + 44.1 – 49.6 = 88.4 days

167 The answer is $19,800.

Sales in	Total sales	Cash sales	Credit sales	Received in May	
	$	$	$		$
April	20,000	8,000	12,000	(97% × 12,000)	11,640
May	20,400	8,160	12,240		8,160
					———
					19,800
					———

168 B

Overtrading is associated with fast-growing companies that have insufficient long-term capital, and rely on short-term liabilities to finance their growth. The finance is largely provided by suppliers (trade payables) and a bank overdraft. As a result, there is an increasing bank overdraft (higher borrowing) and very low or even negative working capital. A typical overtrading enterprise is experiencing rapid growth and rising sales. Although it should be profitable, its problem will be a shortage of cash and liquidity. Cash balances will be not be rising, since the overdraft is increasing.

169 D

An aged analysis for trade payables is an analysis of unpaid invoices from suppliers according to the length of time since the issue of the invoice. It is not a list (therefore answer A and answer B are incorrect), but a table. A spreadsheet might be used to construct the analysis. The analysis can be used to decide which suppliers should be paid, and how much.

An aged analysis for trade receivables is similar, except that it relates to unpaid invoices sent to credit customers. This analysis is used to decide which customers to 'chase' for payment.

170 B

Under the Miller-Orr model, the greater the variability in cash flows, the greater is the spread between the upper and lower cash balance limits. The return point is the lower limit plus one-third of the spread.

171 The answer is $42,000.

Using the Miller-Orr model, the size of the spread between the lower limit and upper limit should be:

$$\text{Spread} = 3\left[\frac{\tfrac{3}{4} \times \text{Transaction cost} \times \text{Variance of cash flow}}{\text{Interest rate}}\right]^{\tfrac{1}{3}}$$

$$= 3\left[\frac{\tfrac{3}{4} \times 40 \times 4,000^2}{0.0004}\right]^{\tfrac{1}{3}}$$

= $31,879. To the nearest $1,000, this is $32,000.

Upper limit = Lower limit + Spread

= $10,000 + $32,000

= $42,000

172 Return point = 2,500 + (9,000 × 1/3) = 5,500

Upper limit = 2,500 + 9,000 = 11,500

$$\text{Spread} = 3 \times \left[\frac{3/4 \times 30 \times 300,000}{0.00025}\right]^{1/3} = 9,000$$

173 The answer is $17,000.

$$\text{Optimal amount} = \sqrt{\frac{2 \times 30 \times (12 \times 20,000)}{0.05}}$$

= $16,970

To the nearest $100, this is $17,000.

174 The answer is 27.86%.

Annual rate of interest = $(100/98)^{(365/30 - 0)} - 1$

= 0.2786 or 27.86%

175 C

The equivalent annual return offered by supplier P is:

$(100/99)^{12} - 1 = 12.82\%$

This is below the minimum required rate of return of 12.85% and should not be accepted.

The equivalent annual return offered by supplier Q is:

$(100/98)^{12/2} - 1 = 12.89\%$

This is just above the minimum required rate of return of 12.85% and therefore should be accepted.

176 The three main services provided by a without recourse factor are:

- sales ledger administration/debt collection

- credit insurance (which is the without recourse element of the service)

- factor finance (providing short-term finance against the security of the unpaid invoices).

177 The answer is 500 units.

Optimal order quantity = $\sqrt{\dfrac{2 \times 200 \times 10,000}{[4 + (3\% \times 400)]}}$

= 500 units

178 B

With JIT purchasing, the objective is to receive deliveries exactly at the time required, so that the ideal inventory level is always 0. Therefore inventory holding costs should be lower. There will be an increased dependence on suppliers to deliver exactly on time, but there will be a risk (probably an increased risk) of inventory shortages due to failure by suppliers to deliver on time. However, since purchases will be made to meet demand requirements, there are likely to be much more frequent deliveries.

179 A

The simple EOQ model formula is:

EOQ $= \sqrt{\dfrac{2cd}{h}}$

where   d = annual demand
        h = cost of holding one unit for one year
        c = cost of placing order

180 C

Interest rates affect the holding costs of inventory which appear in the denominator of the EOQ formula, so a rise in interest rates will increase holding costs and lower the EOQ. Sales appear in the numerator of the expression, so a higher sales volume results in a larger EOQ.

181 C

EOQ $= \sqrt{\dfrac{2C_oD}{C_h}}$

$= \sqrt{\dfrac{2 \times \$185 \times 2,500}{\$25}}$

$= \sqrt{37,000}$

$= 192$ units

Each week $\dfrac{2,500}{52} = 48$ units are required.

Therefore each order of 192 units will last $\dfrac{192}{48} = 4$ weeks.

182 The answer is $895.

$$\sqrt{\frac{2 \times \$15 \times 32,000}{\$1.2}} = \sqrt{800,000} = 894.43 \text{ units}$$

183 C

Invoice discounting is a method of obtaining short-term funds. Specific invoices are 'sold' to a finance organisation, typically a factor, which provides finance up to a proportion (about 70%) of the value of the invoice. The invoice discounter is repaid with interest out of the money from the invoice payment, when it is eventually paid.

184 B

Converting each rate to an equivalent annual rate:

A	$(1.016)^4$	–	$1 = 0.06556$	=	6.556%
B	$(1.035)^2$	–	$1 = 0.07123$	=	7.123%
C	$(1.052)^{12/9}$	–	$1 = 0.06993$	=	6.993%
D				=	7.000%

185 D

If $1 million is invested for one year at 7%, the value of the investment will be $1,000,000 × 1.07 = $1,070,000 after one year.

If $1 million is invested for three months at 6.5% per year and then for nine months at 7.5% per year, this means that the interest for the first three months will be 6.5% × 3/12 = 1.625%, and the interest for the next nine months will be 7.5% × 9/12 = 5.625%. The value of the investment after one year will therefore be:

$1,000,000 × 1.01625 × 1.05625 = $1,073,414.

This is $3,414 more than the income that would be obtained by investing at 7% for the full year. However, there is a risk that interest rates will not rise during the first three months, and XYZ will not be able to invest at 7.5% for the nine months, but only at a lower rate.

186 C

Certificates of deposit are negotiable, i.e. they can be sold by the holder ('bearer') to someone else. The fact that they are in bearer form simplifies the negotiability. When the deposit reaches its maturity date, the bearer of the CD is entitled to the money in the bank deposit with accumulated interest.

187 A

The bill can be made out to a specified person or to 'bearer'. The bearer is the current holder of the bill, who can be anyone who has drawn or subsequently bought the bill (bills are negotiable or transferable). A bill made out to bearer will not have any specific person's name on it as the payee. A bill is made out by the drawer, and should be accepted by the person on whom the bill is drawn (the drawee) who should also pay the bill at maturity. The holder of a term bill can sell the bill at a discount to face value to a bank, i.e. the bill holder can 'discount' the bill with a bank at any time up to maturity of the bill. The bank (or person to whom the bank subsequently sells the bill) is entitled to payment of the full amount of the bill at maturity.

188   A

The customer cannot be asked for immediate payment once a bill of exchange has been accepted.

189   C

The instrument is a bill of exchange drawn on the bank. This is often called a bank bill (as distinct from a commercial bill, which is a bill drawn on a non-bank company). A bill drawn on a bank under a short-term financing arrangement is also known as an acceptance credit.

190   A

Forfaiting is a method of obtaining medium-term export finance, involving the issue of promissory notes by the importer/buyer, which the exporter is able to sell to a forfaiting bank at a discount to obtain finance. Promissory notes are promises to pay a specified amount of money at a specified future date. The importer's promissory notes have settlement dates spread over a number of years, often the expected useful economic life of the imported items. The importer is therefore able to pay for the imported goods over a period of several years, whilst the exporter can obtain immediate payment by selling the promissory notes.

191   Forms of short-term finance generally available to small entities include:

- trade credit

- bank overdraft

- term loan

- factoring

- hire purchase or leasing.

192   The answer is 10.5%.

The yield to maturity must be more than the coupon rate of 7% as the purchase price of the bond is less than maturity value. Using the maths tables to compute the present values of the sums receivable under the bond, the maturity value can be calculated as follows:

$t = 8; r = 10$

$(7 \times 5.335) + (100 \times 0.467) = 37.345 + 46.7 = \$84.045$

$t = 8; r = 11$

$(7 \times 5.146) + (100 \times 0.434) = 36.022 + 43.4 + \$79.422$

By interpolation:

$10\% + ((84.045 - 82.0)/(84.045 - 79.422)) = 10\% + (2.045/4.623) = 10.44\%$

193   The answer is 40.4%.

AL offers 1.5% interest for 16 days

$(100/98.5)^{(365/16)} - 1 =$

$(1.015)^{22.813} - 1 = 40.4\%$

194 A

The cost of placing an order under the EOQ formula includes administrative costs, postage and quality control costs.

195 A

Working capital financing involves deciding the mix of long-term and short-term debt. An aggressive policy involves using short-term finance to fund all the fluctuating current assets, as well as some of the permanent part of the current assets. So answer A is correct. A conservative policy is where all of the permanent assets (i.e. non-current assets and the permanent part of current assets) are financed by long-term funding. Short-term financing is only used for part of the fluctuating current assets. So answer B is incorrect. A moderate policy matches short-term finance to the fluctuating current assets and long-term finance to the permanent part of current assets plus non-current assets. So answer D is also incorrect.

196 The answer is 14.8%.

Annual cost $= (100/98.5)^{(365/(60-20))} - 1$

$= (100/98.5)^{9.125} - 1$

$= 14.8\%$

197 The answer is $8,863.7.

$700 \times$ (Annuity factor for t = 5; r = 10) + 10,000 $\times$ (Discount factor t = 5; r = 10) =

(700×3.791) + ($10,000 \times 0.621$) = 2,653.7 + 6,210 = $8,863.7

198 $

June debts: 345 + 520 + 150 − 200 − 520   295
July debts: 233 − 233   0
Augusts debts: 197 + 231 − 197   231
September debts: 319   319
                                                                            ───
                                                                            845

199 The answer is 7.77%.

Interest $= 0.06 \times 100 = 6$ pa for 10 years

Gain on redemption = 100 − 88 = 12

The yield to maturity is effectively the internal rate of return of the bond, which is found by trial and error. Let us assume a discount rate of 8% for the first calculation:

Time	Cash flow	Discount factor @ 8%	Discounted cash flow
	$		$
T_0	(88)	1	(88)
$T_1 - T_{10}$	6	6.710	40.26
T_{10}	100	0.463	46.3
			─────
			(1.44)

As this gives an NPV close to zero, use 7% for our next calculation:

Time	Cash flow	Discount factor @ 7%	Discounted cash flow
	$		$
T_0	(88)	1	(88)
$T_1 - T_{10}$	6	7.024	42.14
T_{10}	100	0.508	50.8
			4.94

Change in NPV between 7% and 8% is 6.38 (4.94 + 1.44) so, to get an NPV of zero, rate needs to be:

$8\% - 1.44/6.38 = 8 - 0.23 = 7.77\%$

Section 5

ANSWERS TO SECTION B-TYPE QUESTIONS

PRINCIPLES OF BUSINESS TAXATION

200 SALES TAX

A sales tax falls on the final consumer of a product or service. The customer is charged with sales tax on the final selling price. None of the tax burden falls on businesses in the middle of the supply chain because they are able to claim a tax credit for any tax paid on their purchases, and set this off against the tax they have collected on their own sales (outputs).

For example, suppose that A sells raw materials to B for $100 and B converts them into a final product for sale to C at $250. If sales tax is 10%, A will charge $10 in tax to B and pay this to the tax authorities. B will charge $25 in tax to C, but will pay the tax authorities only $15 ($25 on outputs less the credit of $10 on inputs). The tax authorities therefore receive $10 from A and $15 from B, adding up to $25 in total, which is the tax paid by C on the end product.

(a) When a product or service is taxed at 0%, the same rule applies. However, since a business selling zero-rated items will collect no tax on its outputs, but will pay tax on its inputs, the business will be able to claim a refund of tax from the tax authorities.

(b) When a product of service is exempt from tax, a different situation applies. A business selling exempt items is not registered as a tax collector, and is not allowed to claim a credit for the tax it pays on inputs. The exempt business is therefore an end-customer, on which the full burden of the sales tax falls.

201 TAX COLLECTORS FOR THE GOVERNMENT

Memo

To: Non-executive director

From: Management accountant

Date:

Subject: **Taxation**

In addition to paying tax on its own profits, businesses might be involved in assisting the government to collect taxes in a variety of ways.

(a) Businesses are required to collect indirect taxes, such as sales tax (value added tax) and excise duties. Indirect taxes are not levied on specific individuals, and it is therefore necessary to collect the tax at the point where the sale is made.

(b) Businesses also collect tax on the earnings of their employees, by deducting tax due to the government from the gross wages or salaries earned by each employee. The business is also required to provide the employee with documentary evidence of the taxes that it has deducted, so that an employee is able to provide evidence to the government if he or she is required to file a personal tax return for income earned during the tax year (both earned and unearned, and income from capital gains).

(c) Under an imputation system, a tax credit in respect of a dividend is imputed to the shareholder. The business pays tax on its own profits, and so the tax credit imputed to the dividend does not raise any extra tax for the government. Nevertheless, the business assists the government by providing the shareholder with documentary evidence of the tax credit. The shareholders can then use this evidence to sort out their personal tax affairs with the authorities.

(d) When a business pays dividends or interest to a foreign shareholder, it might be required to withhold some of the payment in the form of withholding tax, and pay this to the authorities.

Dividend payments to shareholders are not allowable for tax. A company is a taxable person and a company's income is deemed to be the profit before payment of dividends to its owners. If dividends were an allowable expense against tax, a company could avoid tax entirely simply by paying a dividend equal to its taxable profits for the year. It might be argued that the dividend income is received by the shareholders, who should then be liable for tax on the dividends they have received: however, if this tax rule applied, the collection of tax could be delayed significantly and would be a more complex administrative process. It might also be possible to arrange tax avoidance or tax deferral schemes whereby dividends are paid to a wholly-owned subsidiary which exists simply to receive dividends, pay them on to its own shareholders and pay no tax.

Interest payments by businesses are usually allowable for tax purposes because they are normally made to an entity that is a separate taxable person, who will be liable for tax on the interest income. If interest payments were not allowed for tax purposes, it would then be inappropriate to charge tax on the interest income of the lender, because the income will already have been taxed as 'profit' of the paying company, and it is generally recognised that taxing the same income twice is undesirable (with the exception of income earned in another country).

An exception to this general rule might apply, however, when a company borrows large amounts from other companies in the same group. Interest payments to other group companies might be treated as dividends for tax purposes, and not allowed as a deductible expense for tax purposes.

Signed: Management Accountant

202 LOSS RELIEF

Rules are needed for all aspects of taxation, since taxation systems are inevitably rules-based. The rules that are applied should ideally be fair and should discourage tax avoidance.

Allowing tax relief on losses is a fair tax rule because it takes a longer view of business profits, and does not tax each year's profits or losses in isolation. In this way, a business making the same total taxable profits over a number of years will pay the same tax as another business making the same profits over the same period.

For example, suppose that Entity X makes profits over a three-year period of $20,000, $30,000 and $50,000. If tax is at the rate of 30%, and is charged on the profit for the specific year, the total tax payable over the three years on the total profits of $100,000 would be $30,000 ($6,000 in Year 1, $9,000 in Year 2 and $15,000 in Year 3).

In comparison, suppose Entity Y made a profit of $80,000 in Year 1, a loss of $60,000 in Year 2 and a profit of $80,000 in Year 3. If tax is at the rate of 30%, and is charged on the profit for the specific year, the total tax payable over the three years on the total profits of $100,000 would be $48,000 ($24,000 in Year 1, $0 in Year 2 and $24,000 in Year 3).

One entity would pay more tax than the other, but on the same total profits over the same period.

If taxation is charged on an annual basis on the profits in that year, but there is no relief for losses, companies would be motivated to reduce their tax liabilities by trying to manipulate the taxable profit each year in order to minimise their liability.

It would be possible to deal with the problem by paying back tax to entities on losses incurred in particular years. For example, if an entity makes a loss of $60,000 in a particular year, and the rate of tax is 30%, the tax system could provide for a payment of $18,000 from the government to the entity. However, this would mean compensating the entity for the losses it has made, and this is generally regarded as inappropriate.

For these reasons, rules allowing loss relief are appropriate, so that an entity can claim relief for losses in one year by setting them off against profits in a previous year, or carrying them forward to set off against profits in future years.

The rules should be formulated in a way that prevents tax avoidance. For example, entities might not be allowed to set off capital losses against operating profits in previous years, the current year or future years, because this might encourage the entity to create 'artificial' capital losses in a particular year in order to minimise its tax liability.

203   EXCESS TAX

Within a tax jurisdiction, there are rules governing the deadlines for filing tax returns and for making tax payments. Although tax systems vary between jurisdictions, it is likely that the business will be required to prepare its financial statements for a period before it is required to file a final tax return for the year, and before the actual tax liability is agreed with the tax authorities. The entity must therefore make an estimate of what the tax liability will be, and provide for this in its income statement and balance sheet.

The estimated tax liability might be higher than the actual tax liability that is eventually agreed. In this case, there is an over-provision of tax for the year in the financial statements.

The business entity will report this in its annual financial statements as an element of the tax charge for the year. The over-provision of tax for the previous year is shown as a deduction from the total tax charge for the current year. (The total tax charge is the tax on the current year's profits, minus the over-provision for the previous year plus or minus the change in the deferred tax liability.) Accounting for the over-provision is simply an accounting adjustment, and there is no repayment of taxation involved. The tax authorities are not affected.

In some cases, however, a business entity might actually pay more tax than it should actually be required to pay. For example, the entity might dispute a decision by the tax authorities that a particular expense is not allowable. If it is subsequently conceded that the expense should be allowable, the entity might already have paid more tax than it should actually have been required to pay. In such circumstances, the tax authorities will refund the over-payment of tax.

204 DIVIDENDS

Under the **classical system**, entities are liable for tax on the full amount of their profits, and in addition, shareholders are liable to tax on the full amount of the dividend payments received. In the case of Taxit, the tax payments in total would therefore be as follows:

	$
Tax liability of Taxit on profits (40% × $5,000,000)	2,000,000
Tax liability of shareholders on dividend income (40% × $2,400,000)	960,000
Total tax payable	2,960,000

This type of taxation system will encourage entities to retain profits and avoid dividend payments, because dividends are taxed twice, once as profits of the entity and once as income in the hands of the shareholders.

Under the **full imputation system**, shareholders receive a tax credit for the dividends they receive. They are imputed to have paid tax and to have received a dividend net of the tax. The imputed tax is treated as a tax credit, and shareholders can set this credit against their gross dividend income in computing their tax liability. In a full imputation system, the result is that profits and dividends are only taxed once.

In the case of Taxit, the gross dividend is imputed to be $2,400,000 × 100/60 = $4,000,000 on which there is a tax credit of $1,600,000 (40%). The tax payments in total would therefore be as follows:

	$	$
Tax liability of Taxit on profits (40% × $5,000,000)		2,000,000
Tax liability of shareholders on dividend income (40% × $4,000,000)	1,600,000	
Tax credit	(1,600,000)	
Net tax payable by shareholders		0
Total tax payable		2,000,000

Under a partial imputation system, there is an element of double taxation of dividends and profits, but this is restricted. This occurs when the tax credit given to shareholders is less than the rate of tax at which the shareholders are liable on their income. In the case of Taxit, the gross dividend (given a tax credit of 25%) is imputed to be $2,400,000 × 100/75 = $3,200,000, and the tax credit is $800,000 (25%).

The tax payments in total would therefore be as follows:

	$	$
Tax liability of Taxit on profits (40% × $5,000,000)		2,000,000
Tax liability of shareholders on dividend income (40% × $3,200,000)	1,280,000	
Tax credit	(800,000)	
Net tax payable by shareholders		480,000
Total tax payable		2,480,000

205 TAX ENTRIES (PILOT PAPER)

Note 1: Tax expense

	$
Tax for the year	1,000,000
Balance brought forward at 1 January 20X3	(5,000)
Deferred tax charge	150,000
	1,145,000

Note 2: Deferred tax

	$
Balance at 1 January 20X3	1,600,000
Increase in the year	150,000
Balance at 31 December 20X3	1,750,000

Income statement for the year ended 31 December 20X3 (extract)

Tax expense (note 1) $1,145,000

Balance sheet at 31 December 20X3 (extracts)

Non-current liabilities

Deferred tax (note 2) $1,750,000

Current liabilities

Taxation payable $1,000,000

Tutorial note

The answer shown above is in line with the examiner's answer to this pilot paper question. The answer has, however, provoked considerable debate as it is arguable that the $5,000 balance brought forward should be added to the income statement charge, rather than deducted from it. The correct solution depends on the reading of the question, which appears to be ambiguous. If the debit balance is seen as an over-payment that will be refunded, the above answer is correct. If, however, it is seen as an under-provision which needs to be corrected in the following year, the $5,000 balance should be added.

206 TAX CHARGE

There are several reasons why the income tax charge in the financial statements is not at the same rate as the stated percentage.

(a)   The accounting profit and the taxable profit on which the tax charge is calculated will be different.

   (i)   Some items of income in the financial accounts might be non-taxable, and some items of expenditure might be non-allowable for tax. Non-taxable income and non-allowable expenses create permanent differences between accounting profit and taxable profit.

   (ii)   The amounts allowed for tax purposes for some assets or liabilities are different from their carrying amount in the balance sheet. These differences between accounting value and the tax base value will be eliminated over the life of the asset or liability, when it is eventually disposed of. However, until then, there are temporary differences between accounting value and tax value, which result in differences between accounting profit and taxable profit. These temporary differences give rise to deferred tax in the accounts. The accounting profit after tax is calculated after making a charge (or a credit) for increases or decreases in a deferred tax liability. Deferred tax is an element of the tax charge in the accounts that does not exist for tax purposes.

(b)   The tax charge in a particular year might include an amount for under-provision or over-provision of tax in the previous year. This affects the tax charge in the accounts, but not the actual tax liability for the current year.

The main reasons why the income tax charge in the income statement differs to that in the cash flow statement are that:

(a)   some of the tax liability for the previous year is unpaid at the beginning of the year, but paid during the year, and

(b)   some of the tax liability for the current year is unpaid at the end of the year.

This means that the cash flow figure for tax actually paid is for some of the tax liability in the previous year and some of the tax liability in the current year. This will differ from the current tax charge for the current year. Other differences are due to the change in deferred tax which is not a cash flow, and for the fact that any over-provision or under-provision of tax for the previous year is also not a cash flow, even though it is a part of the tax charge for the year.

207   AB (MAY 05 EXAM)

	Tax allowances			*Depreciation charge*
20X3/X4	$	20X3/X4		$
Cost	250,000	Cost		250,000
Allowance (250,000 × 50%)	(125,000)	Depreciation (250,000 × 20%)		(50,000)
C/f	125,000	C/f		200,000
20X4/X5		20X4/X5		
Allowance (125,000 × 25%)	(31,250)	Depreciation (250,000 × 20%)		(50,000)
C/f	93,750	C/f		150,000

Deferred tax provision:	*at 31 March 20X4*	*at 31 March 20X5*
	$	$
Accounting book value	200,000	150,000
Tax written down value	125,000	93,750
	75,000	56,250
Tax at 30% =	22,500	16,875

Balance sheet at 31 March 20X5
Deferred tax $16,875

Income statement for the year ended 31 March 20X5

Income tax expense – the reduction in deferred tax of $5,625 ($22,500 – $16,875) will reduce the current year's tax charge.

208 DG (NOV 06 EXAM)

	Accounts $	*Tax* $
Purchase 1.10.X2	200,000	200,000
UEL	5	
30.9.X3 – depreciation	(40,000)	(60,000)
	160,000	140,000
30.9.X4 – depreciation	(40,000)	(42,000)
	120,000	98,000
30.9.X5 – depreciation	(40,000)	(29,400)
	80,000	68,600

(i) Deferred tax balance 30.9.X5:

	$
Accounts value	80,000
Tax value	(68,600)
	11,400
@ 20%	2,280

(ii) Accounts profit or loss on disposal

	$
Net book value	80,000
Proceeds	(60,000)
Loss	20,000

(iii) Balancing allowance

	$
Tax written down value	68,600
Proceeds	(60,000)
Balancing allowance	8,600

209 DEFT

Deferred tax note	$m
Deferred tax balance at 1 November 20X3	1.50
Increase for the year (W1)	0.84
Deferred tax balance at 31 October 20X4	2.34
Tax charge	
Current tax	4.70
Deferred tax	0.84
	5.54

Working

	$m
(W1) Increase in provision	
Capital allowances for the year	20.8
Depreciation charge	18.0
Increase in timing differences	2.8
Tax rate	30%
Increase in deferred tax	$0.84 million

210 AVOIDANCE v EVASION (NOV 05 EXAM)

(a) Tax avoidance involves arranging the affairs of an enterprise in such a way as to minimise its tax liability. Tax avoidance is legal.

Tax evasion is the illegal manipulation of the tax system to avoid paying tax, e.g. by falsifying tax returns or claiming fictitious expenses.

(b) Governments can reduce the opportunity for avoidance/evasion by:

- deducting tax at source

- simplifying the structure of the system so that there are a minimal number of reliefs/allowances

- increasing the perceived risk of avoidance/evasion by having an efficient system of auditing tax returns

- imposing penalties and publicising their imposition

- changing social attitudes by creating a system which is perceived as equitable and customer friendly.

211 WITHHOLDING TAX (MAY 06 EXAM)

(a) **Witholding tax**

A withholding tax is a tax deducted at source before a payment is made to the recipient.

Underlying tax

Underlying tax is the tax on the profits out of which a dividend is paid.

(b) The gross amount received by CW is $45,000 \times 100/90 = \$50,000$. The withholding tax is therefore $5,000 ($50,000 \times 10\%$).

(c) After-tax profits of Z are $500,000 - \$100,000 = \$400,000$

Underlying tax is $50,000/\$400,000 \times \$100,000 = \$12,500$

PRINCIPLES OF REGULATION OF FINANCIAL REPORTING

212 CONSULTATIVE PROCESS

The International Accounting Standards Board (IASB) is responsible for issuing International Financial Reporting Standards (IFRS). To issue an IFRS, eight of the 14 members of the IASB must vote in favour. The process begins as follows:

An item is identified that might be the subject of a new IFRS. IASB staff identify the issues associated with the item and consider the application of the IASB Framework. (All IFRSs are based on the IASB Framework.) IASB staff also study national accounting requirements and regulations relating to the item and consult with national accounting standard setters.

The IASB then consults with the Standards Advisory Council (SAC) about whether the item should be added to the IASB's agenda for issuing new standards. An advisory group is then formed to assist and advise the IASB.

The IASB then issues a discussion document for public comment. Once comments are received, the IASB then issues an exposure draft for public comment (containing the basis for the IASB's conclusions on the item).

All comments on the exposure draft are considered, and the IASB then approves and issues the new IFRS (including the basis for conclusions).

213   DEVELOPMENT (MAY 06 EXAM)

The options available include:

(1)   Adopting International Financial Reporting Standards (IFRS) as its local standards.

The advantage of this approach is that it is quick to implement.

The disadvantage is that it may not take into account any specific local traditions or variations.

(2)   Modelling its local accounting standards on the IASB's IFRSs, but amending them to reflect local needs and conditions.

The advantage is that the standards should be more relevant to local needs and compliant with International Standards.

The disadvantage is that it will take longer to implement and requires an adequate level of expertise to exist within the country.

(3)   C could develop its own accounting standards with little or no reference to IFRSs.

The advantage is that any standards developed will be specific to C's requirements.

The disadvantage is that, as C does not yet have any accounting standards, it will be a long time before the project is completed as it is a very slow process. Standards may not be compliant with International Standards. This approach requires expertise, which may not be available in C at present.

214   FAIR PRESENTATION

IAS 1 requires that financial statements should present fairly the financial position, financial performance and cash flows of an enterprise. Another way of expressing this is that the financial statements must give a true and fair view.

The problem arises because IAS 1 does not contain a definition of fair presentation. IAS 1 states that, in virtually all circumstances, applying IASs will result in financial statements that achieve a fair presentation, but this statement highlights the fact that fair presentation is a concept of its own, separable from IASs.

Fair presentation is unavoidably a subjective matter, so that the directors might genuinely believe that a set of financial statements give a fair presentation, while the auditors might genuinely disagree.

The IASB Framework offers some assistance in giving a fair presentation. The Framework states that applying the qualitative characteristics (of relevance, reliability, comparability and understandability) and appropriate accounting standards (e.g. IFRSs) normally results in financial statements that give a fair presentation. Therefore, where an IAS or IFRS exists, that standard should be followed. In accounting areas where no standard currently exists, alternative accounting methods should be tested to assess their delivery of the qualitative characteristics. The accounting policy should be selected that maximises the relevance, reliability, comparability and understandability of the financial statements that are produced.

215   WOT

Item (1)

A liability is a present obligation arising out of a past event that is expected to result in an outflow of resources that embody economic benefits.

Providing for the replacement of non-current assets is not appropriate, because the definition of a liability is not satisfied – and a provision is a liability. There is no current obligation to replace the equipment. It might sell the building, or might simply decide not to replace the equipment at the end of its assumed life.

Tutorial note

Depreciation, which represents a consumption of economic resources through the use of non-current assets, is an expense, and it is appropriate to make an annual depreciation charge for non-current assets (the building and air conditioning and heating system).

The consumption of economic resources is at a different rate for the building and for the air conditioning and heating system. These should be treated as separate assets and depreciated over their relative lives. It could also be argued that providing for the replacement of the asset and charging depreciation would be a form of double-counting of expense.

Item (2)

An asset is a resource controlled by an entity as a result of past events out of which future economic benefits are expected to flow. Development costs for an entity's own benefit meet this definition, provided that there is reasonable probability that future economic benefits will be obtained. IAS 38 specifies the circumstances in which development costs should be capitalised. If the conditions in IAS 38 are met, development costs are a resource built up from which future benefits will probably be obtained: the costs should therefore be capitalised as an intangible asset and amortised over the future periods when the benefits will be obtained.

This applies to WOT's own development costs, but not to the research and development for clients. Here, the situation is different. Although WOT is doing research and development work, it is work in progress for the client. The costs of this R and D should be matched with the revenues it will bring. To the extent it has been invoiced to clients, it will appear as cost of sales in the income statement (not as research and development). Any unbilled costs should appear as a current asset under work in progress.

216 LOSSES

Expenses are defined in the *Framework* as both losses and expenses arising in the course of the ordinary activities of an entity, such as cost of sales, wages costs and depreciation. Losses are defined in the *Framework* to be decreases in economic benefits, and may or may not arise in the ordinary course of activities. A loss can arise, for example, due to an impairment in asset values or to the creation of a liability or an increase in a liability.

When a loss is expected on a long-term contract, a liability arises. This is because the entity has an obligation to complete the contract, and the liability therefore arises out of a present obligation (a contractual requirement) arising out of a past event (agreeing the contract). Another requirement of the *Framework* is that an item should be recognised in the financial statements only if it can be measured with reliability. However, the *Framework* also states cost or value must be estimated, and the use of reasonable estimates is sufficient to provide a reliable measurement.

In the case of the contract referred to in the question, the economic benefits from the contract will be the contract price ($5 million). The obligations to transfer economic benefits as a result of the contract are total costs which are expected to be incurred – a total of $5.3 million. A net 'obligation' arises here of $0.3 million – the expected liability exceeds the amount of the asset. This $0.3 million is recorded as a liability on the balance sheet as part of the amount due to customers (or as a reduction in the amount due from customers).

217 DISAGREEMENT

Strand has recognised (recorded) an asset (a receivable) of $800 million, and also recorded a provision for future costs of $300 million. The effect is that a net profit (before tax) has been recorded in the year to 30 September 20X5 of $500 million. Under the IASB's *Framework*, it is acceptable to recognise an asset and a liability if certain conditions are satisfied:

- The asset or liability must arise out of a past event.

- It must be probable that any future economic benefit associated with the item will flow to or from the entity.

- The item must have a cost or value that can be measured with reliability.

Taking each of these in turn, the following comments can be made:

Arising out of a past event

The agreement with the supplier has been made. It can therefore be argued that there is a past event out of which an asset or liability arises.

Probability of future economic benefit flowing to or from the entity

It is not clear that there is any probability of future economic benefits flowing to or from the entity, because the supplier has the right to cancel the contract without notice. If Strand is unable to provide the goods in accordance with the assurances given to the customer, it is quite possible that the customer will decide to cancel the contract.

Reliable measurement

Since the customer has the right to cancel the order at any time, the future economic benefits flowing into and out of the entity cannot be measured with reliability.

In conclusion, given the definition of assets and liabilities in the Framework, Strand does not appear to be justified in recording the transaction as a sale in the year to 30 September 20X5.

IAS 18

The analysis above has been made with reference to the Framework. IAS 18 *Revenue* addresses the same point more specifically. The transaction should not be recognised as a sale because it fails to meet the recognition criteria for the sale of goods in IAS 18, which include the requirements that:

- the entity should have transferred to the buyer the significant risks and rewards of ownership of the goods (which has not yet occurred)

- the amount of revenue and costs to be incurred can be measured with reliability

- it is probable that the economic benefits associated with the transaction will flow to the entity.

218 EXTERNAL AUDIT (NOV 06 EXAM)

(a) **Objective of an external audit:**

To make an independent report to the shareholders as to whether the financial statements give a true and fair view and whether they have been prepared in accordance with legal regulations (e.g. Companies Act) and accounting standards. There may be additional objectives, depending upon the requirements of local law.

(b) As the performance of construction contracts is the main objective of the company, and as the discrepancy amounts to nearly two-thirds of the value of the reported profit, it is likely that the difference between EA & Co and DC amounts to a fundamental disagreement.

In these circumstances, in accordance with ISA 701 *Modifications to the Independent Auditors' Report*, the audit report would contain an adverse opinion, such as the following:

'As more fully explained in note... , no allowance has been made for future losses that are expected to arise on certain construction contracts currently in progress, as the directors consider that such losses should be offset against future amounts receivable on other long-term contracts. In our opinion, allowance should have been made for foreseeable losses on individual contracts as required by IAS 11 *Construction Contracts*.

If losses had been recognised, the effect would have been to reduce the profit before tax for the year, and the value of the contract work-in-progress at 30 September 20X6 by $2.4m.

In view of the failure to provide for the losses referred to above, in our opinion the financial statements do not give a true and fair view of the company's financial position at 30 September 20X6, nor of the results of its operations for the year then ended.'

219 ACCEPTABLE ACCOUNTING POLICY

Memo

To: Audit committee chairman

From: Management accountant

Date:

Subject: **Accounting policies and the external auditors**

The primary consideration for the auditors in judging the acceptability of an accounting policy is whether, as a result of applying the policy, the financial statements give true and fair view or fair presentation of the financial position and performance of our company, and of changes in its position. A policy will only be considered acceptable if it results in the financial statements giving a true and fair view.

The concept of true and fair is not formally defined within accounting standards or the IASB's *Framework*, but key factors to consider would include:

- compliance with the relevant national legislation

- compliance with relevant international financial reporting standards and interpretations of those standards by IFRIC

- compliance with the IASB's *Framework*.

Auditors will also take account of materiality, which is the 'threshold' quality of financial information. An accounting policy might not be acceptable in general terms, but might nevertheless be acceptable in a specific situation if the effect is not material. This is because the impact of the accounting policy would not be significant, and so would not distort the view presented by the financial statements to such an extent that decisions taken by their users would be affected.

220   ELEMENTS OF FINANCIAL STATEMENTS (MAY 05 EXAM)

The IASB's *Framework* defines the five elements of financial statements as follows:

Assets – an asset is a resource controlled by the entity as a result of past events and from which future economic benefits are expected to flow to the entity.

Liabilities – a liability is a present obligation of the entity arising from past events, the settlement of which is expected to result in an outflow of resources from the entity.

Equity – the residual interest in the assets of the entity after deducting all its liabilities.

Income – increases in economic benefits during the accounting period in the form of inflows or enhancements of assets; or decreases of liabilities that result in increases in equity, other than those relating to combinations from equity participants.

Expenses – decreases in economic benefits during the accounting period in the form of outflows or depletions of assets that result in decreases in equity, other than those relating to distributions to equity participants.

221   QUALITATIVE CHARACTERISTICS (NOV 05 EXAM)

The four principal qualitative characteristics are:

- Understandability – Financial information should be readily understandable by users. Users are assumed to have a reasonable knowledge of business and accounting, and a willingness to study the information with reasonable diligence.

- Relevance – Information must be relevant to the decision-making needs of users. Information is relevant when it influences the economic decisions of users by helping them to evaluate past, present or future economic events, or confirming or correcting their past evaluations.

- Comparability – Users must be able to compare the financial statements of an entity through time in order to identify trends. Users must also be able to compare the finacial statements of different entities to evaluate relative performance and position.

- Reliability – Information is reliable where it is free from material error and bias and can be considered to be a faithful representation of the underlying transactions and events. Reliability can be sub-categorised into faithful representation, substance over form, neutrality, prudence and completeness.

SINGLE COMPANY FINANCIAL ACCOUNTS

222   DF (NOV 06 EXAM)

(1)   **Over-statement due to fraud**

As the error is material in terms of the profit previously reported for the prior year, a prior year adjustment should be made in accordance with IAS 8 *Accounting Policies, Changes in Accounting Estimates and Errors*. This will reduce the prior year profit and retained reserves brought forward by $45,000. The comparative figures in the financial statements would also be restated and the $45,000 would be excluded from the current year's figures. The nature of the error and the amount of the correction must be disclosed in the notes.

(2) **Sale in respect of order received before the year end**

In accordance with IAS 18 *Revenue*, the sale cannot be recognised until significant risks and rewards of ownership have passed to the customer. In this case, whilst the revenue arises from the ordinary course of the company's activities, the costs and revenues can be estimated reliably and it can be anticipated that economic benefit will flow to the company, the risks and rewards of ownership have not been passed to the customer at the year end. Accordingly, the revenue and costs should be excluded from the financial statements for the year ended 30 September 20X6.

223 TAB SEGMENTS

IAS 14 requires that the internal organisational and management structure and internal financial reporting system of an enterprise to its board of directors and CEO should normally be the basis for identifying reportable segments and whether the primary reporting segments are business segments or geographical segments.

A business segment should be a distinguishable part of the entity providing an individual product or service, or a group of related products, that is subject to risks and returns that are different from those of other business segments. Similarly, a geographical segment should be a distinguishable part of the entity providing products or services within an economic environment that is subject to risks and returns that are different from those of other economic environments.

A single business segment cannot include products or services with significantly different risks and returns. Similarly, a geographical segment cannot include operations in economic environments that have significantly different risks and returns. A geographical segment could be a country, group of countries or region within a country.

The dominant source of an entity's risks and returns, business or geographical, should determine whether the primary reporting format is business segments or geographical segments.

Factors to consider in identifying business segments include the nature of the products or services, the nature of the production processes, the type or class of customer for the products or services, and the methods of distribution used.

Factors to consider in identifying geographical segments include the similarity of economic or political conditions, relationships between operations in different geographical areas, closeness of operations and underlying currency risks. A geographical segment can be identified either by the location of its operations (where its products are produced) or by the location of its customers (where its products are sold).

A segment may be presumed significant where the sales revenue, profit or net assets exceed 10% of the business as a whole. However, judgement is required in deciding what the reportable segments should be.

On the basis of the information provided in the question, TAB might identify two geographical segments under the headings 'Europe' and 'Asia', using a 'location of operations' approach. Alternatively it could identify up to five geographical segments (one in each country of location of operations). There is no information in the question to judge whether a 'location of customers' approach might be better.

TAB has five types of products (one for itself and one for each subsidiary). The business segments could therefore be for five segments. However, it might be appropriate to group some of the products into the same segment. Possible candidates for grouping together are textiles and fashion garments, perhaps under the heading 'textiles' or 'textiles and clothing'. In addition it may be reasonable to group car products and kitchen utensils under the heading 'domestic products'.

224 CHANGE

(a) Beta's directors have made a change in accounting policy. This is permitted by IAS 8 if this results in financial statements that show more relevant and reliable information. The change in policy should be applied retrospectively. Beta should present the opening balance of each affected component of equity (in this case the accumulated profits), as if the new accounting policy had always been applied.

In this example, Beta should restate the accumulated profits as at the beginning of Year 8 as if the policy of charging interest on borrowing costs as an expense had always been applied. This will involve an adjustment of the accumulated profits after tax before Year 7 and in Year 7. The adjustments should be shown in the statement of changes in equity for Year 8, to arrive at a re-stated value for the accumulated profits as at the beginning of the year. The value of the assets in the course of construction as at the beginning of Year 8 should also be re-stated.

A note to the accounts should explain the nature of the change in accounting policy, and the reason for the change. In addition, the note should state the effect of the change on profits for the previous year (Year 7) and prior years, for each line item affected in the income statement. In this case, the interest expense/finance charge, taxation on profit and profit after taxation will all be affected, and the note should show the effect of the change on these items.

(b) The income statement for Year 8 will include the following figures for Year 8 and comparable figures for Year 7.

	Year to 31 December	
	Year 8	*(re-stated)*
		Year 7
	$000	$000
Profit before interest and tax	6,000	4,500
Interest	(1,000)	(500)
Profit before tax	5,000	4,000
Tax (at 30%)	(1,500)	(1,200)
Profit	3,500	2,800

Note: The tax charge for Year 7 will already have taken account of the tax relief on the interest expense.

225 INCOME STATEMENT (MAY 06 EXAM)

CE – Income statement for the year ended 31 March 20X6

	$000
Revenue	2,000
Cost of sales	(688)
Gross profit	1,312
Distribution costs	(200)
Administrative expenses	(760)
Profit	352
Finance costs	(190)
Profit before tax	162

Workings

Cost of sales		Administration	
Trial balance	480	Trial balance	260
Depreciation	192	Provision	500
Inventory adjustment	16		
	688		760

226   BJ (NOV 05 EXAM)

IFRS 5 *Non-current Assets Held for Sale and Discontinued Operations* defines a discontinued operation as a component of an entity that has either been disposed of or is classified as held for sale.

The airline operation appears to be a major and separate line of business that is clearly distinguishable from the other business activities of BJ. Its sale therefore requires separate disclosure in the financial statements, as a discontinued operation. The following disclosures are required by IFRS 5 *Non-current Assets Held for Sale and Discontinued Operations*:

(a)   a single amount on the face of the income statement comprising the total of the post-tax profit or loss of the operation and the post-tax gain or loss on the disposal of the assets constituting the discontinued operation

(b)   an analysis of this amount into the revenue, expenses and pre-tax profit or loss; the related income tax expense; the gain or loss on the disposal of the assets of the operation (loss $250 million ($750 – $500)); and the related income tax expense

(c)   the net cash flows attributable to the operating, investing and financing activities of the discontinued operation in the current year

(d)   a description of the operation (airline)

(e)   a description of the facts and circumstances of the sale (sale of fleet on 31 July 20X5)

(f)   the industry and geographical segment in which it is reported (airline operating within Europe).

A provision of $20 million must be made in respect of the severance payments to employees as these constitute a present obligation arising as a result of a past event. The $20 million therefore appears in both the income statement and the balance sheet.

The costs of restructuring the remaining business should be classified as 'restructuring' within continuing activities. A provision of $10 million is required in the financial statements for the year ended 30 September 20X5 as at that date the entity is committed to the restructuring.

227   TANGIBLE NON-CURRENT ASSETS

Property, plant and equipment

	Land	Buildings	Plant and machinery	Under construction	Total
Cost/valuation	$000	$000	$000	$000	$000
Balance at 1 January 20X5	2,743	3,177	1,538	53	7,511
Revaluation of assets	375				375
Disposal of assets			(125)		(125)
Transfers			350	(350)	0
New purchases (balancing figure)	402	526	890	297	2,115
Balance at 31 December 20X5	3,520	3,703	2,653	0	9,876

	Land	Buildings	Plant and machinery	Under construction	Total
Cost/valuation	$000	$000	$000	$000	$000
Depreciation					
Balance at 1 January 20X5	–	612	671	–	1,283
Disposal of assets	–	–	(111)	–	(111)
Depreciation for the year	–	75	212	–	287
Balance at 31 December 20X5	0	687	772	0	1,459
Carrying amount 31 December 20X5	3,520	3,016	1,881	0	8,417
Carrying amount 31 December 20X4	2,743	2,565	867	53	6,228

228 DW

Corrected schedule of the movements on plant

	Cost $m	Depreciation $m
At 1 October 20X4	97.20	32.50
Addition at cost (W1)	21.50	
Disposals (W2)	(15.00)	(9.00)
Depreciation charge for year (W3)		20.74
Balance at 30 September 20X5	103.70	44.24

Workings

(W1) **Addition at cost**

	$million
Basic cost	20.00
Installation	1.00
Testing	0.50
	21.50

(W2) **Disposal**

The accumulated depreciation on the plant disposed of = 20% of $15 million for three years = $9 million. (*Note:* The asset was held at the year ends 30 September 20X2, 20X3 and 20X4; therefore depreciation has been charged for three years.)

(W3) **Annual depreciation charge**

The depreciation charge for the year is 20% of the corrected cost of plant at the year end i.e. 20% × $103.7 million = $20.74 million.

229   BI (NOV 05 EXAM)

Building

	$
Cost	1,000,000
Y/e 30/9/X3 – Depreciation (1,000,000/20)	(50,000)
Y/e 30/9/X4 – Depreciation (1,000,000/20)	(50,000)
NBV	900,000
Revaluation	1,800,000
Credit to revaluation reserve	900,000

Following the revaluation, depreciation must be calculated on the revalued figure. There seems to have been no change to the estimate of the building's life, so 18 years of life remain.

	$
Y/e 30/9/X5	
Valuation b/f	1,800,000
Depreciation (1,800,000/18)	(100,000)
NBV	1,700,000
Revaluation	1,500,000
Debit to revaluation reserve	200,000

As the building had previously been revalued, the impairment loss can be debited to the revaluation reserve rather than being charged to the income statement.

Future depreciation will be based on the revalued figure: $1,500,000/17 years = $88,235 p.a.

Brand

The brand must be valued at the lower of carrying amount ($250,000) and recoverable amount ($200,000), i.e. $200,000. Recoverable amount is the higher of (a) fair value less costs to sell ($200,000) and (b) value in use ($150,000).

Working	$
Cost	500,000
Accumulated amortisation (500,000 × 5/10)	(250,000)
Carrying amount	250,000

The impairment loss of $50,000 ($250,000 – $200,000) must be charged to the income statement in the year ended 30 September 20X5.

230   REVALUATION (NOV 06 EXAM)

	A	B
1.9.W6 Cost	200,000	120,000
Useful economic life	20	15
At first revaluation – 31.8.X1 – NBV	200,000 × 15/20 =150,000	120,000 × 10/15 = 80,000
Revaluation gain/(loss)	30,000	(5,000)
Valuation carried forward	180,000	75,000
At second revaluation – 31.8.X6 – NBV	180,000 × 10/15 = 120,000	75,000 × 5/10 = 37,500
Revaluation gain/(loss)	(20,000)	(7,500)
Revaluation	100,000	30,000

The impairment on B of $7,500 goes to the income statement, as there is no revaluation reserve in respect of that building.

The impairment on A is less than the revaluation reserve of $30,000, so the impairment is booked against the revaluation reserve, leaving a balance on that reserve of $10,000.

231 USEFUL ECONOMIC LIFE (PILOT PAPER)

Memo

To: Transport Manager

From: Trainee Management Accountant

Date:

Subject: **Useful economic life of vehicle**

A requirement of IAS 16 *Property, Plant and Equipment* is that the useful economic life (and the residual value) of each item of property, plant and equipment should be reviewed at least once each year. If there is a change in the estimate, a change in accounting estimate should be made in accordance with IAS 8 *Accounting Policies, Changes in Accounting Estimates and Errors*.

The delivery vehicle is currently valued at cost less accumulated depreciation. At 1 April 20X2, the asset had been held for two years, and its expected useful life was four years. Its carrying value was therefore $10,000, which is $20,000 cost less two years of accumulated depreciation of $5,000 per year.

At 31 March 20X3, the revision to the estimated useful life means that from 1 April 20X2, the asset had four more years of expected useful life. From that date, the asset should therefore be depreciated over its remaining revised expected useful life. The annual depreciation charge from 1 April 20X2 should therefore be $2,500 (= $10,000/4 years).

This means that for the year to 31 March 20X3, the annual depreciation charge should be $2,500. The carrying value of the asset at the beginning of the year, as indicated above, is $10,000. The carrying value at 31 March 20X3 will be:

	$
Vehicle at cost	20,000
Less accumulated depreciation	12,500
Net book value	7,500

232 DECOMMISSIONING (PILOT PAPER)

Memo

To: Production Manager

From: Trainee Management Accountant

Date:

Subject: **Decommissioning costs**

It is a requirement of IAS 16 *Property, Plant and Equipment* that the cost of an item of property, plant or equipment should, on initial recognition of the cost, include an estimate of the future costs of decommissioning work and restoring the site on which the asset is located, if there is an obligation to do this work. For the oil well a future obligation exists, therefore a cost for the future decommissioning work and land restoration must be included in the cost of the asset from 1 March 20X3.

This obligation for future decommissioning costs and land restoration should be measured in accordance with IAS 37 *Provisions, Contingent Liabilities and Contingent Assets*. This states that, when the time value of money is material, which it is in this case, the amount of the future obligation should be discounted to a present value. The discount rate should be a pre-tax rate.

The cost of the new oil well from 1 March 20X3 must therefore include an amount for future decommissioning costs, equal to $20 million discounted from Year 20 to a present value equivalent. There should be a corresponding liability in the balance sheet for the discounted value of the provision.

The asset should be depreciated in accordance with our normal accounting policies, and normal rules of valuation of the asset will apply. For example, the asset will be subject to regular impairment reviews.

There should be an annual review of the provision, and any adjustments to the present value of the provision will be made through the income statement. If there is no inflation and no change in the estimate of costs, the provision should be $20 million by the end of Year 20.

Signed: Trainee Management Accountant

233 HOTELS

Memo

To: Accountant

From:

Date:

Subject: **Accounting treatment of revaluations**

(a)   The carrying amount or net book value of Hotel K at 30 September is $430,000, which is $110,000 higher than its current valuation of $320,000. In compliance with the new accounting policy, Hotel K should be revalued to $320,000. The reduction in the balance sheet valuation of $110,000 represents an impairment loss. This loss should be recognised as a charge in the income statement for the year to 30 September 20X4.

Tutorial note

The hotel has not previously been revalued. If there had been a previous revaluation, the impairment loss could have been set off against the amount of the earlier revaluations of the same property by means of a reduction in the revaluation reserve, rather than treated as a charge in the income statement. However, this situation does not apply in this case.

(b)   Hotel G should be revalued to $650,000 and Hotel H to $820,000 from 1 January 20X4. The valuations should separate the value of the land from the value of the buildings, and depreciation from 1 January 20X4 should be based on the new valuation of the buildings and the estimated remaining useful life of the buildings (50 years for Hotel G and 30 years for Hotel H). A similar accounting treatment should apply to Hotel K from 1 January 20X4.

The transfer to the revaluation reserve for Hotels G and H should be the difference between their carrying amount at 1 January 20X4 (before the revaluation) and their revalued amount. The carrying value of the hotels is their cost less accumulated depreciation to 1 January 20X4. The carrying value of the hotels is reduced by a depreciation charge for the first three months of the year (1 October – 31 December 20X3).

In this way, there will be a depreciation charge for the hotels in the income statement for the full 12 months of the year, the first three months based on the old valuation and the following nine months based on the new valuation.

(c)   The carrying amount or net book value of each hotel at 30 September 20X4 should be the revalued amounts less accumulated depreciation since the revaluations (for the nine months from 1 January 20X4).

234   OAK

The initial measurement of the cost at which the plant should be capitalised is calculated as follows:

	$	$
Basic list price of plant		240,000
Less trade discount of 12.5% on list price		(30,000)
		210,000
Shipping handling and installation costs		2,750
Estimated pre-production testing		12,500
Site preparation costs		
Electrical cable installation ($14,000 – 6,000)	8,000	
Concrete reinforcement	4,500	
Own labour costs	7,500	20,000
Dismantling and restoration costs (15,000 + 3,000)		18,000
Initial cost of plant		263,250

Note: The early settlement discount is a revenue item (and will probably be deducted from administration costs in the income statement). The maintenance cost is also a revenue expense in the income statement, although a proportion of it would be a prepayment at the end of the year of acquisition (the amount would be dependent on the date on acquisition). The $6,000 cost of the specification error must be charged to the income statement.

235   DEVELOPMENT COSTS (MAY 06 EXAM)

(a)   Under IAS 38 *Intangible Assets,* development expenditure can be regarded as an intangible asset if and only if, an entity can demonstrate all of the following:

*   the technical feasibility of completing the asset so that it can be used or sold

*   the intention to complete the asset to use it or sell it

*   the ability to use or sell the asset

*   how the asset will generate future economic benefits

*   the availability of technical, financial and other resources to complete the project to make and use or sell the asset

*   the ability to reliably measure the expenditure on the development of the asset.

(b)   As all of the above criteria seem to have been met by CD's new process:

CD will treat the $180,000 development cost as an intangible non-current asset in its balance sheet at 30 April 20X6. Amortisation will start from 1 May 20X6 when the new process starts operation.

236 SLY

(a)   IAS 2 suggests that the costs of conversion that are included in the cost of inventory should include both fixed and variable production overheads and other overheads, if any, attributable to bringing the product to its present location and condition. Fixed production overheads should be apportioned based on the normal level of activity. Any unallocated overheads should be treated as an expense in the period in which they are incurred.

IAS 2 also states that other costs may be included in the cost of an item of inventory, but only to the extent that they are incurred in bringing the inventory to its present location and condition. In some cases, inventory cost may also include some borrowing costs.

Care should be taken to ensure that only overheads relating to production are included. Those relating to selling are inappropriate, and those relating to administration require special consideration.

(b)   The amount of overhead to be absorbed to SLY's closing work-in-progress may be calculated as follows:

Factory overhead	$
Factory rent, rates and insurance	150,000
Factory security	110,000
Factory heat, light and power	300,000
Depreciation of machinery	200,000
Total overhead	760,000
Normal level of activity	95,000 hours
Recovery rate per hour $760,000/95,000 =	$8 per hour

Factory overhead to be included in inventory cost = 500 hours at $8 = $4,000

It might possibly be appropriate to include some non-factory overhead costs in the inventory valuation. Administration expenses may require inclusion, but the information given is insufficient to establish if this is appropriate in this case. IAS 2 appears to indicate that inclusion of non-production overhead costs should be fairly uncommon.

It is assumed that delivery vehicles are used for deliveries to customers only, and that the depreciation charge on these items is therefore a distribution overhead cost.

237 PREFERENCE SHARES

On a balance sheet, equity interests are distinguished from financial liabilities. IAS 32 includes in the definition of financial liability a contractual obligation to deliver cash or another financial asset, or to exchange financial assets or liabilities with another entity under conditions that might be unfavourable. IAS 32 defines an equity instrument as any contract that shows evidence of a residual interest in the assets of an entity after deducting all of its liabilities.

IAS 32 also requires the component elements of a financial instrument to be distinguished separately as a liability or as equity. There are features present in most classes of preference shares that make them more similar to financial obligations than to equity.

These characteristics of preference shares that make them more like liabilities than equity might be:

- the right to a fixed rate of return (dividend), payable before any dividend can be paid to equity shareholders, and no rights to further participation in profits

- priority over equity shareholders to a return of assets on a winding up/liquidation

- the right to repayment of capital on redemption, in the case of redeemable preference shares.

Even convertible preference shares have such rights, in addition to the right to convert the shares in to equity shares at a future date.

IAS 32 therefore requires that the issuer of any shares should present them on the face of the balance sheet in accordance with their substance rather than their form. The legal form of all shares (ordinary and preference) is that they are shares and so perhaps should be presented as 'issued share capital' on the balance sheet. IAS 32 disagrees: if the substance of a preference share is that it is equivalent to debt, then it should be reported as a non-current liability on the balance sheet. This is an example of the principle of 'substance over form' being applied.

In the case of the entity in the question, to comply with IAS 32, the entity would be required to treat the redeemable preference shares as a liability, and would be required to separate the convertible preference shares into a liability component and an equity component. The irredeemable preference shares might be classified as equity, but there are also reasons for classifying them as liabilities.

238 REDEEMABLE SHARES (MAY 06 EXAM)

(a)

The total finance cost is:	$
Issue costs	192,800
Annual dividend (200,000 × $10 × 5%) × 5	500,000
Redemption cost (200,000 × $10 × 15%)	300,000
	992,800

(b)

	Balance b/fwd	Finance cost 10%	Dividend paid	Balance c/fwd
	$	$	$	$
31/3/X6	1,807,200	180,720	−100,000	1,887,920
31/3/X7	1,887,920	188,792	−100,000	1,976,712
31/3/X8	1,976,712	197,671	−100,000	2,074,383
31/3/X9	2,074,383	207,438	−100,000	2,181,821
31/3/Y0	2,181,821	218,179	−100,000	2,300,000

239 NEWCARS

(a) As a director and a 25% shareholder of both Newcars and Oldcars there is no doubt that Arthur is a related party to both companies. There are two reasons for this:

(i) Arthur is a director of both companies, and all directors are related parties.

(ii) Arthur is also probably a related party because of his shareholding in each company. When an entity is significantly influenced by an individual, the individual is a related party. Holding 20% or more of the shares will generally be considered sufficient to have 'significant influence'.

However, the question is whether Newcars and Oldcars are related parties. On this point, IAS 24 suggests that they are.

A party is a related party if it is significantly influenced by a member of the key management personnel of the entity, including any director. On this basis, Newcars is a related party of Oldcars and Oldcars is a related party of Newcars – provided that Arthur does have significant influence over both companies.

(b) Under IAS 24, both Newcars and Oldcars will have to disclose information about the transactions with a related party sufficient to give the users of the statements an indication of the potential effect of the relationship on the financial statements.

For both Newcars and Oldcars, the following specific information will need to be disclosed:

- the nature of the related party relationship

- the fact that they are both subject to Arthur's influence

- the amount of the transactions

- outstanding amounts to or from the other, and their terms and conditions

- allowances for receivables on those balances and amounts written off as irrecoverable debts due from related parties.

240 CB IMPORTERS (MAY 06 EXAM)

A customer with whom an entity transacts a significant volume of business is not a related party merely by virtue of the resulting economic dependence. XC is therefore not a related party and the negotiated discount does not need to be disclosed.

A party is related to an entity if it has an interest in the entity that gives it significant influence over the entity, such as being a member of the key management personnel of the entity.

As founder member and major shareholder holding 40% of the equity, George is able to exert significant influence and is a related party of CB.

George is also a related party as he is CB's president. He is a member of the key management personnel of CB.

The sale of the property for $500,000 will need to be disclosed, along with its valuation as a related party transaction.

Providers of finance are not related parties simply because of their normal dealings with the entity. However, if a party is a close member of the family of any individual categorised as a related party, they are also a related party. As Arnold is George's son and George is a related party, Arnold is also a related party. The loan from FC will need to be disclosed, along with the details of Arnold and his involvement in the arrangements.

241 CIVIL ENGINEERING COMPANY

Income statement extract

	$000
Revenue	3,000
Costs to be recognised	2,900
	100
Less: Provision for loss	(200)
Loss on contract	(100)

Balance sheet extract

Current liabilities:	
Trade payables (3,400 – 3,000)	400
Amounts due to customers on construction contract (W1)	200

Workings

(W1)	$000
Costs incurred to date	2,900
Less: loss recognised	(100)
	2,800
Progress payments	3,000
Amounts due to customers	200

Tutorial note

It is not certain that the contract price will increase to $10m and so it is assumed that the price will remain at $8m. The costs incurred to date ($2,900) plus the estimated costs to completion ($5,200) exceed the contract price, therefore a loss of $100 must be recognised.

242   AE (MAY 05 EXAM)

	$000	$000
Revenue		60,000
Costs incurred to 31 March 20X5	24,000	
Costs to completion	19,000	
		43,000
Profit		17,000
Income statement:		
Recognise 50% profit		8,500
Revenue recognised 50% of contract value 60,000/2		30,000
Balance sheet:		
Total contact costs incurred		24,000
Recognised profit		8,500
		32,500
Less: Progress payments received		25,000
Gross amount due from customer		7,500

Income statement for the year to 31 March 20X5	$000
Revenue from long-term contract	30,000
Cost of sales (balance)	21,500
Profit	8,500

Balance sheet as at 31 March 20X5	$000
Receivables	
Long-term contract – gross amounts due from customer	7,500

243 NEW PRODUCTS

IAS 38 specifies the appropriate accounting for research and development expenditure. An entity should classify the generation of the asset into a research phase and a development phase. All research costs must be recognised as an expense and written off as incurred. Development costs must be recognised as an intangible non-current asset if they meet specified conditions that demonstrate that the development will generate future economic benefits. Otherwise development costs must be written off as incurred.

In the year ending 31 May 20X2, Phase 1 is a research activity. $75,000 should be charged to the income statement as incurred.

In the year ending 31 May 20X3, Phase 2 might be described as an applied research activity. This is research towards a particular aim. IAS 38 specifies that expenditure on the search for, evaluation and final selection of applications of research findings is an example of research phase expenditure. The $192,000 incurred should be charged to the income statement as incurred.

Phase 3 is a development phase. We must assess whether the conditions listed in IAS 38 apply throughout this phase, or only during the later stages of the phase. A development phase is recognised if all the following conditions apply:

- technical feasibility

- intention to complete the project

- ability to use or sell the developed item

- probability of future economic benefits should be demonstrated

- sufficient resources to complete the project

- expenditure can be measured reliably.

Y is about to launch the product, and we are told that it is commercially viable and that Y has sufficient resources for the foreseeable future, so it looks as though all of the above conditions are satisfied. If the conditions are satisfied throughout Phase 3, all expenditure incurred in Phase 3 should be capitalised, as an intangible non-current asset. In the year ending 31 May 20X4, the $223,000 development costs must be capitalised as an intangible non-current asset in the balance sheet. This will be amortised over future periods to match with the income generated by the new product.

244 BRAND NAME

Brand QQ was acquired as part of Q's business. IAS 38 sets out the conditions under which an intangible asset (such as a brand) can be recognised:

- it must be probable that future economic benefits will flow to the business, and

- the cost of the asset can be measured reliably.

In the situation in the question, both conditions apply. Presumably the valuation of $220,000 on purchase is a reliable measurement of the fair value of the brand at this date, so Brand QQ can be recognised as a purchased intangible non-current asset in Z's balance sheet.

In Z's balance sheet at 31 October 20X4, the brand will be shown as:

	Cost	Accumulated amortisation	Net book value
Non-current assets	$000	$000	$000
Purchased brand	220	–	220

The brand has just been acquired that very day, so it is probably appropriate to charge no amortisation in the year to 31 October 20X4.

In Z's balance sheet at 31 October 20X5, the brand will be shown as:

	Cost	Accumulated amortisation	Net book value
Non-current assets	$000	$000	$000
Purchased brand	220	22	198

The brand will be amortised over 10 years, so $22,000 amortisation will be charged in the income statement for the year to 31 October 20X5.

Revaluation of Brand QQ as at 31 October 20X5 is probably not permissible, since IAS 38 only allows revaluation to a fair value (use of the revaluation model for valuation) when fair value can be determined by reference to an active market. It seems unlikely that an active market would exist for assets such as Brand QQ.

The directors should apply the provisions of IAS 36 to decide whether an impairment review should be carried out on Brand QQ. If there is any indication at 31 October 20X5 that the brand might be impaired, then a review must be undertaken at that date.

245 SCOPE

(a) IAS 38 *Intangible Assets* makes a distinction between expenditure incurred in the research phase of a project and expenditure incurred in the development phase. Research phase expenditure must be written off as incurred. Development phase expenditure must be capitalised as an intangible asset and carried forward in the balance sheet, when the following conditions can be demonstrated:

(i) the technical feasibility of completing the project

(ii) the intention to complete the project and use or sell the developed item

(iii) an ability to use or sell the item

(iv) the generation of probable future economic benefits from the developed item

(v) availability of adequate technical, financial and other resources to complete the project

(vi) ability to measure the expenditure reliably.

The new pulping process does seem to satisfy the conditions listed above, so the costs to date must be carried forward in the balance sheet as an intangible non-current asset.

The attempt to develop a new species of tree definitely fails to satisfy the conditions listed above. It is not commercially viable and may not overall recover its costs, so expenditures on the project must be written off as incurred as research phase costs.

(b) A liability to the employee arising from his injuries is probable, though we are advised that it is not possible to quantify the liability. There are two possible courses of action in accounting for this item. The lawyers should be pressed to make a prudent estimate of the amount of damages, perhaps from preliminary medical reports, and this estimate should then be provided in the accounts, as a provision. If the lawyers still insist that such an estimate is impossible, there is no point in guessing a value. Instead the facts should be disclosed as a contingent liability in a note to the accounts, stating that no liability has currently been provided since a fair estimate is impossible. However, it is important that this note is worded in such a way that no liability is admitted, for this might prejudice the company's position in subsequent legal proceedings.

246 LEGAL CLAIMS

Memo

To: Chief Accountant

From: Assistant

Date:

Subject: **Contingencies**

Claim by the customer

A provision should be made for the claim by the customer if there is a present obligation arising out of a past event that will probably result in a transfer of economic benefits. The facts here indicate that there is a present obligation (a negligence claim) as a result of past events (faulty work). There is also evidence that a transfer of economic benefits is probable. On this basis, a provision for $100,000 should be recorded in order to comply with IAS 37. The amount would be classified as a provision within current liabilities, rather than a sundry payable, as there is uncertainty as to the amount (and possibly the timing) of the payment.

Claim against the sub-contractor

The facts here indicate that there is a 'contingent asset', arising from the probability of establishing a claim against the sub-contractor, which would create a receivable for Z. If a contingent asset could be recognised, it would be disclosed in a note to the financial statements. However, under IAS 37 a contingent asset should be recorded only if its recoverability is virtually certain; disclosure in a note is required only where the outcome is 'probable'. The subcontractor is close to insolvency, suggesting that the benefit is unlikely to be recoverable. Z's financial statements should therefore not disclose the contingent asset at all.

Signed: Assistant

247 EVENTS

(a)   As the success of the claim for damages of $200,000 is probable, it constitutes a present obligation as a result of a past obligating event, and should therefore be accounted for as a provision, in accordance with IAS 37 *Provisions, Contingent Liabilities and Contingent Assets*. A provision is treated as a liability in the balance sheet, and there will be a charge of $200,000 in the income statement for the period. The success of the counter-claim for $120,000 is also considered probable and this should be disclosed as a contingent asset (reimbursement). However, a contingent asset is disclosed in a note to the accounts, and is not treated as an asset in the balance sheet. It is therefore inappropriate and unacceptable to set off the $120,000 counter-claim against the provision for $200,000.

(b)   IAS 10 *Events After the Balance Sheet Date* makes a distinction between adjusting and non-adjusting events after the balance sheet date. Adjusting events provide additional evidence of conditions existing at the balance sheet date, while non-adjusting events relate to conditions that did not exist at the balance sheet date.

The fire broke out in February 20X5. This is after the balance sheet date of 31 December and so is a non-adjusting event. Provided that the financial statements for the year to 31 December 20X4 have not yet been authorised for issue, the effects of the fire, if material, should be reported in a note, so that users can reach a proper understanding of the entity's affairs.

(c)   The major customer went into liquidation on 27 January. However the customer owed some money to FRG as at 31 December and it is now clear that this balance is not recoverable. If the amount owed is material, it should be reported. The liquidation of the customer's business is an adjusting event, and FRG should write off the bad debt in its financial statements prepared to 31 December 20X4. Trade receivables should be reduced by the amount of the bad debt written off, and there should be a charge in the income statement for the bad debt.

248   PROVISIONS (PILOT PAPER)

IAS 37 defines a provision as 'a liability of uncertain timing or amount'. A provision may only be recognised when three conditions are met:

(1)   The entity should have a present obligation arising out of a past event.

(2)   It must be probable that an outflow of economic resources (that embody economic benefits) will be required to settle the obligation, such as a payment of cash.

(3)   A reliable estimate of the obligation must be possible.

A provision is consistent with the definition of a liability provided by the IASB Framework. The Framework states that the essential characteristic of a liability is that the entity has a present obligation arising out of a past transaction or event. It also states that the obligation usually involves the entity giving up economic resources that embody economic benefits, such as a cash payment or transfer of other assets. A liability should also be measurable, and a reliable estimate possible. The Framework states that some liabilities can be measured only by using a substantial degree of estimation, and that these liabilities are often called provisions.

Clearly, the definition of a provision in IAS 37 is consistent with the definition of a liability in the Framework.

249   CLASSIFICATION OF LEASES

IAS 17 defines a finance lease as a lease that transfers substantially all the risks and rewards incidental to ownership of an asset. Whether a lease should be classified as a finance lease or an operating lease depends on the substance of the contract rather than its legal title or form. IAS 17 gives examples of situations that would normally lead to a lease being classified as a finance lease. These include the following:

(a)   The lease term is a major part of the useful economic life of the asset. Here the lease term is four years, whereas the useful economic life of the asset is probably longer.

(b)   The lease transfers ownership of the assets to the lessee at the end of the lease term, or the lessee has the right to buy the asset at the end of the lease term at a price below the asset's fair value. Neither of these conditions appears to apply in this case.

(c)   At the beginning of the lease, the present value of the minimum lease payments amounts to at least substantially all of the fair value of the leased asset. In this case, the present value of the lease payments does equal the fair value of the cars.

The present value test is an important one. Although there are no other factors that suggest strongly that the leases should be finance leases, it is probably appropriate in this case to treat the car leases as finance leases, and account for them accordingly. (It might also be argued that after four years of use by sales representatives, the cars might not have much useful economic life left, in which case the lease term would be for a substantial part of the economic life.)

The fact that TR must pay for all insurance, repairs and maintenance costs during the lease is further evidence that it is a finance lease. These costs are part of the costs incidental to ownership of an asset. If the lessee has to pay these costs, this provides further evidence that the lessee has accepted substantially all of the risks and rewards of ownership.

250 FINANCE LEASE (1) (PILOT PAPER)

The cost of the asset is $88,300. It is assumed that the expected residual value is 0, and that the straight-line method of depreciation is used. The annual depreciation charge is therefore $88,300/5 years = **$17,660**.

		$
Total lease payments (5 years × $21,000)		105,000
Asset cost		88,300
Finance charges on the lease		16,700
Sum-of-the-digits	5 + 4 + 3 + 2 + 1 = 15	
(lease payments annual in arrears)		
Finance charge for each digit		$1,113.33

		$
Finance charge in Year 1	(5 × $1,113.33)	**5,567**
Finance charge in Year 2	(4 × $1,113.33)	**4,453**
Finance charge in Year 3	(3 × $1,113.33)	3,340

Year	Opening liability for lease	Finance charge	Lease payments	Repayment of lease liability	Closing liability for lease
	(1)	(2)	(3)	(3) – (2) = (4)	(5) = (1) – (4)
	$	$	$	$	$
1	88,300	5,567	21,000	15,433	72,867
2	72,867	4,453	21,000	**16,547**	**56,320**
3	56,320	3,340	21,000	**17,660**	**38,660**

Income statement extracts

Year 1

	$
Depreciation	17,660
Finance charge	5,567

Year 2

	$
Depreciation	17,660
Finance charge	4,453

Balance sheet extracts

	End of Year 1	End of Year 2
	$	$
Non-current assets at cost (leased)	88,300	88,300
Accumulated depreciation	17,660	35,320
Net book value	70,640	52,980
Liabilities: amounts due under finance lease		
Non-current liability	56,320	38,660
Current liability	16,547	17,660

251   FINANCE LEASE (2) (MAY 05 EXAM)

(a)   The finance cost in the income statement for the year ended 31 March 20X5 is $9,067.

(b)   Balance sheet as at 31 March 20X5 – extract

Non-current assets – tangible	$
Finance lease	116,000
Less: Depreciation ($116,000/5 \times 2$ years)	46,400
	56,600

Non-current liabilities	
Amounts due under finance lease	$53,200
Current liabilities	
Amounts due under finance lease ($76,400 – $53,200)	$23,200

Workings

	$
Total payments under the lease ($30,000 \times 5$)	150,000
Fair value of the asset	116,000
Finance cost	34,000

Five years sum of digits: $5 + 4 + 3 + 2 + 1 = 15$

Year	Proportion	Finance cost
		$
20X3/X4	5/15	11,333
20X4/X5	4/15	**9,067**
20X5/X6	3/15	6,800

Year	Balance b/fwd	Finance charge	Repayment	Balance c/fwd
	$	$	$	$
20X3/X4	116,000	11,333	(30,000)	97,333
20X4/X5	97,333	9,067	(30,000)	**76,400**
20X5/X6	76,400	6,800	(30,000)	**53,200**

252   FLOODING

Memo

To: Chief Accountant

From:

Date:

Subject: **Accounting for the consequences of the flooding**

We are in the process of preparing the financial statements for the year to March 20X5, but the flooding took place in April 20X5. The flooding is an event after the balance sheet date. It should be categorised as a non-adjusting event, since it concerns conditions that only arose after the balance sheet date, and did not exist at the balance sheet date.

IAS 10 requires the following disclosures to be given for each material non-adjusting event:

- a description of the nature of the event

- an estimate of its financial effect, or a statement that such an estimate cannot be made.

It could be argued that, because the equipment repairs cost and the inventory write-offs were fully insured, no material loss will be suffered. In this case, the flooding is not a material event and does not have to be disclosed.

However, Z will have to buy in inventory while the repairs are taking place, and this will result in a material reduction in profits from what would have been earned from in-house production. The impact of the flooding is therefore material. A note to the financial statements should be included in the financial statements for the year to 31 March 20X5, describing the nature of the flooding, and including the estimated financial effects of all the implications that will flow from the flooding.

MANAGING SHORT-TERM FINANCE

253 SPREADSHEET

Spreadsheet models are used extensively for cash budgeting and cash flow forecasting. There are several reasons for this.

(a) Standard spreadsheet packages are widely available, and it is relatively simple to learn how to construct a model for a cash flow forecast.

(b) Spreadsheet models are easy to use. Once the model has been constructed, the user simply has to enter the data for the input variables in the model.

(c) Once a model has been constructed, it can be used every time a new cash flow forecast is required. It can therefore save large amounts of time.

(d) It is usual to change variables in a forecast. Variables might be changed over time if it becomes apparent that the original estimates and assumptions were incorrect (for example, assumptions about exchange rates, interest rates, sales revenue, and so on). In addition, variables can be altered in order to carry out sensitivity analysis. For example, assumptions about sales revenue growth, the rate of inflation in prices or costs, the level of variable unit costs or fixed period costs, the timing of certain cash flows can all be changed quickly and simply, and a new forecast prepared. Sensitivity analysis helps management to understand the risks in the cash flow forecast and identify the key variables.

(e) Spreadsheet models can be consolidated. For example, if a similar cash flow forecast spreadsheet model is prepared for each profit centre within a company, a consolidated cash flows forecast for the company as a whole can be constructed simply. Changes to a variable in the cash flow model for one profit centre, affecting the forecast of cash flows for that profit centre, will automatically be carried through to alter the figures in the consolidated forecast.

254   AM (MAY 05 EXAM)

	May	June	July
	$000	$000	$000
Cash sales	35	40	40
Receipts from credit sales (W1)	101	104	111
Total receipts	136	144	151
Payments for purchases (W2)	50	54	55
Expenses paid	50	50	50
Equipment			250
Total payments	100	104	355
Net cash	36	40	(204)
Balance b/f	96	132	172
Balance c/f	132	172	(32)

Based on the above figures, AM will not be able to pay for the equipment when it falls due.

Workings

(W1) **Credit sales – receipts**

	Total	May	June	July
	$000	$000	$000	$000
February	100	5		
March	100	30	5	
April	110	66	33	6
May	110		66	33
June	120			72
Totals		101	104	111

(W2) **Credit purchases – payments**

	Total	May	June	July
	$000	$000	$000	$000
March	50	15		
April	50	35	15	
May	55		39	16
June	55			39
Totals		50	54	55

255 CASH FORECASTING (PILOT PAPER)

	Probability	
	0.7	0.3
	$000	$000
Cash at 30 November	+175	+175
Net operating cash flows in December	+700	− 300
Cash at 31 December	+875	− 125
Net operating cash flows in December	− 900	− 900
Cash at 31 January	− 25	− 1,025

Expected cash balance at 31 January = (in $000) $(0.7 \times - 25) + (0.3 \times - 1,025)$

$= - \$325,000.$

The expected overdraft is $325,000.

The Expected Value (EV) of the short-term cash surpluses or deficits is not useful for cash planning because it is not representative of the forecasts of possible actual outcomes. The forecast cash balance is either an overdraft of $25,000 or an overdraft of $1,025,000.

An EV is a useful long-run average for outcomes that will occur many times. However, an EV is not a useful forecast for a 'one-off' event that will not happen again.

A more suitable approach in this case is to make cash forecasts on the basis of each of the two possible outcomes, and make plans and take measures accordingly for each possible outcome.

256 MODELS

Memo

To: Treasurer of local government department

From: Accountant

Date:

Subject: **Operation of the Miller-Orr model**

The Miller-Orr model provides upper and lower cash limits. These are the cash balances at which securities should be purchased (upper cash limit) or sold (lower cash limit).

- We have to maintain a minimum cash balance of $15,000. This is the 'lower limit'.

- When the cash balance falls to this lower limit, securities should be sold to take the cash level up to the 'return point'. The return point is calculated using the model. The return point is one third of the 'spread' higher than the lower limit. The spread is explained below.

- There is a maximum cash holding, also calculated using the model. When the cash balance reaches this level, cash should be used to buy securities, and take the cash level down to the return point. The return point is two-thirds of the spread below the upper limit.

- The model is used to calculate a spread between the upper and lower limits. This is:

$$3 \times \left[\frac{\frac{3}{4} \times \text{Transaction cost} \times \text{Variance of cash flows}}{\text{Interest rate for the same period}} \right]^{1/3}$$

The spread for the department would be:

$$3 \times \left[\frac{\frac{3}{4} \times 25 \times 9,000,000}{0.000236} \right]^{1/3}$$

$= \$26,827$, say $27,000.

- The lower limit is $15,000

- The upper limit is $15,000 + $27,000 = $42,000

- The return point is $15,000 + ($27,000/3) = $24,000

When the cash level reaches the lower limit, the department should sell $9,000 of securities. When it reaches the upper limit, it should buy $18,000 of securities.

257   CASH MANAGEMENT MODELS (NOV 06 EXAM)

(a)   Baumol

$$\text{Optimal sale} = \sqrt{\frac{2 \times \text{Annual cash disbursed} \times \text{Cost per sale}}{\text{Interest rate}}}$$

$$= \sqrt{\frac{2x \times 420,000 \times V25}{0.073}}$$

$$= 16,961$$

(b)   Miller-Orr

$$\text{Spread} = 3 \left[\frac{0.75 \times \text{Transaction cost} \times \text{Variance}}{\text{Interest rate}} \right]$$

$$= 3 \left[\frac{0.75 \times 25 \times 90,000}{\text{Interest rate}} \right]^{1/3}$$

$$= 3 \sqrt[3]{23,116,438}$$

$$= 3 \times 284.87$$

$$= 854.60$$

Under the Miller-Orr model, DJ should sell securities when the cash reaches the lower limit of $1,000. The amount sold should be sufficient to bring the cash back up to the return point, which is equal to the lower limit plus one-third of the spread, so $1,000 + 284.87 = 1,284.57.

258   GOLF CLUBS

Memo

To: The board of Eagle Golf

From: Treasury assistant

Date:

Subject: **Cash problems and cash management**

All the golf clubs have similar cash flow patterns, and reasonably predictable cash flows. The clubs each receive large amounts of cash income from subscriptions, and gradually use up this cash through the course of the year, until there is normally an overdraft by the year-end. The exception is that there are higher demands for cash during the summer months.

We therefore have a cash surplus for much of the year, and the main problem is therefore how much we can safely invest short term, and how much we should hold in cash. If surplus cash is invested, there is also the problem of deciding how much cash to invest each time, how much cash to hold and (when investments have to be sold to obtain more cash), how much to sell each time.

It is recommended that cash management should be centralised in the treasury function, and the golf clubs should not manage their own cash flows independently of each other.

Centralised cash management means that the cash flow problems can be seen as a single problem for Eagle Golf as a whole, rather than as 20 separate problems in the golf clubs. By amalgamating cash balances where possible, higher interest rates on investments and lower interest rates in borrowing should be achievable.

The problem is how to maximise income from investing temporary cash surpluses. Cash surpluses from each club at the beginning of each year should be remitted to the central treasury unit for investment at the best available rates of return. The treasury unit should then monitor the cash requirements of each club, and provide cash to meet the clubs' requirements.

There is some uncertainty in the cash flows of each golf club, with income from the bar and restaurant (and late subscriptions and subscriptions from new members joining in mid-year) adding to income and some unpredictability in cash needs particularly during the summer months. It might therefore be appropriate to establish a cash control system based on the Miller-Orr model.

Each club could be given upper and lower cash holding limits, calculated by a formula in the model. Whenever the cash level at a golf club reaches the minimum level, the cash balance would be restored to a 'return point' level. The cash would be obtained by the central treasury cashing in some of the investments purchased with the temporary cash surpluses at the beginning of the year. There would also be an upper cash control level, above which the cash holdings of the golf club should not be expected to rise.

The aim of the cash management system should be to maximise the annual income from surplus cash, net of the transaction costs of cashing in investments when the cash is eventually required.

Towards the end of the year, when a cash deficit is expected, pooling cash at the central treasury should minimise the size of the division's overdraft requirements. Negotiating an overdraft centrally should also mean a lower interest rate and so lower interest charges.

Because the cash flows of the golf clubs are fairly predictable, it is also recommended that each golf club should have a cash budget, and the golf club manager should be held accountable for cash flows within the club.

Signed: Treasury assistant

259 DF

Annual equivalent rate of interest

$$\left(\frac{100}{97}\right)^{\frac{365}{80}} - 1 = 14.9\%$$

Note: An approximate rate of interest can be calculated as:

$$\frac{3}{(100-3)} \times \frac{365}{(90-10)} \times 100\% = 14.11\%$$

The more exact answer, however, is 14.9%, as shown.

DF would need to consider the following other factors:

(1)   The bank would charge annual interest of 12% which is less than the rate above. This means that it is cheaper to finance the higher receivables by borrowing than it would be to offer the cash settlement discount.

(2)   If DF borrows on overdraft from a bank, there is a risk that the bank might withdraw or reduce the overdraft facility without notice. Borrowing on overdraft might therefore be more risky.

(3)   Cash settlement discounts will increase in line with sales, whereas a bank loan is for a fixed amount or a fixed limit, and additional loans might have to be arranged. The bank will also probably ask for security for a loan in the form of fixed or floating charges.

(4)   Other customers might demand the same settlement discount terms as FF.

(5)   Once it has been established, the cash settlement discount arrangement may be difficult to withdraw at a future time, if DF no longer wants to offer it.

260   FONT

Cost of debt collection service

Reduction in average collection period for receivables = 20 days

Reduction in average trade receivables = 20/365 × $65.5 million = $3.589 million

	$ million
Saving in interest cost of finance (9% × $3.589 million)	0.32
Reduction in irrecoverable debts (50% × $2 million)	1.00
Total benefits	1.32
Fee payable for the service (1% × $67.5 million)	0.68
Net annual benefit from using the service	0.64

261   LOT

The cost/saving implications of all three possible increases in sales will provide the most useful information.

Calculations of the net benefit or loss under each projected possible increase in sales are as follows:

	20%	25%	30%
	$	$	$
Increase in annual sales	960,000	1,200,000	1,440,000
Total annual export sales	5,760,000	6,000,000	6,240,000
Irrecoverable debts			
Current amount (note 1)	51,000	51,000	51,000
New irrecoverable debts (note 2)	86,400	90,000	93,600
Increase in irrecoverable debts	35,400	39,000	42,600
Current export trade receivables	1,000,000	1,000,000	1,000,000
New amount of receivables (note 3)	1,280,000	1,333,333	1,386,667
Increase in export trade receivables	280,000	333,333	386,667
Annual cost at 10% interest	28,000	33,333	38,667
Extra contribution (35% × extra sales)	336,000	420,000	504,000
Advertising costs	(300,000)	(300,000)	(300,000)
Extra administration costs	(30,000)	(40,000)	(50,000)
Increase in irrecoverable debts	(35,400)	(39,000)	(42,600)
Extra cost of financing receivables	(28,000)	(33,333)	(38,667)
Net effect on annual profit	(57,400)	7,667	72,733

Notes:

(1)   Existing credit sales = $4.8m

Less 15% = $4.08m

Irrecoverable debts = 1.25% = $51,000

Current = 1.25% × 85% × $4,800,000 = $51,000

1.5% × $5,760,000 = $86,400
1.5% × $6,000,000 = $90,000
1.5% × $6,240,000 = $93,600

(2)   Current $4,800,000 × (75/360) = $1,000,000

$5,760,000 × (80/360) = $1,280,000
$6,000,000 × (80/360) = $1,333,333
$6,240,000 × (80/360) = $1,386,667

Expected value of change in profit = $(0.20 \times (57,400)) + (0.50 \times 7,667) + (0.30 \times 72,733)$
= +$14,173.

262   SCL

Annual sales $2 million × 12 = £24 million.

			$
Factor's annual fee	(2.5% × $24 million)		(600,000)
Saving in administration costs			300,000
		$	
Current average receivables	($24 million × 90/360)	6,000,000	
Receivables with the factor	(0.20 × $24m × 60/360)	800,000	
Reduction in average receivables		5,200,000	
Savings in interest at 9%			468,000
Factor finance interest	((0.80 × $24m × 60/360 × 10%))		(320,000)
Net annual cost			(152,000)

263   CREDITWORTHY

Forms of credit evaluation tend to vary according to the likely volume of purchases by the customer, and the amount of credit the customer hopes to receive. Credit checks should be more careful and thorough for larger customers. However, some form of credit checking is strongly advisable for all credit customers.

Methods of obtaining information for credit assessment of a potential new customer are:

(1)   A reference from the customer's bank

(2)   Trade references from other suppliers with which the customer already has an established purchasing relationship

(3)   Information from salesmen who have made a personal visit to the customer's premises

(4)   An analysis of the customer's annual report and accounts

(5)   If possible, information should be obtained from trade journals or trade association enquiries

(6)   The services of a credit checking agency might be employed

(7)   The entity might use its own credit scoring technique, which it applies to information provided by the customer to establish a credit score.

It is generally good business practice to begin by offering a limited amount of credit to new business customers, and to consider increasing the credit limit gradually over time, once a good business relationship with the customer has been established, and the customer has demonstrated an ability to pay what it owes on time.

264   EXCESSIVE CREDIT

Memo

To: Financial controller

From:

Date:

Subject: **Credit collection procedures**

Preventing customers from taking excessive credit

In order to prevent customers from taking excessive credit, the problem amongst existing customers needs to be reduced and procedures put in place to stop other customers taking excess credit.

Strict follow-up procedures should be applied for chasing payments on all overdue debts. For example, if a payment is overdue after 30 days a telephone call might be made to the customer, followed by a formal letter 10 days later, and so on.

If the threat of legal action is used, we must carry out the threat.

It might be appropriate to employ individuals with the specific task of collecting overdue payments. If necessary, they should be given training in debt collection procedures and techniques.

Existing customers whose payments are overdue

We should identify the scale of the problem. How many customers are taking excess credit and how much?

An aged analysis of receivables should be produced and analysed regularly. This will show all credit customers, the balance outstanding per customer and the balance split into the differing age categories, for example less than 30 days, between 30 and 60 days, and so on. This can be used to identify the slow payers and which customers have taken/are about to take excessive credit.

Customers taking excessive credit should be telephoned to find out why they are late in paying, and should be asked to pay. For telephone calls to be effective, the call should be made to the individual with the authority to make the payment and the call should end with an agreed payment plan.

If the client has not paid because of a missing invoice, or an unsettled dispute over the invoice, the problem should be dealt with. A duplicate invoice should be sent where appropriate, and the manager responsible should be asked to deal with any unresolved dispute as a matter of urgency.

New customers

Strict policies and procedures should be applied new customers to ensure that they pay promptly. We should ensure that credit terms are clearly stated on all sales orders, sales invoices and statements.

265 BF (NOV 05 EXAM)

(a) EOQ $= \sqrt{\dfrac{2cd}{h}}$

Where   d   =   annual demand

h   =   cost of holding one unit for one year

c   =   cost of placing order

Therefore: $\sqrt{\dfrac{2 \times 25 \times 65,000}{3}} = 1,041$

(b) Total cost using the EOQ of 1,041:

	$
Purchase cost (65,000 × $10)	650,000
Procurement cost (65,000/1,041 × $25)	1,561
Holding cost (1,041/2 × $3)	1,562
Total annual costs	653,123

Total cost if order size increased to 2,000:

	$
Purchase cost (65,000 × $9.80)	637,000
Procurement cost (65,000/2,000 × $25)	813
Holding cost (2,000/2 × $3)	3,000
Total annual costs	640,813

It is therefore worth increasing the order size as it will reduce costs by $12,310 a year.

266 PRINCIPLES OF SHORT-TERM INVESTMENT

To: Board of directors

From: Assistant Treasurer

Date:

Subject: **Short-term investments**

In selecting short-term investments for surplus cash, several criteria or principles should be considered.

Maturity

Many financial instruments are for a fixed maturity (term to settlement). At maturity, there is a payment of principal, possibly with interest, to the investor. Examples of investments with a fixed maturity include bonds, certificates of deposit and bills. A principle of short-term investment is that, to avoid risk, the selected investments should have a maturity that matches the desired term of investment.

Tutorial note

For example, if GIL wishes to invest its cash for nine months, suitable investments would be those maturing in nine months. If investments have a longer maturity than the investment period, they will have to be sold off before maturity, giving rise to a risk of loss due to a fall in the market value of the instrument. If investments have a shorter maturity than the desired term of investment, the money will have to be re-invested when the investments mature, and there is a risk that investment yields might have fallen.

In practice, however, it is often difficult to find suitable investments that match the investment period, or the investment period itself is uncertain. As a consequence, selected investments often have a longer or shorter maturity than the expected investment period.

Return

Investors should seek the best return possible, but only for an acceptable level of risk. Higher yielding investments are often more risky, in the sense that there could be a risk of default or a risk of a fall in the value of the investment.

Security and risk

Investors in short-term investments are often looking for a secure investment. This is an investment that does not have a high risk of default, where it is a debt instrument, or is not exposed to a risk of a fall in market value, where it is a marketable investment.

Liquidity

Investors in short-term investments should prefer liquid investments. A liquid investment is one that can be sold readily at a fair market price, without any risk of significant loss from having to sell at the chosen time. Liquid financial markets are large and active markets, and some investments are more liquid than others.

Building a portfolio to spread the investment risk

The risk of losses or disappointing returns on investments can be reduced by investing in a diversified portfolio of different investments. The principle is that some investments might perform better than expected and others worse, but the overall return on the portfolio is more likely to be close to expectation.

Foreign exchange risk

It might also be added that, although it is possible to invest in foreign currency investments, there will be an exposure to foreign exchange risk (the risk of a fall in investment value and the value of returns due to adverse exchange rate movements).

Treasury bills

Treasury bills are risk-free investments, because they are issued by the government, so that default will not occur. However, yields on Treasury bills are lower than on higher risk investments. In addition, the typical maturity of Treasury bills is 91 days, which means that their maturity is shorter than the planned investment term for the money. The market for Treasury bills, however, is large and liquid.

Corporate bonds

Corporate bonds can be a fairly high-risk investment. The risks arise both from the risk of default by the corporate bond issuer, and also from the risk of movements in the market price of bonds (if there is a rise or fall in general interest rates). To compensate investors for the risk, yields can be relatively high. Most bonds have a long remaining term to maturity, and investing in long-term instruments for the short term means that they will have to be sold to cash in the investment at the end of the investment period. The market for corporate bonds is not particularly liquid, although the bonds of some corporate issuers are more liquid than the bonds of others.

Investing exclusively in Treasury bills or corporate bonds would be inadvisable, because the investment risk would be reduced by building a portfolio of diversified investments – possibly containing some bills and some corporate bonds.

Signed: Assistant Treasurer

267   AD (MAY 05 EXAM)

			Days
Raw materials inventory	$\dfrac{\text{Raw materials inventory}}{\text{Purchases}}$	$111/641 \times 365 =$	63.2
Production time	$\dfrac{\text{Work in progress}}{\text{Cost of sales}}$	$63/898 \times 365 =$	25.6
Finished goods inventory	$\dfrac{\text{Finished goods inventory}}{\text{Cost of sales}}$	$102/898 \times 365 =$	41.4
Receivables days	$\dfrac{\text{Trade receivables}}{\text{Credit sales}}$	$216/992 \times 365 =$	79.5
Payables days	$\dfrac{\text{Payables}}{\text{Purchases}}$	$97/641 \times 365 =$	(55.2)
Working capital cycle			154.5

268   BH (NOV 05 EXAM)

(a)   The coupon rate is the interest rate payable on the face (nominal) value of the bond.

The yield to maturity (redemption yield) is the effective yield on a redeemable security, taking into account both the interest yield and any gain or loss due to the fact that it was purchased at a price different to the redemption value.

(b)   The annual interest payable on the bond is $70 ($1,000 × 7%).

There are two ways of calculating the redemption yield on a bond:

(i)   Calculate the internal rate of return of the relevant cash flows, including buying the bond at time zero:

Time		*CF*	*DF@7%*	*PV*	*DF@10%*	*PV*
0	*(MV)*	(850)	1	(850)	1	(850)
1-5	I	70	4.100	287	3.791	265
5	R	1000	0.713	713	0.621	621
				150		36

Yield = IRR ≈ 7 + (10-7)×150/(150-36) = approximately 11%

(ii)   Find the rate that equates the present value of the future receipts with the market value, using trial and error:

Rate	*PV of future receipts*
7%	(70 × 4.100) + (1,000 × 0.713) = 1,000
10%	(70 × 3.791) + (1,000 × 0.621) = 886
11%	(70 × 3.696) + (1,000 × 0.593) = 852, close enough

Tutorial note

The wording of the question is wrong – either BH issued the bond and will repay the face value later, **or** BH bought the bond and will receive the face value as redemption.

269   RISK AND YIELD (NOV 06 EXAM)

Notes on risk and effective yield of potential investments:

Treasury bills

Treasury bills reflect the credit rating of the country, so are generally low risk. However, as the risk is low, the investment is relatively attractive, such that the rate of interest is generally relatively low. In this case a yield of $10 would be earned over three months, which is an effective interest rate of only 1% per quarter.

Yield is achieved through a combination of interest payments and a growth in the value of the bill over time.

Equities

The value of equities can go down as well as up. In this case, the equity index has increased for the last 14 months. However, this cannot be taken as a guarantee of future continued good performance.

The risk associated with a particular share depends upon the risk associated with the market in general and the risk associated with the particular company. In this case, the proposed companies are multinationals, which can result in a lower risk due to diversification.

Due to the higher risk associated with equities, the yield is generally relatively high.

Bank deposit

A bank deposit is an investment in the business of the bank. However, banks are generally very secure, such that it is normally assumed that the investment will be recovered in full.

As with treasury bills, the yield is low to reflect the low risk, so carries a low rate of interest. However, in this case, the company would be required to give 30 days' notice of any withdrawals. This gives the bank more certainty and is reflected in an increased return on the deposit, in the form of an increased interest rate.

Section 6

ANSWERS TO SECTION C-TYPE QUESTIONS

SINGLE COMPANY FINANCIAL ACCOUNTS

270 UJM

Tutorial note

The irrecoverable debts and increase in the allowance for receivables should be classified as administrative expenses. The impairment of the building is also an administrative cost, since buildings depreciation is treated as an administrative cost.

(a) **UJM**

Income statement for the year ended 31 March 20X7

	$000
Revenue	101,050
Cost of sales (W1)	(72,200)
Gross profit	28,850
Administrative expenses (W3)	(14,121)
Distribution costs	(1,600)
Profit from operations	13,129
Finance cost (W4)	(500)
Profit before tax	12,629
Income tax expense	(5,660)
Net profit for the period	6,969

UJM

Balance sheet as at 31 March 20X7

	$000	$000
Assets		
Non-current assets		
Property, plant and equipment (W5)		59,000
Current assets		
Inventory	6,100	
Trade receivables (W6)	10,679	
Bank	4,200	
		20,979
Total assets		79,979

	$000	$000
Equity and liabilities		
Capital and reserves		
Ordinary share capital		25,000
Share premium account		17,650
Revaluation reserve (3,000 – 1,000)		2,000
Accumulated profits (W7)		9,880
		54,530
Non-current liabilities		
5% loan notes		10,000
Current liabilities		
Trade payables	9,539	
Current tax payable	5,660	
Accrued interest	250	
		15,449
Total equity and liabilities		79,979

Workings

(W1) **Cost of sales**

	$000
As in the trial balance	66,200
Depreciation charge, plant and machinery: 20% × 30,000	6,000
	72,200

(W2) **Impairment of buildings**

The balance on the revaluation reserve is $3,000,000. This represents revaluations in the past of the land and buildings. The land has been revalued by $2,000,000 ($6,000,000 – $4,000,000). The buildings must therefore have been revalued by $1,000,000.

	$000
Buildings at March 20X6 valuation	50,000
Accumulated depreciation at 31 March 20X6	(5,000)
Carrying amount at 31 March 20X6	45,000
Depreciation charge in year to 31 March 20X7 (2% × 50,000)	(1,000)
Carrying amount at 31 March 20X7	44,000
Revalued amount at 31 March 20X7	39,000
Impairment of buildings	5,000

This impairment loss can be set off initially against any amount in the revaluation reserve relating to the buildings. This is $1,000,000. The revaluation reserve is therefore reduced by $1,000,000, and the balance of the impairment loss, $4,000,000, is treated as a charge in the income statement for the year (administrative expense).

(W3) **Administrative expenses**

	$000	$000
As in the trial balance		5,900
Depreciation of buildings (see W2)		1,000
Impairment of buildings (see W2)		4,000
Bad debt		3,059
Allowance for receivables:		
31 March 20X7: [5% × (14,300 − 3,059)]	562	
31 March 20X6	400	
Increase in allowance		162
Total administrative expenses		14,121

(W4) **Finance cost**

Loan note interest = 5% × 10,000 = 500.

Of this, 250 has been paid and 250 is accrued or payable.

(W5) **Property, plant and equipment**

	$000
Plant and machinery at cost	30,000
Accumulated depreciation, 31 March 20X6	(10,000)
Depreciation charge 20X7	(6,000)
Carrying amount, 31 March 20X7	14,000
Land at valuation	6,000
Buildings at valuation	39,000
Total non-current assets (carrying amount)	59,000

(W6) **Trade receivables**

	$000
As in the trial balance	14,300
Bad debt written off	(3,059)
Allowance for receivables (W3)	(562)
	10,679

(W7) **Accumulated profits**

	$000
At 31 March 20X6	4,411
Profit for the year	6,969
Dividend paid	(1,500)
At 31 March 20X7	9,880

(b)   **Y**

Cash flow statement for the year ended 31 December 20X4

	$000	$000
Cash flows from operating activities		
Net profit before taxation	196	
Adjustments for:		
Depreciation	59	
Loss on disposal of non-current assets	9	
Interest expense	14	
	⎯	
	278	
Increase in inventory (12 – 10)	(2)	
Increase in trade receivables (34 – 26)	(8)	
Increase in trade payables (21 – 15)	6	
	⎯	
Cash generated from operations	274	
Interest paid	(14)	
Income taxes paid (W1)	(55)	
Net cash from operating activities	⎯	205
Cash flows from investing activities		
Purchase of non-current assets	(45)	
Proceeds from sale of non-current assets (W2)	6	
Net cash used in investing activities	⎯	(39)
Cash flows from financing activities		
Proceeds from issue of share capital (W3)	16	
Repayment of loan (100 – 250)	(150)	
Dividends paid	(36)	
Net cash used in financing activities	⎯	(170)
		⎯
Net decrease in cash and cash equivalents		(4)
Cash and cash equivalents at beginning of period (all cash at bank)		28
		⎯
Cash and cash equivalents at end of period (all cash at bank)		24
		⎯

Workings

(W1) **Tax paid**

	$000	$000
Tax liability at 31 December 20X3		
Deferred tax	16	
Income tax	24	
	⎯	
		40
Tax charge for the year		62
		⎯
		102
Tax liability at 31 December 20X4		
Deferred tax	20	
Income tax	27	
	⎯	
		(47)
		⎯
Tax paid during the year		55
		⎯

(W2) **Sale of non-current asset(s)**

	$000	$000
Non-current assets at cost, 31 December 20X4	798	
Cost of asset acquired during the year	(45)	
	753	
Non-current assets at cost, 31 December 20X3	780	
Cost of asset disposed of during the year		27
Accumulated depreciation, 31 December 20X4	159	
Depreciation charge for the year	(59)	
	100	
Accumulated depreciation, 31 December 20X3	112	
Accumulated depreciation on asset disposed of		12
Net book value (carrying amount) of asset disposed of		15
Loss on disposal		(9)
Sale proceeds		6

(W3) **Issue of share capital**

	$000
Share capital and share premium at 31 December 20X4: (180 + 18)	198
Share capital and share premium at 31 December 20X3: (170 + 12)	(182)
Proceeds from issue of shares	16

271   MOP

MOP

Income statement for the year ended 30 September 20X5

	Note	$m	$m
Revenue			2,970
Cost of sales (W3)	(1)		(1,067)
Gross profit			1,903
Distribution costs		(148)	
Administrative expenses		(64)	(212)
			1,691
Finance costs			(72)
Profit before tax	(2)		1,619
Taxation	(3)		(69)
Profit after tax			1,550

MOP

Balance sheet as at 30 September 20X5

	Note	$m	$m
Assets			
Non-current assets:			
Tangible	(5)		3,908
Current assets			
Inventories (W2)		38	
Receivables		980	
Cash and cash equivalents		98	1,116
Total assets			5,024
Equity and liabilities			
Capital and reserves			
Issued capital			600
Accumulated profits			2,382
			2,982
Non-current liabilities			
Interest bearing borrowings		1,618	
Deferred taxation		277	
			1,895
Current liabilities			
Trade payables		27	
Taxation		120	
			147
Total equity and liabilities			5,024

Notes to the financial statements:

(1) **Related party transactions**

The company buys goods from Seller, a company which is 98% owned by one of MOP's directors. Purchases during the year amounted to $43 million, all under Seller's normal terms and conditions. The amount owed to Seller at 30 September 20X5 amounted to $3 million.

Tutorial note

Seller is a related party within the definition of IAS 24. If there have been transactions with a related party, the entity should disclose the related party relationship and information about the transactions and outstanding balances necessary for an understanding of the potential effects of the relationship on the financial statements.

---

(2) **Profit on ordinary activities**

Profit is stated after charging depreciation of $207 million.

Tutorial note

IAS 1 states that when the income statement classifies expenses by function, additional information on the nature of expenses should be disclosed in a note, including depreciation and amortisation expense, and employee benefits expense.

---

(3)   **Taxation**

The taxation charge in the income statement comprises:

	$m
Taxation on the profit for the year	120
Over-provision in respect of the previous year	(37)
Deferred tax income (W4)	(14)
	69

(4)   **Proposed dividend**

A final dividend of $150 million has been proposed.

Tutorial note

IAS 1 requires that the amount of any dividends declared or proposed after the balance sheet date but before the financial statements are issued should be disclosed in a note.

---

(5)   **Movements on non-current assets**

Tangible non-current assets

	Property $m	*Plant and equipment* $m	*Total* $m
Cost			
At 1 October 20X4 (W5)	4,456	759	5,215
Additions	–	160	160
Disposals	–	(125)	(125)
At 30 September 20X5	4,456	794	5,250
Depreciation			
At 1 October 20X4 (W5)	811	402	1,213
Depreciation for the year (W1)	89	118	207
Disposals		(78)	(78)
At 30 September 20X5	900	442	1,342
Carrying amount (net book value)			
1 October 20X4	3,645	357	4,002
30 September 20X5	3,556	352	3,908

Workings

(W1) Depreciation and non-current assets

Depreciation

A full annual charge for depreciation is charged in the year of acquisition and none in the year of disposal. Depreciation for the year to 30 September 20X5 is therefore based on figures in the trial balance, which already reflect acquisitions and disposals that have occurred during the year:

	Property			Plant and equipment
	$m			$m
Cost	4,456	Cost		794
		Accumulated depreciation		(324)
Carrying amount				470
Depreciation rate	2%			25%
Depreciation charge	= 89			= 118

Tutorial note

It might seem odd that the property cost is not separated into land (not depreciated) and buildings. Presumably, the property consists entirely of depreciable assets, and so excludes land. For example, it might represent long leaseholds.

Sale of plant and equipment (***Note:*** This has already been recorded in the trial balance)

	$m
Cost	125
Less Accumulated depreciation	(78)
Carrying amount of plant sold	47

The $11m presented in the trial balance is a loss on sale.

Tutorial note

The opening balance of assets at cost is calculated as the balancing figure, after adjusting the 30 September 20X5 figures for the cost of acquisitions and disposals during the year.

The opening balance for accumulated depreciation for plant and equipment is the trial balance figure, plus the accumulated depreciation on the assets disposed of during the year: 324 + 78 = 402.

(W2) **Inventory valuation**

IAS 2 requires inventories to be valued at the lower of cost or net realisable value (NRV) *on an item by item basis.* Hence, the correct valuation is:

	Cost	NRV	Lower
	$m	$m	$m
Current inventory			
Purchase price	26		
Manufacturing overhead*	7		
	33	51	33
Obsolete inventory			
Purchase price	6		
Manufacturing overhead	2	5	
	8	5	5

* Non-manufacturing overheads are *not* included.

Total inventory valuation = 33 + 5 = 38

Inventory needs to be adjusted by (45 – 38) = 7. This is an extra charge to cost of sales.

(W3) **Cost of sales**

	$000
As in the trial balance	842
Depreciation of property (W1)	89
Depreciation of plant and equipment (W1)	118
Loss on disposal of plant and equipment (W1)	11
Impairment loss, inventory (W2)	7
	1,067

(W4) **Deferred taxation**

The provision required at 30 September 20X5 needs to be calculated by comparing the accounting carrying values and tax written down values as follows:

	Property	*Plant and equipment*	*Total*
	$000	$000	$000
Carrying value in the accounts	3,556	352	3,908
Tax written-down value			2,985
			923
Tax rate = 30%			
Deferred tax liability at 30 September 20X5			277
Deferred tax liability at 30 September 20X4			291
Reduction in deferred tax in the year			14

(W5) **Accumulated profits**

	$000
At 30 September 20X5	1,132
Profit for the year	1,550
Dividend paid	(300)
At 30 September 20X6	2,382

272 HI RETAIL

Hi Retail

Income statement for the year ended 30 September 20X2

	$000
Sales revenue	9,415
Cost of sales (W1)	(5,304)
Gross profit	4,111
Distribution costs	(314)
Administrative expenses (W3)	(760)
Profit from operations	3,037
Finance cost (10% × 1,000)	(100)
Investment income received	37
Profit before tax	2,974
Income tax expense (W4)	(1,205)
Net profit for the year	1,769

Note: The increase in the value of the investment during the year was $30,000 ($522,000 – $492,000). However, this is a non-current investment; therefore the increase in value is treated as a movement in the revaluation reserve, and is not reported as part of the profit for the year.

In contrast, if the investment had been a current asset, the increase in value by $30,000 to a fair value of $522,000 would have been included in the profit for the year (IAS 39).

Hi Retail

Balance sheet as at 30 September 20X2

	$000	$000
Non-current assets		
Buildings (W5)	9,460	
Equipment and fixtures (W5)	396	
Investments	522	
		10,378
Current assets		
Inventory	822	
Trade receivables (852 – 45)	807	
Bank and cash	959	
		2,588
Total assets		12,966
Capital and reserves		
Issued share capital ($1 ordinary shares, fully paid)	4,000	
Share premium (W6)	2,388	
Revaluation reserve (W7)	202	
Accumulated profits (W8)	3,369	
		9,959
Non-current liabilities		
10% loan notes 20X9	1,000	
Deferred tax	281	
Provision for legal damages	100	
		1,381
Current liabilities		
Trade payables	396	
Accrued loan note interest (100 – 50)	50	
Income tax payable	1,180	
		1,626
Total equity and liabilities		12,966

Statement of changes in equity for the year ended 30 September 20X2

	Share capital $000	*Share premium* $000	*Revaluation reserve* $000	*Accum. Profits* $000	*Total* $000
Balance at 30 Sept 20X1	3,200	788 (W6)	172	2,400	6,560
Surplus on revaluation of investments			30		30
Net profit for the year				1,769	1,769
Dividends paid				(800)	(800)
Issue of share capital	800	1,600			2,400
Balance at 30 Sept 20X2	4,000	2,388	202	3,369	9,959

Workings

(W1) **Cost of sales**

	$000
As in the trial balance	4,491
Depreciation of buildings 3% × $11,200	336
Depreciation of equipment 20% × ($2,625 − $210)	483
Less: Gain on disposal of equipment (W2)	(6)
	5,304

(W2) **Disposal of non-current asset**

Cost of equipment	210
Accumulated deprecation to the date of disposal	(205)
Carrying amount at the date of disposal	5
Net disposal proceeds	11
Gain on disposal	6

(W3) **Administrative expenses**

	$000
As in the trial balance	615
Irrecoverable debt written off	45
Provision: Damages likely to be payable	100
	760

(W4) **Income tax expense**

	$000
Due for the year	1,180
Deferred tax increase ($281 − $256)	25
	1,205

(W5) Tangible non-current assets

	Buildings	*Equipment and fixtures*
	$000	$000
Cost or valuation at 30 September 20X2	11,200	2,625
Accumulated depreciation at 30 Sept 20X1	(1,404)	(1,741)
Net book value of asset disposed of		(5)
Depreciation charge for the year	(336)	(483)
Carrying amount at 30 September 20X2	9,460	396

(W6) Share premium account

Shares in issue at 30 September 20X2	4,000,000
Issued in 1 for 4 rights issue [× 1/(1 + 4)]	800,000
Shares in issue before the rights issue	3,200,000

	$000
Addition to share premium from rights issue	1,600
(800,000 shares × $(3 – 1) per share)	
Share premium after the rights issue (trial balance)	2,388
Share premium before the rights issue	788

(W7) Revaluation reserve

	$000
As in the trial balance	172
Revaluation of non-current investment (522 – 492)	30
	202

(W8) Accumulated profits

	$000
As in the trial balance	2,400
Profit for the year	1,769
Dividends paid	(800)
	3,369

273   AZ FINANCIAL STATEMENTS (PILOT PAPER)

AZ Income statement for the year ended 31 March 20X3

	$000
Revenue	124,900
Cost of sales (W1)	(99,735)
	25,165
Other income	1,200
Distribution costs (W2)	(9,573)
Administrative expenses (W3)	(16,045)
Other expenses	(121)
	626
Interest cost (W4)	(1,278)
Loss before tax	(652)
Tax expense	(15)
Loss for the period	(667)

AZ Statement of changes in equity for the year ended 31 March 20X3

	Share capital $000	Share premium $000	Accumulated profit $000	Total $000
Balance at 31 March 20X2	19,000	0	14,677	33,677
Issue of shares	1,000	500		1,500
Share issue costs		(70)		(70)
Net loss for the period			(667)	(667)
Dividends			(1,000)	(1,000)
Balance at 31 March 20X3	20,000	430	13,010	33,440

AZ: Balance sheet as at 31 March 20X3

Assets	$000	$000	$000
Non-current assets	*Cost*	*Dep'n*	*Net book value*
Property, plant and equipment (W5)	34,035	14,306	19,729
Current assets			
Inventory		5,180	
Trade and other receivables (W6)		9,330	
Cash		26,250	
			40,760
Total assets			60,489

	$000	$000	$000
Equity and liabilities			
Capital and reserves			
Issued capital		20,000	
Share premium		430	
Accumulated profits		13,010	
			33,440
Non-current liabilities			
7% loan notes (redeemable 20X7)		18,250	
Provision		25	
			18,275
Current liabilities			
Trade and other payables		8,120	
Accruals (W4)		639	
Current tax payable		15	
			8,774
Total equity and liabilities			60,489

Tutorial notes

1   *Share capital.* The trial balance includes the share premium and share issue expenses for the issue of shares during the year. The trial balance must therefore also show the nominal value of the issued share capital **after** the share issue. It follows that if there were 20 million shares after the issue and 1 million shares issued during the year, the balance on the issued share capital account at the beginning of the year was for 19 million shares. This is also consistent with the fact that the dividend payment of $0.05 in February was $1,000,000 in total (= 20 million shares × $0.05).

2   *Restructuring costs.* These are shown as an expense in the trial balance (= debit balance) for costs incurred. There is no existing provision for restructuring costs in the trial balance (which would be a credit balance). These costs should be charged as an expense in the income statement for the year. They are included in the suggested solution as 'other expenses'.

3   *Compensation payable.* The information in the question points strongly to the requirement to include the likely compensation payable as a provision. There is no indication when this money will be payable, and the provision has been included in the balance sheet as a non-current liability. In the income statement, the expense is included within administrative expenses: (debit Administrative expenses, credit Provision).

Workings

(W1) **Cost of sales**

	$000
Opening inventory	4,852
Cost of goods manufactured	94,000
	98,852
Closing inventory	(5,180)
	93,672
Depreciation of plant and equipment (20% × 30,315)	6,063
Total cost of goods sold	99,735

(W2) Distribution costs

	$000
Trial balance figure	9,060
Depreciation of vehicles [25% × (3,720 – 1,670)]	513
	9,573

(W3) Administrative expenses

	$000
Trial balance figure	16,020
Provision for compensation payment	25
	16,045

(W4) Interest cost

The only interest cost is for the loan notes, and the annual cost is 7% × $18,250,000 = $1,277,500. The interest paid in the trial balance is $639,000, which is one half of the annual interest cost. This suggests that the interest for the second six months of the year has not yet been paid, but is payable very soon.

In the income statement, the interest cost should be (in $000) 1,278. In the balance sheet, there should be a liability for interest (in $000) of 639. This should be shown either as an amount payable or as an accrued interest charge. The suggested solution shows the liability separately as an accrual, but this amount could be included within the total for trade and other payables.

(W5) Property, plant and equipment

	Cost		Accumulated depreciation	Net book value
	$000		$000	$000
Plant and equipment	30,315	(6,060 + 6,063)	12,123	18,192
Vehicles	3,720	(1,670 + 513)	2,183	1,537
	34,035		14,306	19,729

(W6) Trade and other receivables

	$000
Trade receivables (trial balance)	9,930
Allowance for trade receivables	(600)
	9,330

274   AF (MAY 05 EXAM)

AF

Income statement for the year ended 31 March 20X5

		$000
Revenue		8,210
Cost of sales	(W1)	(3,957)
Gross profit		4,253
Income from investments		68
Administrative expenses		(1,540)
Distribution costs		(1,590)
Profit from operations		1,191
Finance cost (1,500 × 6%)		(90)
Profit before tax		1,101
Income tax expense (250 + 110)		(350)
Profit for the period		751

AF

Balance sheet as at 31 March 20X5

	$000	$000	$000
Non-current assets			
Property, plant and equipment (3,594 + 1,393)			4,987
Available for sale investments			1,750
Current assets			
Inventory		1,320	
Trade receivables		1,480	
Cash and cash equivalent		822	
			3,622
Total assets			10,359
Equity and liabilities			
Equity			
Share capital		4,500	
Share premium		1,380	
Revaluation reserve (330 + 11)		440	
Retained earnings (W5)		864	
Total equity			7,184
Non-current liabilities			
6% Loan	1,500		
Deferred tax (710 + 100)	810		
Total non-current liabilities		2,310	
Current liabilities			
Trade and other payables (W6)	615		
Tax payables	250		
Total current liabilities	865		
Total liabilities		3,175	
Total equity and liabilities		10,359	

Workings

(W1)   **Cost of sales**

	$000	$000
Cost of goods		3,463
Add depreciation – buildings (W2)		96
– plant and equipment (W3)		348
Operating lease (W4)		50
		3,957

(W2)   **Buildings**

	$000	$000
Land and building at cost		5,190
Less: Depreciation for year b/f	1,500	
Depreciation for year (5,190 – 2,000) × 3%	96	(1,596)
Net book value		3,594

(W3) **Plant and equipment**

Plant and equipment cost		3,400
Depreciation b/fwd	1,659	
Depreciation for year (3,400 − 1,659) × 20%	348	2,007
Net book value		1,393

(W4) **Operating lease**

Total payments (4 × 62,500)	250
Allocated evenly over 5 periods (250/5)	50 a

Tutorial note

The new lease is an operating lease, therefore the full cost must be charged to the income statement over the five years of the lease. The useful economic life of the asset is irrelevant.

(W5) **Retained earnings**

Balance b/fwd	388
Profit for the year	751
	1139
Less: Dividend paid	(275)
	864

(W6) **Trade and other payables**

Trade payables	520
Operating lease accrual	50
Finance cost	45
	615

275 BG (NOV 05 EXAM)

Income statement for the year ended 30 September 20X5

	$000
Sales revenue	1,017
Cost of sales (W1)	(860)
Gross profit	157
Investment income	11
	168
Administrative expenses (239 − 190 provision release)	(49)
Profit from operations	119
Finance costs	(15)
Profit before tax	104
Income tax expense (W2)	(88)
Net profit for the year	16

Statement of changes in equity for the year ended 30 September 20X5

	Share capital $000	Share premium $000	Revaluation reserve $000	Accumulated profits $000	Total $000
Balance at 30 September 20X4	200	40	30	226	496
Revaluation of property			20		20
Net profit for the year				16	16
Dividends paid				(60)	(60)
Balance at 30 September 20X5	200	40	50	182	472

Balance sheet as at 30 September 20X5

	$000	$000
Assets		
Non-current assets		
Tangible assets (W3)		232
Available for sale investments		225
		457
Current assets		
Inventory	37	
Receivables	141	
Cash at bank and in hand	147	
		325
Total assets		782
Equity and liabilities		
Capital and reserves		
Issued share capital		200
Share premium account		40
Revaluation reserve		50
Accumulated profits		182
		472
Non-current liabilities		
Long-term loans	150	
Deferred tax (50 + 15)	65	
		215
Current liabilities		
Trade payables	24	
Accrued interest	7	
Income tax	64	
		95
Total equity and liabilities		782

Workings

(W1) **Cost of sales**

	$000
Cost of cleaning materials consumed	101
Direct operating expenses	548
Depreciation ($752 \times 20\%$)	150
Vehicle lease rentals	61
	860

(W2) **Income tax**

	$000
Income tax on profits for the year	64
Under-provision in respect of previous years	9
Deferred tax	15
	88

(W3) **Tangible non-current assets**

	Equipment and fixtures $000
Cost at 30 September 20X5	752
Accumulated depreciation:	
At 30 September 20X4	370
Charge for year	150
At 30 September 20X5	520
Net book value:	
At 30 September 20X5	232

276 V

V

Income statement for the year ended 30 September 20X4

	$000
Sales revenue	9,800
Cost of sales (W1)	(1,750)
Gross profit	8,050
Distribution costs (W2)	(945)
Administrative expenses (W3)	(770)
Profit from operations	6,335
Finance costs	(5)
Profit before tax	6,330
Income tax expense (W6)	(1,945)
Net profit for the year	4,385

V

Balance sheet at 30 September 20X4

	$000	$000
Assets		
Non-current assets		
Tangible assets (W5)		10,340
Current assets		
Inventory	520	
Receivables	910	
Cash at bank and in hand	90	
		1,520
Total assets		11,860
Equity and liabilities		
Capital and reserves		
Issued share capital		1,000
Revaluation reserve (760 + 1,530)		2,290
Accumulated profits (W7)		5,050
		8,340
Non-current liabilities		
Long-term loans	500	
Deferred tax	690	
		1,190
Current liabilities		
Trade payables	470	
Application and allotment	110	
Income tax	1,750	
		2,330
Total equity and liabilities		11,860

Workings

	$000
(W1) Cost of sales	
Opening inventory	480
Purchases	1,660
Closing inventory	(520)
Depreciation on warehouse buildings (6,500 × 2%)	130
	1,750
(W2) Distribution costs	
Warehouse and delivery wages	350
Sales commissions	180
Sundry distribution costs	310
Depreciation on vehicles ((700 − 280) × 25%)	105
	945

(W3) Administrative expenses

Sundry administration expenses	85
Administration staff salaries	240
Legal fees and damages	270
Depreciation on computer $((900 - 200) \times 25\%)$	175
	770

(W4) Revaluation of property

Carrying value of warehouse premises at 30 September 20X3	
Valuation	8,500
Less accumulated depreciation	(400)
	8,100
Depreciation charge for the year (W1)	(130)
Carrying amount before revaluation	7,970
New valuation (2.5 million + 7 million)	9,500
Revaluation	1,530

The accumulated depreciation of $530,000 (400 + 130) is reduced to zero, and the buildings are shown in the balance sheet at their new value, $7 million. The land is revalued to $2.5 million.

(W5) Tangible non-current assets

	Premises	Computer network	Delivery vehicles	Total	
	$000	$000	$000	$000	
Cost or valuation:					
At 30 September 20X3	8,500	900	700	10,100	
Revaluation	1,000	0	0	1,000	
At 30 September 20X4	9,500	900	700	11,100	
Accumulated depreciation:					
At 30 September 20X3		400	200	280	880
Charge for year		130	175	105	410
Revaluation		(530)	–	–	(530)
At 30 September 20X4		0	375	385	760
Net book value:					
At 30 September 20X3		8,100	700	420	9,220
At 30 September 20X4		9,500	525	315	10,340

(W6) Income tax

	$000
Income tax on profits for the year	1,750
Under-provision in respect of previous years	45
Deferred tax (690 – 540)	150
	1,945

(W7) **Accumulated profits**

	$000
Balance at 30 September 20X3	1,265
Net profit for the year	4,385
Dividends paid	(600)
Balance at 30 September 20X4	5,050

277   DM (NOV 06 EXAM)

Income statement for the year ended 30 September 20X6

	$000
Sales revenue	602
Cost of sales (84 + 285 – 93 + 26)(W1)	(302)
Gross profit	300
Distribution costs (46 + 20)(W1)	(66)
Administrative expenses (91 + 9) (W1)	(100)
Profit from operations	134
Finance costs (11 + 7)(W3, W4)	(18)
Profit before tax	116
Income tax expense (24 + 15)	(39)
Net profit for the year	77

Statement of changes in equity for the year ended 30 September 20X6

	Share capital $000	Share premium $000	Accumulated profits $000	Total $000
Balance at 30 September 20X5	200	0	32	232
Share issue	100	50		150
Net profit for the year			77	77
Dividends paid			(25)	(25)
Balance at 30 September 20X6	300	50	84	434

Balance sheet as at 30 September 20X6

	$000	$000
Assets		
Non-current assets		
Tangible assets (W2)		631
Current assets		
Inventory	93	
Receivables	6	
Cash at bank and in hand	43	
		142
Total assets		773
Equity and liabilities		
Capital and reserves		
Issued share capital		300
Share premium account		50
Accumulated profits		84
		434
Non-current liabilities		
Finance lease creditor	66	
Long-term loans	140	
Deferred tax (40 + 15)	55	
		261
Current liabilities		
Trade and other payables (29 + 7)	36	
Finance lease creditor	18	
Income tax	24	
		78
Total equity and liabilities		773

Workings

(W1) **Depreciation**

	$000
Buildings $(500 - 200) = 300 \times 0.03$	9
Plant and equipment $(211 - 80) \times 0.2$	26
Vehicles 0.2×100	20
	55

(W2) **Tangible assets**

	$000
Land and buildings at cost	500
Plant and equipment at cost	211
Depreciation brought forward – buildings	(45)
Depreciation brought forward – plant and equipment	(80)
Depreciation for period – above	(55)
Finance lease assets (W3)	100
	631

(3) **Lease**

Total payments = 27,000 × 5 = 135,000

Exceeds cost so suggests finance lease. Also, term of lease is equal to economic life, therefore, assume finance lease.

	$000
Cost	100
Depreciation	(20)
	80

	$000
Initial creditor	100
Interest accrued at 10.92%	11
Less payment	(27)
Total lease creditor	84

Payable within one year:	
Payment in next period	27
Less interest accruing in next period	
84 × 0.1092	(9)
	18

Payable in more than one year	
84 − 18	66

(4) **Interest on loan**

6% × 10/12 × 140 = 7

278 C CASH FLOW

(a) **C: Cash flow statement for the year ended 31 March 20X4**

	$000	$000
Profit before taxation		982
Adjustments for:		
Depreciation (W1)		456
Amortisation of development expenditure		18
Finance cost		45
Profit on sale of non-current asset (W2)		(11)
Increase in provisions (400 − 120)		280
		1,770
Increase in trade receivables (712 − 401))		(311)
Increase in inventory (1,337 − 864)		(473)
Increase in trade payables (626 − 552)		74
Cash generated from operations		1,060
Interest paid (W3)		(29)
Taxation paid (W4)		(188)
Net cash from operating activities		843

	$000	$000
Cash flows from investing activities		
Purchase of property, plant and equipment (W5)	(2,827)	
Development expenditure paid (W6)	(39)	
Interest received (W7)	34	
Net cash used in investing activities		(2,832)
Cash flows from financing activities		
Proceeds from issue of ordinary shares (W8)	1,500	
Proceeds from new loans raised (1,006 – 410)	596	
Equity dividends paid	(350)	
Net cash from financing activities		1,746
Net decrease in cash and cash equivalents		(243)
Cash and cash equivalents at 31 March 20X3		759
(730 + 7 + 22)		
Cash and cash equivalents at 31 March 20X4 (0 + 489 + 27)		516

Workings

(W1) **Depreciation**

There are two methods of calculating the depreciation charge for tangible non-current assets:

Method 1

	Buildings	*Plant, machinery and equipment*	*Total*
	$000	$000	$000
Cost or valuation as at 31 March 20X4	3,063	2,188	
Accumulated depreciation at start of year		(671)	
Accumulated depreciation on asset sold		380	
Carrying value before 20X4 depreciation		1,897	
Depreciation rate	2.5%	20%	
Depreciation for the year, in $000	76.6	379.4	456

Method 2

	$000
Tangible assets at cost or valuation, 31 March 20X4	8,887
(3,636 + 3,063 + 2,188)	
Carrying value at 31 March 20X4 (balance sheet)	7,724
Accumulated depreciation at 31 March 20X4	1,163
Accumulated depreciation at 31 March 20X3 (416 + 671)	(1,087)
Accumulated depreciation on asset disposed of	380
Therefore depreciation charge for the year	456

(W2) **Gain or loss on sale of non-current asset**

	$000
Cost of machinery disposed of	400
Accumulated depreciation	(380)
Carrying amount at time of disposal	20
Disposal proceeds	31
Gain on disposal	11

There is a receivable for the $31,000 in the balance sheet at 31 March 20X4. This means that the cash received from the disposal during the year was $0.

(W3) **Interest paid**

	$000
Interest payable at the beginning of the year	4
Finance charge for the year	45
	49
Interest payable at the end of the year	(20)
Interest payments during the year	29

(W4) **Taxation paid**

	$000	$000
Tax liability at the beginning of the year		
Deferred tax	291	
Current tax	188	
		479
Taxation charge for the year		197
		676
Tax liability at the end of the year		
Deferred tax	254	
Current tax	234	
		(488)
Taxation paid during the year		188

(W5) **Purchase of property, plant and equipment**

	$000
Property, plant and equipment:	
At carrying amount, 31 March 20X4 (3,636 + 3,063 + 2,188)	8,887
At carrying amount, 31 March 20X3 (3,186 + 1,663 + 1,161)	6,010
	2,877
Revaluation of land	(450)
Cost of machinery disposed of during the year	400
Therefore payments to acquire property, plant and equipment	2,827

(W6) **Payments for development expenditure**

	$000
Carrying value at 31 March 20X3	90
Amortisation charge for the year	(18)
	72
Carrying value at 31 March 20X4	111
Therefore amount paid for development expenditure	39

(W7) **Interest received**

Interest receivable was $34,000 at the beginning of the year and $0 at the end of the year. There is no interest receivable in the income statement; therefore cash receipts for interest during the year must be $34,000.

(W8) **Proceeds from issue of ordinary shares**

	$000	$000
Share capital and share premium at the beginning of the year		
Ordinary shares	1,500	
Share premium	500	
		2,000
Share capital and share premium at the end of the year		
Ordinary shares	2,000	
Share premium	1,500	
		3,500
Cash received from share issue		1,500

(b) **Analysis of cash and cash equivalents**

	At 31 March 20X4 $000	At 31 March 20X3 $000
Bank	489	7
Cash	27	22
Current asset investment	0	730
	516	759

279 TEX CASH FLOW STATEMENT (PILOT PAPER)

Tutorial notes

1   The cash flow statement can be prepared using either the direct or the indirect method, because the information is provided for either method to be used. The only exception is that there is no information available to separate the cash paid to suppliers from the cash paid to and on behalf of employees. Both the direct and indirect methods are shown in this solution. The direct method is more complicated in the question, but you need to learn both methods.

2   In order to prepare a cash flow statement, we need to work out the depreciation charge for the year, the gain or loss on disposal of non-current assets and the amount of taxation paid. Since these workings are essential, they are shown at the beginning of the solution.

3   Proposed dividends cannot be shown in the balance sheet or the statement of changes in equity (or, in this question, the income statement) **unless** they have been declared before the balance sheet date. It is very unusual to declare a final dividend before the balance sheet date, but this is the situation described in the question. There is also a proposed dividend in the opening balance sheet, indicating that it is normal practice for this company to declare a final dividend before the balance sheet date. The amount of dividends actually paid must therefore be calculated from the balance sheet liabilities for dividend and the dividend shown in the income statement.

Workings

(W1) **Non-current asset purchases**

	Property $000	Plant $000	Total $000
Cost at the beginning of the year	8,400	10,800	
Disposal (at cost)	–	(2,600)	
	8,400	8,200	
Cost at the end of the year	11,200	13,400	
Purchases during the year	2,800	5,200	8,000

(W2) **Depreciation**

	Property $000	Plant $000	Total $000
Accumulated depreciation at the beginning of the year	1,300	3,400	
Accumulated depreciation on disposal	–	(900)	
	1,300	2,500	
Accumulated depreciation at the beginning of the year	1,540	4,900	
Depreciation charge for the year	240	2,400	2,640

(W3) **Gain or loss on disposal**

	$000
Cost of asset disposed of	2,600
Accumulated depreciation on asset	(900)
Net book value of asset disposed of	1,700
Cash from disposal	730
Loss on disposal	970

(W4) **Tax paid**

	$000	$000
Tax liability at the beginning of the year		
Current tax payable	685	
Deferred tax	400	
		1,085
Income tax expense for the year		1,040
		2,125
Tax liability at the end of the year		
Current tax payable	1,040	
Deferred tax	600	
		(1,640)
Tax paid		485

(W5) **Dividends paid**

	$000
Declared dividends at the beginning of the year	600
Dividend for the year	1,100
	1,700
Declared dividends at the end of the year	(700)
Dividends paid	1,000

(W6) **Cash receipts from customers**

	$000
Trade receivables at the beginning of the year	800
Revenue for the year	15,000
	15,800
Trade receivables at the end of the year	(1,500)
Cash received	14,300

(W7) Cash paid to suppliers and to and on behalf of employees

	$000
Inventory at the end of the year	1,600
Cost of sales	9,000
	10,600
Inventory at the beginning of the year of the year	(1,100)
	9,500
Trade payables at the beginning of the year	800
Trade payables at the end of the year	(700)
	9,600
Other operating expenses	2,300
	11,900
Depreciation for the year (W2)	(2,640)
Loss on disposal of non-current asset (W3)	(970)
Cash paid	8,290

Direct method

TEX: Cash flow statement for the year ended 30 September 20X3

	$000	$000
Cash flows from operating activities		
Cash receipts from customers (W6)	14,300	
Cash payments to suppliers and employees (W7)	(8,290)	
Cash generated from operations	6,010	
Interest paid	(124)	
Taxation paid (W4)	(485)	
Net cash flows from operating activities		5,401
Cash flows from investing activities		
Purchase of property, plant and equipment (W1)	(8,000)	
Proceeds from the sale of plant	730	
		(7,270)
Cash flows from financing activities		
Proceeds from the issue of share capital		
(10,834 – 7,815)	3,019	
Repayment of borrowings	(1,200)	
Dividends paid (W5)	(1,000)	
		819
Net increase in cash and cash equivalents		(1,050)
Cash and cash equivalents at the beginning of the year		1,200
Cash and cash equivalents at the end of the year		150

Notes:

(1)   Cash and cash equivalents included in the cash flow statement include the following amounts:

	30 September 20X3	30 September 20X2
	$000	$000
Cash in bank	150	1,200

(2)   During the year, the company acquired property, plant and equipment with a total cost of $8,000,000. These were paid for in cash.

Alternative solution: indirect method

TEX: Cash flow statement for the year ended 30 September 20X3

	$000
Cash flows from operating activities	
Profit before taxation	3,576
Adjustments for:	
Depreciation (W2)	2,640
Loss on disposal of plant (W3)	970
Interest expense	124
	7,310
Increase in inventory	(500)
Increase in trade receivables	(700)
Decrease in trade payables	(100)
Cash generated from operations	6,010
Interest paid	(124)
Taxation paid (W4)	(485)
Net cash from operating activities	5,401

The rest of the cash flow statement is identical to the statement produced using the direct method.

280   DIRECT AND INDIRECT

(a)   **B**

Cash flow statement for the year ended 31 December 20X4

	$000	$000
Cash flows from operating activities		
Net profit before taxation	303	
Adjustments for:		
Depreciation	74	
Loss on disposal of non-current assets	4	
Interest expense	23	
	——	
Operating profit before working capital changes	404	
Increase in inventories (19 – 16)	(3)	
Increase in receivables (40 – 30)	(10)	
Increase in payables (31 – 24)	7	
	——	
Cash generated from operations	398	
Interest paid (W1)	(29)	
Income taxes paid (W2)	(75)	
Net cash from operating activities	——	294
Cash flows from investing activities		
Purchase of plant and equipment	(98)	
Proceeds from sale of plant (W3)	2	
Net cash used in investing activities	——	(96)
Cash flows from financing activities		
Proceeds from issue of share capital (W4)	91	
Repayment of loans (70 – 320)	(250)	
Dividends paid	(52)	
Net cash used in financing activities	——	(211)
		——
Net decrease in cash and cash equivalents		(13)
Cash and cash equivalents at beginning of period		
(all cash at bank)		32
		——
Cash and cash equivalents at end of period (all cash at bank)		19
		——

Workings

(W1) **Interest paid**

	$000
Accrued interest at the beginning of the year	8
Interest charge for the year	23
	——
	31
Accrued interest at the end of the year	(2)
	——
Payments for interest charges in the year	29
	——

(W2) **Income taxes paid**

	$000	$000
Beginning of the year		
Deferred tax	7	
Current taxes payable	55	
	―	
Tax liability at the beginning of the year		62
Tax charge for the year		87
		―
		149
End of the year		
Deferred tax	16	
Current taxes payable	58	
	―	
Tax liability at the end of the year		(74)
		―
Payments of tax in the year		75
		―

(W3) **Disposals of non-current assets**

	$000
Cost of non-current asset disposed of	18
Accumulated depreciation on this asset	(12)
	―
Carrying amount of asset disposed of	6
Loss on disposal	4
	―
Sale value of asset	2
	―

(W4) **Issue of shares**

	$000	$000
Beginning of the year		
Issued share capital	152	
Share premium	80	
	―	
		232
End of the year		
Issued share capital	182	
Share premium	141	
	―	
		323
		―
Cash received from share issue(s) in the year		91
		―

(b)   **Direct method**

Y

Cash flow statement for the year ended 31 December 20X4

	$000	$000
Cash flows from operating activities		
Cash receipts from customers (W5)	480	
Cash paid to suppliers and employees (W6)	(82)	
	———	
Cash generated from operations	398	
Interest paid (W1)	(29)	
Income taxes paid (W2)	(75)	
	———	
Net cash from operating activities		294

Workings

(W5) **Cash receipts from customers**

	$000
Opening trade receivables	30
Sales for the year	490
	———
	520
Closing trade receivables	(40)
	———
Cash received from customers	480
	———

(W6) **Cash paid to suppliers and employees**

	$000	$000
Closing inventory at 31 December 20X4	19	
Raw materials consumed	49	
	———	
	68	
Opening inventory at 31 December 20X3	(16)	
	———	
Purchases of raw materials		52
Opening trade payables at 31 December 20X3		24
Closing trade payables at 31 December 20X4		(31)
		———
Payments to suppliers		45
Staff costs		37
		———
Payments to suppliers and employees		82
		———

281   AG (MAY 05 EXAM)

AG

Cash flow statement for the year ended 31 March 20X5

	$000	$000
Cash flows from operating activities		
Profit before taxation	255	
Adjustments for:		
Depreciation	720	
Development expenditure amortisation	80	
Finance cost	45	
Gain on disposal of non-current tangible asset (W2)	(23)	
Operating profit before working capital changes		1,077
Increase inventory	(110)	
Increase in trade receivables	(95)	
Increase in trade payables	130	
Increase in accrued expenses (W6)	10	
		(65)
Cash generated from operations		1,012
Interest paid (W7)	(120)	
Income taxes paid (W5)	(200)	(320)
Net cash from operating activities		692
Cash flows from investing activities		
Purchase of property, plant and equipment (W1)	(370)	
Proceeds from sale of equipment	98	
Development expenditure (W3)	(50)	
Net cash used in investing activities		(322)
Cash flows from financing activities		
Proceeds from issue of share capital (W4)	1,050	
Repayment of loans	(1,000)	
Equity dividends paid	(100)	
Net cash used in financing activities		(50)
Net increase in cash and cash equivalents		320
Cash and cash equivalents at 1 April 20X4		232
Cash and cash equivalent at 31 March 20X5		552

Workings

(W1)   **Purchase of property, plant and equipment**

	$
Balance b/fwd	4,800
Disposals	(75)
	4,725
Revaluation	125
	4,850
Depreciation for year	(720)
	4,130
Balance c/fwd	4,500
Purchases	370

(W2)   **Gain on disposal of property plant and equipment**

	$
Net book value	75
Cash	98
Gain	23

(W3)   **Development expenditure**

	$
Balance b/fwd	400
Amortised in year	80
	320
Balance c/fwd	370
New expenditure	50

(W4)   **Proceeds from issue of share capital**

		$
31 March 20X5	Share capital + share premium (2,600 + 750)	3,350
31 March 20X4	Share capital + share premium (1,900 + 400)	2,300
Received		1,050

(W5)   **Income taxes paid**

	$	$
Balance b/fwd – corporate income tax	190	
– deferred tax	200	
		390
Income statement		140
		530
Balance c/fwd – corporate income tax	80	
– deferred tax	250	330
Tax paid		200

(W6) **Accrued expenses**

	$	$
Balance b/fwd	172	
Interest b/fwd	(87)	
		85
Balance c/fwd	107	
Interest c/fwd	(12)	
		95
		10

(W7) **Interest paid**

	$
Balance b/fwd	87
P & L	45
	132
Balance c/fwd	12
Paid	120

282 RED

Red

Cash flow statement for year ended 31 March 20X6

	$ million	$ million
Cash flows from operating activities		
Net profit before taxation	116	
Adjustments for:		
Depreciation	37	
Amortisation of development expenditure $(5 - 3)$	2	
Profit on sales of non-current assets $(21 - 19)$	(2)	
Interest receivable	(3)	
Finance charge	7	
	157	
Decrease in inventories $(120 - 148)$	28	
Increase in receivables $(152 - 116)$	(36)	
Increase in payables $(216 - 135)$	81	
Cash generated from operations	230	
Interest paid (W4)	(3)	
Interest element of finance lease payments	(3)	
Income taxes paid (W3)	(23)	
Net cash from operating activities		201
Cash flows from investing activities		
Purchase of tangible non-current assets (W1)	(97)	
Receipts from sale of tangible non-current assets	21	
Purchase of investments	(80)	
Interest received $(2 + 3 - 1)$	4	
Net cash used in investing activities		(152)
Cash flows from financing activities		
Proceeds from issuance of share capital	19	
(10 million shares × $2) less issue costs $1 million		
Payment of finance lease liabilities (W2)	(18)	
Redemption of bonds	(20)	
Dividends paid	(20)	
Net cash used in financing activities	—	(39)
Net increase in cash and cash equivalents		10
Cash and cash equivalents at the beginning of the year *(Note 1)*		1
Cash and cash equivalents at the end of the year *(Note 1)*		11

Notes:

(1) **Cash and cash equivalents**

	31 March 20X6 $ million	*31 March 20X5* $ million
Cash at bank	4	21
Loan notes repayable on demand	15	0
Bank overdraft	(8)	(20)
	11	1

Workings

(W1) **Tangible non-current assets**

	$000
Carrying amount at 31 March 20X5	196
Additions to finance leases	28
Revaluations	7
Disposals (at carrying amount)	(19)
Depreciation for the year	(37)
	175
Carrying amount at 31 March 20X6	272
Therefore purchases in the year	97

(W2) **Finance leases**

It is assumed that the non-current liabilities for finance leases in the balance sheet relate to the lease obligation itself (capital, rather than lease interest).

	$000
Lease obligation at 31 March 20X5 (42 + 3)	45
Additions to finance leases	28
	73
Lease obligation at 31 March 20X6 (50 + 5)	55
Therefore repayments of lease obligations	18

(W3) **Tax paid**

	$000	$000
Income tax liability at 31 March 20X5		12
Deferred tax at 31 March 20X5		8
		20
Tax charge for the year		32
		52
Income tax liability at 31 March 20X6	17	
Deferred tax at 31 March 20X6	12	
		29
Tax paid		23

(W4) **Interest paid**

		$000
Interest liability at 31 March 20X5		2
Finance charge	7	
Lease interest component	(3)	
Interest charge for the year	——	4
		6
Interest liability at 31 March 20X5		(3)
Interest paid		3

283 CJ (MAY 06 EXAM)

CJ – Cash flow statement for the year ended 31 March 20X6

	$000	$000
Cash flows from operating activities		
Profit before taxation	4,398	
Adjustments for:		
Other income	(200)	
Depreciation	4,055	
Finance cost	1,302	
Gain on disposal of plant (W2)	(23)	
	9,532	
Increase in inventory	(214)	
Increase in trade receivables	(306)	
Increase in trade and other payables (W6)	420	
Cash generated from operations	9,432	
Interest paid (W3)	(1,602)	
Income taxes paid (W4)	(1,796)	
Net cash from operating activities		6,034
Cash flows from investing activities		
Purchase of property, plant and equipment (W1)	(2,310)	
Investment income received	180	
Proceeds from sale of equipment	118	
Proceeds from disposal of available for sale investments (W5)	620	
Net cash used in investing activities		(1,392)
Cash flows from financing activities		
Proceeds from issue of share capital (W7)	10,000	
Repayment of interest bearing borrowings	(6,000)	
Equity dividends paid	(800)	
Net cash from financing activities		3,200
Net increase in cash and cash equivalents		7,842
Cash and cash equivalents at 1 April 20X5		(880)
Cash and cash equivalents at 31 March 20X6		6,962

Workings

(W1)

Net book values	Property	Plant	Available for sale investments
	$000	$000	$000
Balance b/fwd	18,000	10,000	2,100
Revaluation	1,500	0	0
	19,500	10,000	2,100
Disposal	0	(95)	(600)
Depreciation for year	(2,070)	(1,985)	0
	17,430	7,920	1,500
Acquired in year (to balance)	1,730	580	0
Balance c/fwd	19,160	8,500	1,500

Total purchases = 1,730 + 580 = 2,310

(W2) **Gain on disposal of plant**

	$000	$000
Net book value	95	
Cash received	118	
Gain	23	

(W3) **Interest paid**

Balance b/fwd	650
Finance cost in income statement	1,302
	1,952
Balance c/fwd	(350)
Interest paid in year	1,602

(W4) **Tax paid**

Balance b/fwd – Current tax	1,810	
Deferred tax	800	2,610
Income statement charge		2,099
		4,709
Balance c/fwd – Current tax	1,914	
Deferred tax	999	2,913
Paid in year		1,796

(W5) **Proceeds from disposal of available for sale investments**

Disposal per (W1)	600
Add gain on disposal	20
	620

(W6) Increase in trade payables

Trade and other payables balance b/fwd		1,700
Less: Interest b/fwd		(650)
		1,050
Trade and other payables balance c/fwd	1,820	
Less: Interest c/fwd	(350)	1,470
Increase in trade payables		420

(W7) Proceeds from issue of equity share capital

Equity shares	5,000
Share premium	5,000
	10,000

284 DN (NOV 06 EXAM)

Cash flow statement for the year ended 31 October 20X6

	$000	$000
Cash flows from operating activities		
Profit before tax		790
Adjustments for:		
Depreciation (100 + 230)		330
Profit on disposal		(5)
Interest payable		110
		1,225
Increase in inventories (190 – 140)		(50)
Increase in receivables (340 – 230)		(110)
Increase in payables (105 – 85)		20
		1,085
Interest paid (W8)		(130)
Tax paid (W9)		(120)
Net cash from operating activities		835
Cash flows from investing activities		
Additions to tangible assets (W1)	(677)	
Disposal proceeds in respect of tangible assets (W2)	15	
		(662)
Cash flows from financing activities		
Bank loan repaid (W3)	(2,000)	
New loan (W3)	1,500	
Share issue (W6)	600	
Dividend (W7)	(400)	
		(300)
Net decrease in cash and cash equivalents		(127)
Cash and cash equivalents at 1 November 20X5		45
Cash and cash equivalents at 31 October 20X6		(82)

Workings

(W1)

Plant and equipment (NBV)

B/f	1,405	Depreciation	230
Additions (balance)	677	Disposal	10
		c/f	1,842
	2,082		2,082

(W2)

Disposal proceeds	15,000
NBV 60,000 × 1/6	(10,000)
Profit on disposal	5,000

(W3)

Bank loans

Repaid	2,000	B/f	2,000
C/f	1,500	New loan	1,500
	3,500		3,500

(W4) **Payables**

	20X6	20X5	
Trade payables	105	85	To movement on payables
Interest	55	75	To interest working
Tax	70	50	To tax working
Bank overdraft	82	0	To cash and cash equivalents

(W5)

Property

B/f	2,800		
Revaluation	400	Depreciation	100
		C/f	3,100
	3,200		3,200

(W6)

Equity and share premium

		B/f	1,000
		Proceeds from share issue	600
C/f – equity	1,300		
C/f – share premium	300		
	1,600		1,600

(W7) **Dividend**

Profit after tax	650
Movement on retained earnings 1,660 – 1,410	250
Therefore, dividend	400

Check $0.2 \times 2 \times 1,000 = 400$

(W8)

Interest creditor

		B/f	75
Paid	130	Income statement	110
C/f	55		
	185		185

(W9)

Tax creditor

		B/f	50
Paid	120	Income statement	140
C/f	70		
	190		190

Section 7

MAY 2007 EXAM QUESTIONS

SECTION A – 40 MARKS

[The indicative time for answering this section is 72 minutes.]

Answer ALL 15 sub-questions.

QUESTION ONE

1.1   DH has the following two legal claims outstanding:

- A legal action against DH claiming compensation of $700,000, filed in February 2007. DH has been advised that it is probable that the liability will materialise.

- A legal action taken by DH against another entity, claiming damages of $300,000, started in March 2004. DH has been advised that it is probable that it will win the case.

How should DH report these legal actions in its financial statements for the year ended 30 April 2007?

	Legal action against DH	*Legal action taken by DH*
A	Disclose by a note to the accounts	No disclosure
B	Make a provision	No disclosure
C	Make a provision	Disclose as a note
D	Make a provision	Accrue the income

(2 marks)

1.2   Country X uses a Pay-As-You-Earn (PAYE) system for collecting taxes from employees. Each employer is provided with information about each employee's tax position and tables showing the amount of tax to deduct each period. Employers are required to deduct tax from employees and pay it to the revenue authorities on a monthly basis.

From the perspective of the government, list THREE advantages of the PAYE system.

(3 marks)

1.3   DS uses the Economic Order Quantity (EOQ) model. Demand for DS's product is 95,000 units per annum. Demand is evenly distributed throughout the year. The cost of placing an order is $15 and the cost of holding a unit of inventory for a year is $3.

How many orders should DS make in a year?

(3 marks)

1.4   According to the International Accounting Standards Board's *Framework for the Preparation and Presentation of Financial Statements*, what is the objective of financial statements?

Write your answer in no more than **35** words.   **(2 marks)**

1.5   The International Standard on Auditing 701 *Modifications to the Independent Auditor's Report*, classifies modified audit reports into 'matters that do not affect the auditor's opinion' and 'matters that do affect the auditor's opinion'. This latter category is further sub-divided into three categories.

List these THREE categories.   **(3 marks)**

1.6   DY's trade receivables balance at 1 April 2006 was $22,000. DY's income statement showed revenue from credit sales of $290,510 during the year ended 31 March 2007.

DY's trade receivables at 31 March 2007 were 49 days.

Assume DY's sales occur evenly throughout the year and that all balances outstanding at 1 April 2006 have been received.

Also, it should be assumed all sales are on credit, there were no irrecoverable debts and no trade discount was given.

How much cash did DY receive from its customers during the year to 31 March 2007?

A $268,510

B $273,510

C $312,510

D $351,510   **(2 marks)**

1.7   DD purchased an item of plant and machinery costing $500,000 on 1 April 2004, which qualified for 50% capital allowances in the first year, and 20% each year thereafter, on the reducing balance basis.

DD's policy in respect of plant and machinery is to charge depreciation on a straight line basis over five years, with no residual value. On 1 April 2006, DD decided to revalue the item of plant and machinery upwards, from its net book value, by $120,000.

Assuming there are no other capital transactions in the three year period and a tax rate of 30% throughout, calculate the amount of deferred tax to be shown in DD's income statement for the year ended 31 March 2007, and the deferred tax provision to be included in its balance sheet at 31 March 2007.   **(4 marks)**

1.8   On 31 March 2007, DT received an order from a new customer, XX, for products with a sales value of $900,000. XX enclosed a deposit with the order of $90,000.

On 31 March 2007, DT had not completed credit referencing of XX and had not despatched any goods. DT is considering the following possible entries for this transaction in its financial statements for the year ended 31 March 2007:

(i)   include $900,000 in income statement revenue for the year

(ii)   include $90,000 in income statement revenue for the year

(iii)   do not include anything in income statement revenue for the year

(iv)   create a trade receivable for $810,000

(v)   create a trade payable for $90,000.

According to IAS 18 *Revenue Recognition*, how should DT record this transaction in its financial statements for the year ended 31 March 2007?

A   (i) and (iv)

B   (ii) and (v)

C   (iii) and (iv)

D   (iii) and (v)   **(2 marks)**

1.9   **Excise duties are deemed to be most suitable for commodities that have certain specific characteristics.**

List THREE characteristics of a commodity that, from a revenue authority's point of view, would make that commodity suitable for an excise duty to be imposed.   **(3 marks)**

1.10   **During its 2006 accounting year, DL made the following changes.**

Which ONE of these changes would be classified as 'a change in accounting policy'as determined by IAS 8 *Accounting Policies, Changes in Accounting Estimates and Errors*?

A   Increased the bad debt provision for 2006 from 5% to 10% of outstanding debts

B   Changed the treatment of borrowing costs from capitalising borrowing costs incurred on capital projects to treating all borrowing costs as an expense in the year incurred

C   Changed the depreciation of plant and equipment from straight line depreciation to reducing balance depreciation

D   Changed the useful economic life of its motor vehicles from six years to four years

                                                                                (2 marks)

1.11 DR has the following balances under current assets and current liabilities:

Current assets	$
Inventory	50,000
Trade receivables	70,000
Bank	10,000

Current liabilities	$
Trade payables	88,000
Interest payable	7,000

DR's quick ratio is

A   0.80 : 1

B   0.84 : 1

C   0.91 : 1

D   1.37 : 1   **(2 marks)**

1.12 Which ONE of the following is most likely to increase an entity's working capital?

A   Delaying payment to trade payables

B   Reducing the credit period given to customers

C   Purchasing inventory on credit

D   Paying a supplier and taking an early settlement discount   **(2 marks)**

1.13 Details from DV's long-term contract, which commenced on 1 May 2006, at 30 April 2007 were:

	$000
Invoiced to client for work done	2,000
Costs incurred to date:	
Attributable to work completed	1,500
Inventory purchased, but not yet used	250
Progress payment received from client	900
Expected further costs to complete project	400
Total contract value	3,000

DV uses the percentage of costs incurred to total costs to calculate attributable profit.

Calculate the amount that DV should recognise in its income statement for the year ended 30 April 2007 for revenue, cost of sales and attributable profits on this contract according to IAS 11 *Construction Contracts*.   **(4 marks)**

1.14 **Country Y has a sales tax system which allows entities to reclaim input tax paid.**

In Country Y the sales tax rates are:

Zero rated	0%
Standard rated	15%

DE runs a small retail store. DE's sales include items that are zero rated, standard rated and exempt.

DE's electronic cash register provides an analysis of sales. The figures for the three months to 30 April 2007 were:

	Sales value, excluding sales tax
	$
Zero rated	11,000
Standard rated	15,000
Exempt	13,000
Total	39,000

DE's analysis of expenditure for the same period provided the following:

	Expenditure, excluding sales tax
	$
Zero rated purchases	5,000
Standard rated purchases relating to standard rate outputs	9,000
Standard rated purchases relating to exempt outputs	7,000
Standard rated purchases relating to zero rated outputs	3,000
	24,000

Calculate the sales tax due to/from DE for the three months ended 30 April 2007.

(2 marks)

1.15 **A bond has a current market price of $83. It will repay its face value of $100 in 7 years' time and has a coupon rate of 4%.**

If the bond is purchased at $83 and held, what is its yield to maturity?

(4 marks)

(Total for Question One: 40 marks)

SECTION B – 30 MARKS

[The indicative time for this section is 54 minutes.]

Answer ALL 6 sub-questions. Each sub-question is worth 5 marks.

QUESTION TWO

(a)   Country Z has the following tax regulations in force for the years 2005 and 2006 (each year January to December):

- Corporate income is taxed at the following rates:

    - $1 to $10,000 at 0%;

    - $10,001 to $25,000 at 15%;

    - $25,001 and over at 25%.

- When calculating corporate income tax, Country Z does **not** allow the following types of expenses to be charged against taxable income:

    - entertaining expenses

    - taxes paid to other public bodies

    - accounting depreciation of non-current assets.

- Tax relief on capital expenditure is available at the following rates:

    - buildings at 4% per annum on straight line basis

    - all other non-current tangible assets are allowed tax depreciation at 27% per annum on reducing balance basis.

DB commenced business on 1 January 2005 when all assets were purchased. No first year allowances were available for 2005.

Non-current assets cost at 1 January 2005

	$
Land	27,000
Buildings	70,000
Plant and equipment	80,000

On 1 January 2006, DB purchased another machine for $20,000. This machine qualified for a first year tax allowance of 50%.

DB's Income statement for the year to 31 December 2006

	$
Gross profit	160,000
Administrative expenses	81,000
Entertaining	600
Tax paid to local government	950
Depreciation on buildings	1,600
Depreciation on plant and equipment	20,000
Distribution costs	20,000
	35,850
Finance cost	1,900
Profit before tax	33,950

Required:

Calculate DB's corporate income tax due for the year 2006.   **(5 marks)**

(b)   On 1 April 2005, DX acquired plant and machinery with a fair value of $900,000 on a finance lease. The lease is for five years with the annual lease payments of $228,000 being paid in advance on 1 April each year. The interest rate implicit in the lease is 13.44%. The first payment was made on 1 April 2005.

Required:

(i)   Calculate the finance charge in respect of the lease that will be shown in DX's income statement for the year ended 31 March 2007.

(ii)   Calculate the amount to be shown as a current liability and a non-current liability in DX's balance sheet at 31 March 2007.

(All workings should be to the nearest $000.)   **(5 marks)**

(c)   The *Framework for the Preparation and Presentation of Financial Statements* (*Framework*) was first published in 1989 and was adopted by The International Accounting Standards Board (IASB).

Required:

Explain the purposes of the *Framework*.   **(5 marks)**

(d)   On 1 June 2006, the directors of DP commissioned a report to determine possible actions they could take to reduce DP's losses. The report, which was presented to the directors on 1 December 2006, proposed that DP cease all of its manufacturing activities and concentrate on its retail activities.

The directors formally approved the plan to close DP's factory. The factory was gradually shut down, commencing on 5 December 2006, with production finally ceasing on 15 March 2007. All employees had ceased working or had been transferred to other facilities in the company by 29 March 2007. The plant and equipment was removed and sold for $25,000 (net book value $95,000) on 30 March 2007.

The factory land and building was being advertised for sale, but had not been sold by 31 March 2007. The net book value of the land and building at 31 March 2007, based on original cost, was $750,000. The estimated net realisable value of the land and building at 31 March 2007 was $1,125,000.

Closure costs incurred (and paid) up to 31 March 2007 were $620,000.

The cash flows, revenues and expenses relating to the factory were clearly distinguishable from DP's other operations. The output from the factory was sold directly to third parties and to DP's retail outlets. The manufacturing facility was shown as a separate segment in DP's segmental information.

Required:

With reference to relevant International Accounting Standards, explain how DP should treat the factory closure in its financial statements for the year ended 31 March 2007.   **(5 marks)**

(e)   DN currently has an overdraft on which it pays interest at 10% per year. DN has been offered credit terms from one of its suppliers, whereby it can either claim a cash discount of 2% if payment is made within 10 days of the date of the invoice or pay on normal credit terms within 40 days of the date of the invoice.

Assume a 365-day year and an invoice value of $100.

Required:

Explain to DN, with reasons and supporting calculations, whether it should pay the supplier early and take advantage of the discount offered.   **(5 marks)**

(f)   DF, a sports and fitness training equipment wholesaler, has prepared its forecast cash flow for the next six months and has calculated that it will need $2 million additional short-term finance in three months' time.

DF has an annual gross revenue of $240 million and achieves a gross margin of 50%. It currently has the following outstanding working capital balances:

- $16 million trade payables

- $20 million trade receivables

- $5 million bank overdraft.

DF forecasts that it will be able to repay half the $2 million within three months and the balance within a further three months.

Required:

Advise DF of possible sources of funding available to it.   **(5 marks)**

(Total: 30 marks)

SECTION C – 30 MARKS

[The indicative time for this section is 54 minutes.]

ANSWER THIS QUESTION

QUESTION THREE

DZ is a manufacturing entity and produces one group of products, known as product Y.

DZ's trial balance at 31 March 2007 is shown below:

	$000	$000
8% loan 2020 (see note (xiv))		2,000
Administration expenses	891	
Bank and cash	103	
Cash received on disposal of land		1,500
Cash received on disposal of plant		5
Cost of raw materials purchased in year	2,020	
Direct production labour costs	912	
Distribution costs	462	
Equity shares $1 each, fully paid		1,000
Income tax (see note (xi))	25	
Inventory of finished goods at 31 March 2006	240	
Inventory of raw materials at 31 March 2006	132	
Land at valuation at 31 March 2006	1,250	
Loan interest paid – half year	80	
Plant and equipment at cost at 31 March 2006	4,180	
Production overheads (excluding depreciation)	633	
Property at cost at 31 March 2006	11,200	
Provision for deferred tax at 31 March 2006 (see note (xii))		773
Provision for depreciation at 31 March 2006: (see notes (iv) and (v))		
Property		1,900
Plant and equipment		2,840
Research and development (see note (vi))	500	
Retained earnings at 31 March 2006		2,024
Revaluation reserve at 31 March 2006		2,100
Revenue		8,772
Trade payables		773
Trade receivables	1,059	
	23,687	23,687

Further information:

(i)   The property cost of $11,200,000 consisted of land $3,500,000 and buildings $7,700,000.

(ii)   During the year, DZ disposed of non-current assets as follows:

- A piece of surplus land was sold on 1 March 2007 for $1,500,000.

- Obsolete plant was sold for $5,000 scrap value on the same date.

- All the cash received is included in the trial balance.

Details of the assets sold were:

Asset type	Cost	Revalued amount	Accumulated depreciation
Land	$500,000	$1,250,000	$0
Plant and equipment	$620,000		$600,000

(iii) On 31 March 2007, DZ revalued its properties to $9,800,000 (land $4,100,000 and buildings $5,700,000).

(iv) Buildings are depreciated at 5% per annum on the straight line basis. Buildings, depreciation is treated as 80% production overhead and 20% administration.

(v) Plant and equipment is depreciated at 25% per annum using the reducing balance method, the depreciation being treated as a production overhead.

(vi) Product Y was developed in-house. Research and development is carried out on a continuous basis to ensure that the product range continues to meet customer demands. The research and development figure in the trial balance is made up as follows:

	$000
Development costs capitalised in previous years	867
Less: Amortisation to 31 March 2006	534
	333
Research costs incurred in the year to 31 March 2007	119
Development costs (all meet IAS 38 *Intangible Assets* criteria) incurred in the year to 31 March 2007	48
Total	500

(vii) Development costs are amortised on a straight line basis at 20% per annum.

(viii) Research and development costs are treated as cost of sales when charged to the income statement.

(ix) DZ charges a full year's amortisation and depreciation in the year of acquisition and none in the year of disposal.

(x) Inventory of raw materials at 31 March 2007 was $165,000. Inventory of finished goods at 31 March 2007 was $270,000.

(xi) The directors estimate the income tax charge on the year's profits at $811,000. The balance on the income tax account represents the underprovision for the previous year's tax charge.

(xii) The deferred tax provision is to be reduced to $665,000.

(xiii) No interim dividend was paid during the year.

(xiv) The 8% loan is a 20-year loan issued in 2000.

Required:

(a) Prepare DZ's property, plant and equipment note to the accounts for the year ended 31 March 2007. **(6 marks)**

(b) Prepare the income statement and a statement of changes in equity for the year to 31 March 2007 and a balance sheet at that date, in a form suitable for presentation to the shareholders and in accordance with the requirements of International Financial Reporting Standards.

(All workings should be to the nearest $000.) **(24 marks)**

Notes to the financial statements are NOT required (except as specified in part (a) of the question), but ALL workings must be clearly shown. Do NOT prepare a statement of accounting policies.

(Total: 30 marks)

(Total for Section C: 30 marks)

Section 8

ANSWERS TO MAY 2007 EXAM QUESTIONS

SECTION A

QUESTION ONE

1.1 C

The legal action against DH gives rise to a probable liability and a provision is therefore required. The legal action taken by DH gives rise to a probable asset and therefore should be disclosed as a note.

1.2 From the perspective of the government. Three advantages of the PAYE system are:

- Tax is collected regularly throughout the year, giving rise to a cash flow advantage

- There is less risk of default as individuals do not need to budget for their tax payments

- The administrative costs are largely passed to the employers.

1.3 The answer is 98

$$Q = \sqrt{\frac{2C_o D}{C_h}}$$

$$\sqrt{\frac{2 \times 15 \times 95,000}{3}} = 974.68$$

$95,000/975 = 97.4.$

1.4 The Framework states that 'the objective of financial statements is to provide information about the financial position, performance and changes in financial position of an enterprise that is useful to a wide range of users in making economic decisions'.

1.5 Matters that do affect the auditor's opinion are subdivided into:

- qualified opinion

- adverse opinion

- disclaimer of opinion.

1.6 B

	$
Balance b/fwd	22,000
Credit sales	290,510
	312,510
Less: Balance c/fwd ($290,510 × 49/365)	(39,000)
Receipts	273,510

1.7 The answer is $36

Tax base	$000	*Accounting book value*	$000
Cost	500	Cost	500
31/3/05 First year allowance 50%	250	31/3/05 Depreciation	100
	250		400
31/3/06 20%	50	31/3/06 Depreciation	100
	200		300
31/3/07 20%	40	Revaluation	120
	160		420
		31/3/07 Depreciation	140
			280

	31/3/06	*31/3/07*
	$000	$000
Accounting book value	300	280
Tax base	200	160
Temporary difference	100	120
Deferred tax at 30%	30	36

Income statement, increase (36 – 30) = 6
Balance sheet – deferred tax provision 2007   36

1.8 D

DT should not record any revenue as it has not yet transferred the risks and rewards of ownership of the goods to XX. However, as it has received a deposit, it should create a trade payable for $90,000.

1.9 From the revenue authority's point of view, a commodity is suitable for an excise duty to be imposed if:

- there are few large producers/suppliers
- demand is inelastic with no close substitutes
- sales volumes are large
- it is easy to define the products to be covered by the tax.

1.10 B

A change from capitalising a cost to treating it as a revenue expense would be classified as a change in accounting policy under IAS 8.

1.11 B

(70,000 + 10,000) : (88,000 + 7,000)

80,000 : 95,000

0.84 : 1

1.12 D

Paying a supplier and taking an early settlement discount will increase an entity's working capital because the bank balance will fall by a smaller amount than the reduction in the trade payables.

1.13

	$000
Total cost	
Cost incurred on attributable work	1,500
Inventory not yet used	250
Expected further costs	400
	2,150
Cost incurred on attributable work	1,500
% complete 1,500/2,150 = 69.76% (round to 70%)	
Total contract revenue	3,000
Total cost	2,150
Total profit	850
Income statement figures for contract	
Revenue (3,000 × 70%)	**2,100**
Cost of sales	**1,500**
Profit	**600**

1.14 The answer is $450.

Outputs: 15,000 × 15% =	2,250
Inputs: (9,000 + 3,000) × 15% =	1,800
Net payment due from DE	450

Sales tax relating to exempt items cannot be reclaimed and is ignored.

1.15 The answer is 7.2%

Using t = 7 and r = 6 and 8, from tables

(4×5.582) and $(100 \times 0.665) = 22.328 + 66.5 = 88.828$

(4×5.206) and $(100 \times 0.583) = 20.824 + 58.3 = 79.124$

$$6 + \left\{ \frac{88.828 - 83.00}{88.828 - 79.124} \right\} \times 2 = 6 + \left\{ \frac{5.828}{9.704} \times 2 \right\}$$

$6 + 1.20 = 7.20\%$

SECTION B

QUESTION TWO

(a) **DB – Corporate income tax**

	2006
	$
Profit before tax per accounts	33,950
Add back:	
Entertaining	600
Local government tax	950
Depreciation on buildings	1,600
Depreciation on plant and equipment	20,000
	57,100
Less tax depreciation	
Building (70,000 × 4%)	2,800
Plant and equipment (W1)	25,768
Taxable profit	28,532

			Tax $
Taxable at 15%	(25,000 – 10,000) =	15,000	2,250
Taxable at 25%	(28,532 – 25,000) =	3,532	883
Corporate income tax 2006			3,133

(W1)

	Plant and equipment	New plant	Total
	$	$	$
Cost	80,000		
2005 tax depreciation @ 27%	21,600		
	58,400		
2006 tax depreciation @ 27%	15,768		15,768
Cost		20,000	
2006 first year allowance @ 50%		10,000	10,000
	42,632	10,000	25,768

(b) (i) Finance charge for year ended 31 March 2007 = $72,000

(ii)

	$000
Current liability (606 – 378) =	228
Non-current liability	378

Working

Year ended 31 March	Bal b/fwd $000	Payment $000	Sub-total $000	Interest $000	Bal c/fwd $000
2006	900	(228)	672	90	762
2007	762	(228)	534	72	606
2008	606	(228)	378	51	429
2009	429	(228)	201	27	228
2010	228	(228)	0	0	0

(c) The purposes of the *Framework* are to:

- assist the Board in the development of future IFRSs and in its review of existing IFRSs

- assist the Board in promoting harmonisation of regulations, accounting standards and procedures relating to the presentation of financial statements by providing a basis for reducing the number of alternative treatments permitted by IFRSs

- assist national standard-setting bodies in developing national standards

- assist preparers of financial statements in applying IFRSs and in dealing with topics that have yet to be covered in an IFRS

- assist auditors in forming an opinion as to whether financial statements conform with IFRSs

- assist users of financial statements that are prepared using IFRSs

- provide information about how the IASB has formulated its approach to the development of IFRSs.

(d) IFRS 5 defines a 'discontinued activity' as one that:

- represents a major line of business

- is part of a single co-ordinated plan, and

- has either been discontinued by the year end or the assets transferred to 'held for sale'.

DP seems to have satisfied these criteria as the directors are committed to the factory closure, but it has not been completed by the year end.

The assets for sale should therefore be classified as non-current assets 'held for sale' and shown separately on the balance sheet in the year to 31 March 2007.

The total cost of the manufacturing facility for the year ended 31 March 2007 must be shown separately in the income statement under the heading 'discontinued activities'. The total cost must include the turnover and operating costs of the manufacturing facility for the year, together with the closure costs of $620,000 incurred to date and the $70,000 loss incurred on the disposal of the plant and equipment.

Assets classified as 'held for sale' are not depreciated. Non-current assets classified as 'held for sale' must be carried at the lower of net book value or fair value less costs to sell. Therefore the net book value of $750,000 will be shown as 'held for sale'.

(e) Taking the discount is equivalent to receiving interest at a rate of 27.86%. Therefore if DN needs to increase its overdraft to make the payment, it is beneficial to do so as long as the interest rate charged is less than 27.86%.

Alternatively, it would be beneficial for DN to use any surplus cash in its current account or cash in any short-term investments yielding less than 27.86%,.

Workings

If DN pays $98 on day 10 instead of day 40, it will need to borrow $98 for 30 days.

The effective annual interest rate is:

$$\frac{365}{30} = 12.1667\%$$

$$1 + r = \left\{\frac{100}{98}\right\}^{12.1667}$$

$$1 + r = 1.2786$$

$$r = 0.2786 \text{ or } 27.86\%$$

(f) DF could obtain short-term finance from any of the following sources:

- by increasing the overdraft

- by taking out a short-term loan

- by taking additional credit from suppliers

  DF currently has trade payable days outstanding of 49 days (16/120 x 365). An increase of $2 million to $18 million would be 55 days (18/120 x 365), This needs to be viewed against the credit period offered by the suppliers. If 60 days' credit is offered, this would be acceptable. If only 45 days is offered, the increase would probably not be acceptable and could cause problems obtaining future credit.

- by improving the receivables collection period:

  DF's trade receivables collection period is currently 30 days (20/240 × 365), which is quite low. So this is unlikely to be a viable option as it would involve reducing the trade receivables collection period to 27 days (18/240 × 365).

- by factoring or invoice discounting. However, this is a long-term solution. It is not suitable for raising a one-off amount.

SECTION C

QUESTION THREE

(a)   **DZ – Property, plant and equipment**

Cost/valuation	Land	Property Land	Buildings	Plant & Equipment	Total
	$000	$000	$000	$000	$000
Balance at 31 March 2006	1,250	3,500	7,700	4,180	16,630
Disposals	(1,250)	0	0	620	(1,870)
	0	3,500	7,700	3,560	14,760
Revaluation	0	600	(2,000)	0	(1,400)
	0	4,100	5,700	3,560	13,360
Depreciation					
Balance at 31 March 2006	0	0	1,900	2,840	4,740
Disposals	0	0	0	–600	–600
	0	0	1,900	2,240	4,140
Revaluation adjustment	0	0	(1,900)	0	(1,900)
Charge for year	0	0	285	330	615
	0	0	285	2,570	2,855
Net book value at 31 March 2007	0	4,100	5,415	990	10,505
Net book value at 31 March 2006	1,250	3,500	5,800	1,340	11,890

Workings:

Depreciation

Buildings

$5,700 \times 5\%$	=	285
Split: Production 80%	=	228
Admin 20%	=	57

Machinery and equipment

Reducing balance = $3,560 - 2,240 = 1,320$

$1,320 @ 25\% = 330$

Total production depreciation = $228 + 330 = 558$

(b)   **DZ – Income statement for the year ended 31 March 2007**

		$000	$000
Revenue			8,772
Cost of sales	(W1)		(4,377)
Gross profit			4,395
Gain on disposal of non-current asset	(W2)		250
Administrative expenses	(W3)	(948)	
Distribution costs		(462)	(1,410)
Profit from operations			3,235
Finance cost			(160)
Profit before tax			3,075
Income tax expense	(W4)		(728)
Profit for the period			2,347

DZ – Balance sheet at 31 March 2007

	$000	$000	$000
Non-current assets			
Property, plant and equipment (answer (a))			10,505
Intangible assets – development costs (W5)			198
Current assets			
Inventory (W6)		435	
Trade receivables		1,059	
Cash and cash equivalents		103	
			1,597
Total assets			12,300
Equity and liabilities			
Equity			
Share capital		1,000	
Revaluation reserve		1,850	
Retained earnings		5,121	
Total equity			7,971
Non-current liabilities			
8% loan	2,000		
Deferred tax (W4)	665		
Total non-current liabilities		2,665	
Current liabilities			
Trade and other payables (W7)	853		
Tax payable (W4)	811		
Total current liabilities		1,664	
Total liabilities			4,329
Total equity and liabilities			12,300

DM – Statement of changes in equity for the year ended 31 March 2007

	Equity shares	Revaluation reserve	Retained earnings	Total
	$000	$000	$000	$000
Balance at 1 April 2006	1,000	2,100	2,024	5,124
Realised revaluation gain (W8)		(750)	750	0
Revaluation in year		500		500
Profit for period			2,347	2,347
Balance at 31 March 2007	1,000	1,850	5,121	7,971

Workings

(W1) **Cost of sales**

	$000
Inventory raw materials at 1 April 2006	132
Purchases	2,020
	2,152
Less inventory raw materials at 31 March 2007	(165)
	1,987
Direct labour	912
Production overheads	633
Depreciation	558
Production cost	4,090
Inventory finished goods at 1 April 2006	240
	4,330
Less inventory finished goods at 31 March 2007	(270)
Loss on disposal of machinery (W2)	15
Research and development cost (W5)	302
Total	4,377

(W2) **Gain on disposal of non-current assets**

Land –	book value	1,250
	Less – receipt	1,500
	Gain	250
Machinery – book value		20
	Less – receipt	5
	Loss	(15)

Tutorial notes

The gain on the sale of the land could be deducted from expenses. However, as it is a material amount, it has been shown separately on Income statement.

The loss on the disposal of the machinery has been treated as an adjustment of previous depreciation and added to the cost of sales figure.

(W3) Administration expenses

Per trial balance	891
Depreciation	57
	948

(W4) Income tax expense

Income tax for year		811
Previous year balance		25
		836
Deferred tax		
Balance 1 April 2006	773	
Balance 31 March 2007	(665)	
		(108)
Income statement		728

(W5) Intangible assets – research and development

Cost balance 1 April 2006		867
Add incurred in year		48
		915
Less amortisation for year at 20%		(183)
Less amortisation b/fwd at 1 April 2006		(534)
Balance 31 March 2007		198

Amortisation for the year	183
Research cost	119
Charge to Income statement	302

(W6) Inventory

Raw materials	165
Finished goods	270
	435

(W7) Trade and other payables

Trade payables	773
Interest due on loan	80
	853

(W8) **Realised gain on disposal**

Land disposed of	
original cost	500
revalued amount	1,250
Realised gain	750

Section 9

NOVEMBER 2007 EXAM QUESTIONS

SECTION A – 40 MARKS

[The indicative time for answering this section is 72 minutes.]

ANSWER *ALL* 15 SUB-QUESTIONS

QUESTION ONE

1.1 **The International Accounting Standards Board's (IASB) *Framework for the Preparation and Presentation of Financial Statements* (*Framework*), sets out four qualitative characteristics of financial information.**

Two of the characteristics are relevance and comparability. List the other TWO characteristics. **(2 marks)**

1.2 **IAS 16 *Property, Plant and Equipment* requires an asset to be measured at cost on its original recognition in the financial statements.**

EW used its own staff, assisted by contractors when required, to construct a new warehouse for its own use.

Which ONE of the following costs would NOT be included in attributable costs of the non-current asset?

A   Clearance of the site prior to work commencing

B   Professional surveyors' fees for managing the construction work

C   EW's own staff wages for time spent working on the construction

D   An allocation of EW's administration costs, based on EW staff time spent on the construction as a percentage of the total staff time **(2 marks)**

1.3   An external auditor gives a qualified audit report that is a 'disclaimer of opinion'.

This means that the auditor:

A   has been unable to agree with an accounting treatment used by the directors in relation to a material item

B   has been prevented from obtaining sufficient appropriate audit evidence

C   has found extensive errors in the financial statements and concludes that they do not show a true and fair view

D   has discovered a few immaterial differences that do not affect the auditor's opinion

(2 marks)

1.4   The trial balance of EH at 31 October 2007 showed trade receivables of $82,000 before adjustments.

On 1 November 2007 EH discovered that one of its customers had ceased trading and was very unlikely to pay any of its outstanding balance of $12,250.

On the same date EH carried out an assessment of the collectability of its other trade receivable balances. Using its knowledge of its customers and past experience EH determined that the remaining trade receivables had suffered a 3% impairment at 31 October 2007.

What is EH's balance of trade receivables, as at 31 October 2007?

A $66,202

B $67,290

C $67,657

D $79,540

(2 marks)

1.5   EX is preparing its cash forecast for the next three months.

Which ONE of the following items should be left out of its calculations?

A   Expected gain on the disposal of a piece of land

B   Tax payment due, that relates to last year's profits

C   Rental payment on a leased vehicle

D   Receipt of a new bank loan raised for the purpose of purchasing new machinery

(2 marks)

1.6 **The following details relate to EA:**

- it was incorporated in Country A

- it carries out its main business activities in Country B

- its senior management operate from Country C and effective control is exercised from Country C.

Assume countries A, B and C have all signed double tax treaties with each other, based on the OECD model tax convention.

In which country will EA be deemed to be resident for tax purposes?

A   Country A

B   Country B

C   Country C

D   Both Countries B and C   **(2 marks)**

1.7 **Treasury shares are defined as:**

A   equity shares sold by an entity in the period

B   equity shares repurchased by the issuing entity, not cancelled before the period end

C   non-equity shares sold by an entity in the period

D   equity shares repurchased by the issuing entity and cancelled before the period end   **(2 marks)**

1.8 **EE reported accounting profits of $822,000 for the period ended 30 November 2007. This was after deducting entertaining expenses of $32,000 and a donation to a political party of $50,000, both of which are disallowable for tax purposes.**

EE's reported profit also included $103,000 government grant income that was exempt from taxation. EE paid dividends of $240,000 in the period.

Assume EE had no temporary differences between accounting profits and taxable profits.

Assume that a classical tax system applies to EE's profits and that the tax rate is 25%.

What would EE's tax payable be on its profits for the year to 30 November 2007?

    (2 marks)

1.9 **EG purchased a property for $630,000 on 1 September 2000. EG incurred additional costs for the purchase of $3,500 surveyors' fees and $6,500 legal fees. EG then spent $100,000 renovating the property prior to letting it. All of EG's expenditure was classified as capital expenditure according to the local tax regulations.**

Indexation of the purchase and renovation costs is allowed on EE's property. The index increased by 50% between September 2000 and October 2007. Assume that acquisition and renovation costs were incurred in September 2000. EG sold the property on 1 October 2007 for $1,250,000, incurring tax allowable costs on disposal of $2,000.

Calculate EG's tax due on disposal assuming a tax rate of 30%.   **(3 marks)**

1.10 **A government wanted to encourage investment in new non-current assets by entities and decided to change tax allowances for non-current assets to give a 100% first year allowance on all new non-current assets purchased after 1 January 2005.**

ED purchased new machinery for $400,000 on 1 October 2005 and claimed the 100% first year allowance. For accounting purposes ED depreciated the machinery on the reducing balance basis at 25% per year. The rate of corporate income tax to be applied to ED's taxable profits was 22%.

Assume ED had no other temporary differences.

Calculate the amount of deferred tax that ED would show in its balance sheet at 30 September 2007. **(3 marks)**

1.11 **EP sells refrigerators and freezers and provides a one-year warranty against faults occurring after sale.**

EP estimates that if all goods with an outstanding warranty at the balance sheet date need minor repairs the total cost would be $3 million. If all the products under warranty needed major repairs the total cost would be $12 million.

Based on previous years' experience, EP estimates that 85% of the products will require no repairs, 14% will require minor repairs and 1% will require major repairs.

Calculate the expected value of the cost of the repair of goods with an outstanding warranty at the balance sheet date. **(3 marks)**

1.12 **List FOUR advantages of forfaiting for an exporter.**

(4 marks)

1.13 **A bond has a coupon rate of 7%. It will repay its face value of $1,000 at the end of six years. The market expects this type of bond to have a yield to maturity of 10%.**

What is the current market value of the bond? **(4 marks)**

1.14 **EB has an investment of 25% of the equity shares in XY, an entity resident in a foreign country.**

EB receives a dividend of $90,000 from XY, the amount being after the deduction of withholding tax of 10%.

XY had profits before tax for the year of $1,200,000 and paid corporate income tax of $200,000.

How much underlying tax can EB claim for double taxation relief? **(3 marks)**

1.15 **EV had inventory days outstanding of 60 days and trade payables outstanding of 50 days at 31 October 2007.**

EV's inventory balance at 1 November 2006 was $56,000 and trade payables were $42,000 at that date.

EV's cost of goods sold comprises purchased goods cost only. During the year to 31 October 2007, EV's cost of goods sold was $350,000.

Assume purchases and sales accrue evenly throughout the year and use a 365-day year. Further assume that there were no goods returned to suppliers and EV claimed no discounts.

Calculate how much EV paid to its credit suppliers during the year to 31 October 2007.

(4 marks)

(Total for Question One: 40 marks)

SECTION B – 30 MARKS

[The indicative time for this section is 54 minutes.]

ANSWER *ALL* 6 SUB-QUESTIONS.

QUESTION TWO

(a)   On 1 September 2007, the Directors of EK decided to sell EK's retailing division and concentrate activities entirely on its manufacturing division.

The retailing division was available for immediate sale, but EK had not succeeded in disposing of the operation by 31 October 2007. EK identified a potential buyer for the retailing division, but negotiations were at an early stage. The Directors of EK are certain that the sale will be completed by 31 August 2008.

The retailing division's carrying value at 31 August 2007 was:

	$000
Non-current tangible assets – property, plant and equipment	300
Non-current tangible assets – goodwill	100
Net current assets	43
Total carrying value	443

The retailing division has been valued at $423,000, comprising:

	$000
Non-current tangible assets – property, plant and equipment	320
Non-current tangible assets – goodwill	60
Net current assets	43
Total carrying value	423

EK's directors have estimated that EK will incur consultancy and legal fees for the disposal of $25,000.

Required:

(i)   Explain whether EK can treat the sale of its retailing division as a 'discontinued operation', as defined by IFRS 5 *Non-current Assets Held for Sale and Discontinued Operations*, in its financial statements for the year ended 31 October 2007. **(3 marks)**

(ii)   Explain how EK should treat the retailing division in its financial statements for the year ended 31 October 2007, assuming the sale of its retailing division meets the classification requirements for a disposal group (IFRS 5). **(2 marks)**

(Total: 5 marks)

(b)   EF is an importer and imports perfumes and similar products in bulk. EF repackages the products and sells them to retailers. EF is registered for sales tax.

EF imports a consignment of perfume priced at $10,000 (excluding excise duty and sales tax) and pays excise duty of 20% and sales tax on the total (including duty) at 15%.

EF pays $6,900 repackaging costs, including sales tax at 15% and then sells all the perfume for $40,250 including sales tax at 15%.

EF has not paid or received any sales tax payments to/from the tax authorities for this consignment.

Required:

(i)   Calculate EF's net profit on the perfume consignment.

(ii)   Calculate the net sales tax due to be paid by EF on the perfume consignment.

(5 marks)

(c)   The trade receivables ledger account for customer X is as follows:

		Debits	Credits	Balance
01-Jul-07	Balance b/fwd			162
12-Jul-07	Invoice AC34	172		334
14-Jul-07	Invoice AC112	213		547
28-Jul-07	Invoice AC215	196		743
08-Aug-07	Receipt RK 116 (Balance + AC34)		334	409
21-Aug-07	Invoice AC420	330		739
03-Sep-07	Receipt RL162 (AC215)		196	543
12-Sep-07	Credit note CN92 (AC112)		53	490
23-Sep-07	Invoice AC615	116		606
25-Sep-07	Invoice AC690	204		810
05-Oct-07	Receipt RM223 (AC420)		330	480
16-Oct-07	Invoice AC913	233		713
25-Oct-07	Receipt RM360 (AC615)		116	597

Required:

(i)   Prepare an aged analysis showing the outstanding balance on a monthly basis for customer X.   **(3 marks)**

(ii)   Explain how an aged analysis of receivables can be useful to an entity.   **(2 marks)**

(Total: 5 marks)

(d)   EJ publishes trade magazines and sells them to retailers. EJ has just concluded negotiations with a large supermarket chain for the supply of a large quantity of several of its trade magazines on a regular basis.

EJ has agreed a substantial discount on the following terms:

•   the same quantity of each trade magazine will be supplied each month

•   quantities can only be changed at the end of each six-month period

•   payment must be made six monthly in advance.

The supermarket paid $150,000 on 1 September 2007 for six months supply of trade magazines to 29 February 2008. At 31 October 2007, EJ had supplied two months of trade magazines. EJ estimates that the cost of supplying the supermarket each month is $20,000.

Required:

(i)   State the criteria in IAS 18 *Revenue Recognition* for income recognition.   **(2 marks)**

(ii)   Explain, with reasons, how EJ should treat the above in its financial statements for the year ended 31 October 2007.   **(3 marks)**

(Total: 5 marks)

(e)   The objective of IAS 24 *Related Party Disclosures* is to ensure that financial statements disclose the effect of the existence of related parties.

Required:

With reference to IAS 24, explain the meaning of the terms 'related party' and 'related party transaction'.   **(5 marks)**

(f)   ES estimates from its cash flow forecast that it will have $120,000 to invest for 12 months.

ES is considering the following investments:

(i)   Purchase of fixed term bonds issued by a 'blue chip' entity quoted on the local stock exchange. The bonds have a maturity date in 12 months' time and pay 12.5% interest on face value. The bonds will be redeemed at face value in 12 months' time. ES will incur commission costs on purchasing the bonds of 1% of cost. The bonds are currently trading at $102 per $100

(ii)   An internet bank is offering a deposit account that pays interest on a monthly basis at 0.8% per month.

Required:

Identify which is the most appropriate investment for the year, giving your reasons.

(5 marks)

(Total for Section B: 30 marks)

SECTION C – 30 MARKS

[The indicative time for this section is 54 minutes.]

ANSWER THIS QUESTION

QUESTION THREE

EY is an office and industrial furniture manufacturing entity that specialises in developing and using new materials and manufacturing processes in the production of its furniture.

The balance sheet below relates to the previous year, 31 October 2006, which is followed by a summary of EY's cash book for the year to 31 October 2007.

EY Balance sheet at 31 October 2006

		$000	$000	$000
Non-current assets				
Development costs	– cost	1,000		
	– amortisation	200	800	
Property, plant and equipment	– cost	7,300		
	– depreciation	1,110	6,190	6,990
Current assets				
Inventory		1,200		
Trade receivables		753		
Cash and cash equivalents		82		
			2,035	
				9,025
Equity and liabilities				
Equity				
Share capital			3,000	
Revaluation reserve			600	
Retained earnings			1,625	
				5,225
Non-current liabilities				
Loan notes		2,260		
Deferred tax		180		
			2,440	
Current liabilities				
Trade and other payables		573		
Tax payable		670		
Interest payable		117		
			1,360	
Total liabilities				3,800
				9,025

EY's summarised cash book for the year ended 31 October 2007

	Note	*Receipts/(Payments)* $000
Cash book balance at 1 November 2006		82
Expenditure incurred on government contract	(i)	(600)
Interest paid during the year	(ii)	(160)
Administration expenses paid		(500)
Research and development costs	(iii)	(1,600)
Income tax	(iv)	(690)
Purchase cost of property, plant and equipment	(v)	(3,460)
Final dividend of 25c per share for year ended 31 October 2006		(750)
Receipt for disposal of land	(vi)	1,200

Summarised cash book continued:

Cash received from customers	7,500
Payments to suppliers of production materials, wages and other production costs	(3,000)
Distribution and selling costs	(730)
Cash received from increase in loan notes	2,500
Cash book balance at 31 October 2007	(208)

Notes:

(i)   The government contract is a long-term project for the supply of a new type of seating for government offices involving the development of new materials. The total contract value is $1,400,000. The expenditure includes all costs incurred during the first year of the contract. The project leader is confident that the remainder of the work will cost no more than $400,000. The contract provides that EY can charge for the proportion of work completed by 31 October each year. The percentage of cost incurred to total cost should be used to apportion profit/losses on the contract.

(ii) Interest outstanding at 31 October 2007 was $130,000.

(iii) During the year EY spent $1,600,000 on research and development. This comprised three projects:

- cost in the year $300,000 – funded research projects carried out at the local university

- cost in the year $500,000 – development of a new type of laminate expected to be a very profitable product line. The final development phase has just finished, and production of the laminate is expected from January 2008

- cost in the year $800,000 – development of a new type of artificial wood, to replace real wood in some furniture and help reduce EY's use of wood. The development produced a good substitute for wood, but was five times more expensive and hence not viable.

Capitalised development expenditure is amortised on the straight line basis over five years and treated as a cost of sale.

(iv) Income tax due for the year was estimated by EY at $420,000.

(v)   The property, plant and equipment balance at 31 October 2006 was made up as follows:

	Land	Premises	Plant & equipment	Total
	$000	$000	$000	$000
Cost/valuation	2,000	1,500	3,800	7,300
Depreciation	0	350	760	1,110
Net book value	2,000	1,150	3,040	6,190

During the year EY purchased new premises at a cost of $1,600,000, and new plant and equipment for $1,860,000. Premises are depreciated on the straight line basis at 6% per year, and plant and machinery are depreciated on the reducing balance at 15% per year and are treated as a cost of sale. EY charges a full year's depreciation in the year of acquisition. No assets were fully depreciated at 31 October 2006.

(vi)   Land originally costing $600,000, which had previously been revalued to $1,000,000, was sold during the year for $1,200,000.

(vii)   A bonus issue of shares was made on the basis of one new share for every six shares held.

(viii)   Deferred tax is to be increased by $42,000.

(ix)   Balances at 31 October 2007 included:

Trade receivables	$620,000
Outstanding trade payables	$670,000
Inventory	$985,000

Required:

Prepare the income statement and a statement of changes in equity for the year to 31 October 2007 and a balance sheet at that date, in a form suitable for presentation to the shareholders and in accordance with the requirements of International Financial Reporting Standards. (All workings should be to the nearest $000.)

Notes to the financial statements are NOT required, but all workings must be clearly shown. Do NOT prepare a statement of accounting policies.

(30 marks)

(Total for Section C: 30 marks)

Section 10

ANSWERS TO NOVEMBER 2007 EXAM QUESTIONS

SECTION A

QUESTION ONE

1.1 Understandability, reliability

1.2 D

The allocation of EW's administration costs would not be included as these costs are not directly incurred as a result of carrying out the construction.

1.3 B

The auditor has been prevented from obtaining sufficient appropriate audit evidence.

1.4 C

$(\$82,000 - 12,250) \times 97\% = \$67,657$

1.5 A

The expected gain on the disposal of a piece of land should be omitted. It is the cash proceeds that should be included, when they are expected to be received.

1.6 C

Effective management and control is the over-riding test under the OECD model tax convention.

1.7 B

Treasury shares are equity shares repurchased by the issuing entity, not cancelled before the period end.

1.8 The answer is $200,250.

The accounting profit should be reported before recognising any dividends paid and, under a classical tax system, it is irrelevant whether or not profits are distributed.

	$
Accounting profit	822,000
Add: Entertaining expenses	32,000
Donation to political party	50,000
Less: Government grant income	(103,000)
	————
	801,000
	————
Tax @ 25%	200,250
	————

1.9 The answer is $41,400.

		$
Disposal proceeds		1,250,000
Less: Costs of disposal		(2,000)
		————
		1,248,000
Acquisition costs:		
Purchase cost	630,000	
Costs arising on purchase	10,000	
Renovation costs	100,000	
	————	
		(740,000)
Indexation – 50%		(370,000)
		————
		138,000
		————
Tax @ 30%		41,400
		————

1.10 The answer is $49,500.

ED has depreciated the asset more quickly for tax than it has done for accounts purposes, such that it should recognise a deferred tax liability, calculated as follows:

	$
Cost	400,000
Depreciation 30/9/06	(100,000)
	————
	300,000
Depreciation 30/9/07	(75,000)
	————
Written down value	225,000
Tax written down value	0
Gross timing difference	225,000
	————
Deferred tax liability @ 22%	49,500
	————

1.11 The answer is $540,000.

In a warranty situation, there are a large number of anticipated repetitions, so it is reasonable to determine the expected value by applying percentages.

Accordingly, the expected value of the cost of repair can be calculated as follows:

	$
$0 × 85%	0
$3 million × 14%	420,000
$12 million × 1%	120,000
	540,000

1.12 Four advantages of forfaiting:

- Trade receivables can be converted into cash.

- There is no recourse to the exporter, so there is no need to recognise a contingent liability.

- Any foreign exchange or interest rate exposure is removed.

- It provides a source of finance that does not affect the ability of the company to borrow or use its overdraft facility.

1.13 The answer is $868.85.

	$
Value in six years' time	1,000
Yield to maturity	10%
Annual interest @ 7% =	70

Market value = Annuity value of interest + Discounted value of redemption

$(70 × 4.355) + (1,000 × 0.564) = 304.85 + 564 = 868.85$

1.14 The answer is $20,000.

	$
Gross dividend = 90,000/0.9	100,000
Underlying tax paid in respect of dividend:	
$\dfrac{200,000}{(1,200,000 - 200,000)} × 100,000$	20,000

EB will be able to claim double taxation relief of $20,000, provided that its actual tax liability on the dividend income is of at least that amount.

1.15   The answer is $345,589.

	$
Owed to credit suppliers at 1 November 2006	42,000
Cost of goods sold	350,000
Less: Opening inventory reflected in cost of goods sold	(56,000)
Add: Closing inventory deducted from cost of goods sold	
60/365 × 350,000	57,534
Less: Amounts owed to credit suppliers at 31 October 2007	
50/365 × 350,000	(47,945)
Amount paid to credit suppliers during the year to 31 October 2007	345,589

SECTION B

QUESTION TWO

(a) (i) EK can treat the sale of its retailing division as a 'discontinued operation' as defined by IFRS 5 *Non-current Assets Held for Sale and Discontinued Operations* as it is 'held for sale'. There is a plan to dispose of the separate major line of business as a single transaction, such that the economic value of the assets will be realised by selling, rather than continuing to use them.

(ii) The assets should be recognised at the lower of:

- the value under normal accounting standards

- the value on sale, being the fair value less the costs of sale.

This may result in an impairment loss, which should be recognised.

Once this valuation exercise has been performed, no depreciation or amortisation should be recognised.

The trading performance of the continuing divisions should be shown in the income statement (or disclosed by way of note), as well as the overall performance, so that readers can evaluate the likely impact of the disposal.

(b)

	(i) Profit $	*(ii)* Sales tax $
Sale price	40,250	
Less: Sales tax @ 15%	(5,250)	(5,250)
	35,000	
Cost of goods	(10,000)	
Excise duty @ 20%	(2,000)	
Sales tax on purchase @ 15%		(1,800)
Repackaging	(6,900)	
Sales tax @ 15%	900	(900)
	17,000	2,550

(c) (i)

	Less than 30 days (October)	*31–60 days (September)*	*61–90 days (August)*	*91–120 days (July)*
14.7 credit note				160
25.9		204		
16.10	233			
	233	204	0	160

(ii) An aged analysis of receivables allows a company to focus its collection efforts to enforce its credit terms. It makes it more obvious whether an increase/decrease in a balance is due to changed activity levels or a change in payment policy by a customer. This makes it easier for the company to assess whether it should carry on doing business, how it should set credit limits and whether it needs to take any action in respect of large balances.

(d)   (i)   The criteria for income recognition under IAS 18 *Revenue Recognition* are:

- the risks and rewards of ownership must have passed to the purchaser

- the seller no longer controls the goods

- the revenue can be measured reliably

- there is reasonable certainty of payment

- the related costs can be measured reliably.

(ii)   The payment made by the supermarket covered the six months to 28 February 2008 so that, at the year end, EJ had supplied two months' worth. Accordingly, EJ should recognise revenue of $150,000 \times 2/6 = 50,000$.

The related costs are $20,000 per month, so $40,000.

Accordingly, EJ should include a gross profit on this contract in its results for the year to 31 October 2007 of $10,000.

(e)   A related party is:

- an entity that directly, or indirectly through one or more intermediaries, controls, is controlled by, or is under the same control as a second entity; or

- an entity that has an interest in the second entity that gives it significant influence; or

- an entity that has joint control over the second entity; or

- an associate

- a joint venture in which the entity is a venturer

- a member of the key management personnel of the entity or parent

- any close relation of the personnel in any of the above.

A related party transaction is a transfer of resources or obligations between related parties, regardless of whether a price is charged.

(f)   Bonds:

	$
Cost, including commission @ 1%	120,000
Cost less commission $120,000 \times 100/101 = \$118,812$	
Value on redemption $118,812 \times 100/102$	116,482
Interest @ 12.5% on 116,482	14,560
Return	11,042

Internet bank:

Interest @ 0.8% per month – so there will be 12 interest periods during the year.

Value in 12 months' time $= 120,000 (1 + 0.008)^{12} = \$12,041$

The internet bank offers the most appropriate investment based on the return generated. As both investments are relatively low risk, return is an appropriate basis for the decision.

SECTION C

QUESTION THREE

EY Balance sheet at 31 October 2007

	$000	$000	$000
Non-current assets			
Development costs — cost	1,500		
— amortisation	400	1,100	
Property, plant and equipment — cost (W5)	9,760		
— depreciation (W5)	2,031	7,729	8,829
Current assets			
Inventory	985		
Long-term contracts (W1)	840		
Trade receivables	620		
			2,445
			11,274
Equity and liabilities			
Equity			
Share capital		3,500	
Revaluation reserve (W5)		200	
Retained earnings (see Statement of changes)		1,164	
			4,864
Non-current liabilities			
Loan notes (W10)	4,760		
Deferred tax (W7)	222		
		4,982	
Current liabilities			
Trade and other payables	670		
Short term borrowings	208		
Tax payable (W4)	420		
Interest payable (W2)	130		
		1,428	
Total liabilities			6,410
			11,274

Income statement for the year to 31 October 2007

	$000
Revenue (W12)	8,207
Cost of sales (W11)	5,933
Gross profit	2,274
Distribution costs	730
Administrative expenses	500
Profit	1,044
Finance costs (W2)	173
Profit before tax	871
Income tax expense (W13)	482
Profit for the period	389

Statement of changes in equity for the year to 31 October 2007

	Share capital $000	Revaluation reserve $000	Retained earnings $000
Balance at 31 October 2006	3,000	600	1,625
Transferred to profit/(loss) on sale		(400)	400
Profit for the period			389
Dividends			(750)
Issue of share capital	500		(500)
	3,500	200	1,164

Workings:

(W1) **Government contract**

	$000	$000
Contract value		1,400
Costs year 1	600	
Remaining	400	
		(1,000)
		400
Profit to recognise, given contract 60% complete = 0.6 × 400,000		240
Carrying value		840

(W2) Interest payable

		$000
B/f		117
Paid		(160)
C/f		(130)
Charge		173

(W3) Research & development

	$000
Funded R&D year 1 – no certainty of valuable outcome – expense	300
Artificial wood – expense as not viable	800
	1,100
Amortisation on existing R&D – straight line	200
	1,300
Laminate – sufficient certainty of generating profits – capitalise	500

No amortisation yet as production has not started

(W4) Income tax

	$000
B/f payable	670
Paid	(690)
Increase in prior year liability	20
Current year charge	420
C/f payable	420

(W5) Property, plant and equipment

	Land	Premises 6% SL	Plant 15% RB	Total
	$000	$000	$000	$000
Cost b/f	2,000	1,500	3,800	7,300
Addition		1,600	1,860	3,460
Disposal	(1,000)			(1,000)
	1,000	3,100	5,660	9,760
Depreciation b/f	0	(350)	(760)	(1,110)
	0	(186)	(735)	(921)
	0	(536)	(1,495)	(2,031)
NBV c/f	1,000	2,564	4,165	7,729

Revaluation reserve:

	$000
B/f	600
Revaluation realised	(400)
C/f	200
Disposal proceeds	1,200
Revaluation	(400)
Cost	(600)
Profit (W14)	200

(W6) Bonus issue 1:6

New shares = 3,000/6 = 500

Transfer from retained reserves

Share capital c/f = 3,500

(W7) Deferred tax

	$000
B/f	180
Increase	42
C/f	222

(W8) Debtors

	$000
B/f	(753)
Received	7,500
C/f	620
Sales	7,367

(W9) Creditors

	$000
B/f	573
Paid	3,000
C/f	670
Purchases	3,097

(W10) Loan notes

	$000
B/f	2,260
Additional	2,500
	4,760

(W11) **Cost of sales**

	$000
Depreciation	921
Profit on sale of land – following treatment of depreciation	(200)
Amortisation	200
R&D costs – following treatment of amortisation (W3)	1,100
Expenditure on Government contract	600
Opening inventory	1,200
Closing inventory	(985)
Purchases (W9)	3,097
	5,933

(W12) **Revenue**

	$000
Sales – debtors working (W8)	7,367
Government contract – working (W1) = 600 + 240	840
	8,207

(W13) **Tax charge**

	$000
Increase in prior year charge	20
Current year charge	420
Increase in deferred tax	42
	482